WAGES AND HOURS

A Volume in the
CRIME, LAW, AND DEVIANCE
Series

Ronnie Steinberg

WAGES

AND

HOURS

LABOR AND REFORM
IN TWENTIETH-CENTURY
AMERICA

Rutgers University Press

NEW BRUNSWICK, NEW JERSEY

The author is pleased to acknowledge permission to use excerpts from the following works:

History of Labor in the United States, 1896-1932: Labor Legislation, Vol. III, by Elizabeth Brandeis. Copyright © 1953 by Macmillan Publishing Co., Inc., renewed 1963 by Mary E. Lescobier and Elizabeth Brandeis. Reprinted by permission of Macmillan Publishing Co., Inc.

Principles of Labor Legislation, 4th rev. ed., by John R. Commons and John B. Andrews. Copyright © 1936 by Harper and Row, Publishers, Inc. Reprinted by permission of Harper and Row, Publishers, Inc.

"The Social Meaning of Industrialization: Some Theoretical Propositions," *Social Problems* 27 (April 1980): 448-466, by Ronnie Steinberg Ratner. Copyright © 1980 by the Society for the Study of Social Problems. Reprinted by permission of the Society for the Study of Social Problems.

TO
RICHARD MAISEL
TEACHER AND FRIEND

AND

IN MEMORY OF
HELEN L. STEINBERG
AND
JEFF A. STEINBERG

CONTENTS

LIST OF FIGURES

LIST OF TABLES

PREFACE

As with most projects, this study has taken on several different forms over the past five years. The original impetus for the research arose from a controversy within the women's movement—whether so-called protective labor laws were beneficial to the working woman or whether such laws curtailed her opportunity to move into better and higher-paying positions. This debate, which had a fifty-year history, resurfaced in the late 1960s and early 1970s when the majority of politically active feminists placed the adoption of the Equal Rights Amendment at the top of their list of political demands. In this context, the reason for the renewed salience of protective labor laws was obvious: a constitutional amendment granting legal equality to men and women would invalidate the presumed benefits previously offered to women because of a subordinate legal status.

My question was equally straightforward: would legal equality prove symbolic rather than substantive? Would, in fact, women in blue-collar and service occupations, for example, lose real protections in the labor market in exchange for the inadequate formal, legal rights covering men in blue-collar and service occupations? I was interested, then, in ascertaining the actual impact of these laws on the employment opportunities of women. In addition, I wondered if the impact of these laws had changed over time. A legal impact study, however, required prior research on the growth and change in the laws. Consequently, what was originally to have been a major independent variable—that is, protective labor laws—became instead the central dependent variable to be described and explained.

Once the focus of investigation had been modified, other changes followed. These laws took on added significance as I saw their relevance to writings by, for example, Karl Marx, T. H. Marshall, and Reinhard Bendix on the growth of institutions of worker self-protection. The scope of this investigation then shifted from women workers to workers in general, and I chose to analyze the subset of protective labor laws that set explicitly terms of the labor contract such as wages and hours.

As I began the project, I discovered that legal statutes lent themselves to quantitative analysis. Because wage and hour standards laws have existed in some states since the 1870s, they are suited to historical analysis. Because they were enacted by state legislatures as well as by Congress, they are also suited to comparative analysis. I chose to organize and distill key features of the provisions of these laws by using a social indicators approach.

A topic that originally had emerged from my direct involvement in movements for political change thus evolved into a quantitative case study of the dynamics of a particular set of social reforms in the United States over the twentieth century. While this study seemed, at the time, to be less immediately relevant than a legal impact study of protective labor laws, it certainly adds considerably to our understanding both of the treatment of women in the labor market in the twentieth century and of the link between labor laws for women and children and labor laws for all employees. Moreover, it is one of the first systematic sociological studies to describe in detail the growth of a set of social reforms in an advanced industrial democracy. This investigation of the growth of social legislation took on an added personal meaning because it combined my substantive interests in employed women, social stratification, and the nature of social policy in the welfare state, with my methodological interest in developing and analyzing historical time series data.

This research could not have been completed without the financial support of several institutions, the facilities generously offered by several universities and research institutions, and finally, the encouragement and assistance of many people. While working on this research, I gained many new colleagues and friends. The Employment and Training Administration of the United States Department of Labor provided an ample dissertation grant, and Ann Greenberg and Martha Dunne of the Office of Sponsored Research at New York University reduced my administrative responsibilities under this grant to a bare minimum. Additional support was provided by a grant from the Russell Sage Foundation Program on Law and Society. Through this program, I was able to spend two years at outstanding law schools taking courses and writing the major portion of the original version of this book. Had it not been for this generous financial support, I would not have been able to undertake what turned out to be a major effort in data collection and analysis.

The Russell Sage Program at Yale Law School directed by Stanton Wheeler and the Visiting Scholar Program at Harvard Law School directed by Jerome A. Cohen and David Smith provided me with comfortable and stimulating surroundings in which to complete the research and the writing of the first draft. In addition, the Center for Research on Women at Wellesley College and the Center for Women in Government provided office space and collegiality while I finished the several revisions.

Carol Parke, documents librarian of the Government Publication Collection at the Sterling Library at Yale University, and Michele Sullivan, assistant documents librarian, taught me how to penetrate the maze of government publications. This remains an invaluable skill. Gene P. Coakley III, supervisor of circulation services at the Yale Law School Library, saved me hours of time.

Jeffrey Berlant, Bliss Cartwright, Carolyn Elliott, William C. Elliott, Diane Polise Garra, Michael Harrington, Charles Perrow, Sidney Ratner, Edwin Schur, Patricia Cayo Sexton, Stephen Wasby, and Stanton Wheeler read and commented on earlier drafts. I am grateful also to Jonathan Kelly and Bernard Lentz for their incisive reviews and critiques of the coding rules. While I did not make all the changes suggested to me, their comments strongly influenced the questions I addressed and the inferences I drew from the analyzed data. Of course, all responsibility for the final scope and shape of the study remains with me.

Furthermore, I was enormously grateful to many women who not only typed portions of the manuscript, but managed to show good-natured tolerance, flexibility, and a sense of humor despite frequent delays on my part: Glenna Ames, Vanessa Beale, Tracy Sluicer, and Judith Paquette. The bulk of the typing was done by Patricia Mitchell and Kathy Stutsrim, who both demonstrated incredible patience and persistence. Susan Hunt edited portions of an earlier draft, and Susan Gesell, among other editorial tasks, organized the bibliography.

I would especially like to thank several people for the help, encouragement, and support they provided throughout this project. David Greenberg reviewed the manuscript with great care and made useful comments about style, substance, and technique. Similarly, the enthusiasm and constructive suggestions of Mayer Zald, who reviewed the manuscript at an early stage, were extremely helpful. The final draft owes much to their perceptive reading and criticism of the earlier versions. Paul Burstein and I spent many afternoons debating various issues addressed in this book, especially the measurement of legislative change. These conversations clarified my thinking, which facilitated the writing of those sections of the book. Richard Wilson ran the computer programs that combined the matrices of legal information and labor force data to form the time series necessary for the data analysis. Since Rick and I share an interest in social policy and social reform and the political economy of state formation, his comments on several chapters in an earlier draft were especially helpful. R. Stephen Warner assisted in this project during its crucial initial and final stages. In an important conversation, he helped me carve out and focus the research questions and steered me toward the appropriate theoretical writings. He studied the final manuscript with great care and made important suggestions that significantly strengthened the final draft.

It is very hard for me to pinpoint the specific ways in which Jonathan Ratner contributed to the completion of this study, because his involvement touched all facets of it. He was clearly my most persistent critic and champion. His sharp analytical skills and editing ability were often put to work, and he contributed greatly to the development and refinement of many of the arguments. His thoughtful understanding during completion of this project was indispensable.

Finally, I am deeply grateful to Richard Maisel. The idea that the provisions of legislation could be analyzed using a social indicators approach was his. Once I had elected to follow his approach, he spent many hours teaching me how to develop coding rules, adapt existing data sets to new problems, develop hypotheses, and design methods to test them, as well as how to analyze data. Because of him, the process of completing this project contributed substantially to my intellectual development.

Professor Maisel had high standards which he repeatedly encouraged me to meet. How closely this work meets his criteria I leave for him to judge. For my part, I found the process of trying, though sometimes trying, also highly satisfying.

ABBREVIATIONS

AM:	All minors
EP:	Equal pay laws
FA:	Female adults
FM:	Female minors
MA:	Male adults
MH:	Maximum hours laws
MM:	Male minors
MW:	Minimum wage laws
NW:	Night-work laws
OT:	Overtime laws
T/C/PU:	Transportation, communications, and public utilities
WP/WC:	Wage payment/wage collection laws

I
INTRODUCTION AND METHODOLOGY

1

"AND ON THE SEVENTH DAY"

Over a century ago, as the United States turned from civil war to business, the bulk of its national output flowed from its granaries. By 1889 industrial production had supplanted agriculture as the factories for the first time claimed more workers than the fields (Dillard, 1967:356). During the 1880s, manufacturing came to contribute more to the national product than did agriculture (Gallman and Howle, 1971:26). These dramatic changes proclaimed market capitalism at work.[1] The prospect of larger than average returns encouraged entrepreneurs to invest their financial resources in capital purchases and to launch and expand industrial enterprises (Edwards, 1979; Ulman, 1955). These new workplaces were the source not only of larger quantities of goods and services, many of them new, but of new social relationships as well.

Historians like Samuel Hays regarded this social transformation as being the essence of industrialization as it was *experienced* by Americans in the mid- to late nineteenth and early twentieth centuries: "The expansion of economic relationships from personal contacts within a village community to impersonal forces in the nation and the entire world; the standardization of life accompanying the standardization of goods and of methods of production; increasing specialization in occupations with the resulting dependence of people upon each other to satisfy their wants; a feeling of insecurity as men faced the vast and rapidly changing economic forces that they could not control; the decline of interest in non-material affairs and the rise of the acquisition of material wealth as the major goals in life" (1957:4). Nowhere was this transformation more evident than in the changed status of laborers; for between 1850 and 1920, America became a nation of employees (Grey and Peterson, 1974:347).

Within these new work settings, employers and workers often found that their interests conflicted. Differences arose around such central terms of employment as the level of wages, the length of the working day, and the conditions of work. In the past, similar conflicts typically had been contained within the more personal and traditional relations between master and worker in small-scale commerce and manufacture or had been dissipated by the mobility of labor. By contrast, industrial production entailed a scale of enterprise and a market for labor that eroded or precluded personal and traditional relations between capitalist entrepreneur and worker[2] (Edwards, 1979; Grey and Peterson, 1974:347–348; see also Braverman, 1974). The tensions could no longer be dissipated by the possibility of a worker leaving a particular firm or region.

Moreover, the worker found his or her legal status as a free laborer an insufficient vehicle for the redress of grievances. This legal status was rooted in nineteenth-century legal doctrine, especially the concept of freedom of contract in which government supported free bargaining between individuals in the marketplace. Freedom of contract was, in turn, the judicial (and, to a lesser extent, legislative) expression of the ideology of laissez-faire, the dominant political philosophy underlying the merger of democracy and capitalism in the United States (Fine, 1976; Paul, 1969). Those who subscribed to the doctrine of freedom of contract believed that each employee and each employer entered into the making of the labor contract as equals. In 1897, for instance, the Supreme Court held that "'liberty embraced the right of the citizen . . . to earn his livelihood by any lawful calling; and for that purpose to enter into all contracts which may be proper, necessary, and essential.'" In 1908, to cite another example, it declared: "'The right of a person to sell his labor upon such terms as he deems proper is, in its essence, the same right of the purchaser of labor to prescribe the conditions upon which he will accept such labor'" (as quoted in Hamilton, 1931:450, 452; Wilensky and Lebeaux, 1965:38).

Such a system of exchange and rewards is quite appealing in theory. In practice, however, workers found that the laissez-faire system—which offered them the right to unconstrained property transactions—resulted in their being constrained to accept, without negotiation or compromise, the terms and conditions of employment set forth by the employer (Commons, 1968; Commons and Andrews, 1936; Pound, 1909). In their struggles to achieve an adequate labor contract, employees discovered that, as individuals, they could not successfully fight the employer. "The contract by which he sold to the capitalist his labour-power [Marx has written] proved, so to say, in black and white that he disposed of himself freely. The bargain concluded, it is discovered that he was no 'free agent,' that the time for which he is free to sell his labour-power is the time for which he is forced to sell it" (Marx, 1906:330). "For modern contract," T. H. Marshall (1965:96) has also concluded, "is essentially an agreement between men who are free and equal in status, though not necessarily in power." The employee faced her or his inequality in the labor market armed only with a set of legal rights more appropriate to a preindustrial society in which work was carried out by independent entrepreneurs and skilled craftsmen.

To offset adverse power imbalances, the worker struggled to achieve self-protection through several channels: first, workers organized into groups in order to bargain collectively over the terms of employment. The workers' purpose, of course, was to strengthen their control over the price and hours for which they sold their labor. Consequently, they attempted to create a system of collective freedom of contract. Where once the law sanctioned the participation of workers only as individuals in contractual relationships, now the law—the workers felt—should acknowledge the union (a corporate entity) as a legitimate party to a contract. T. H. Marshall (1965:104) has called trade unionism "a secondary system of political citizenship," in which employees use the important political resource of organization and, if necessary, mobilization and mass withdrawals, to achieve advantageous employment contracts.

Workers also looked to the government for protection. Ironically, the American state, committed in rhetoric and in law to further, in Robert Nozick's (1974) phrase, "capitalist acts among consenting adults," became the instrument sought by workers and others to intervene in the market transactions between owner and employee. Statutes (associated with the rise of the welfare state) were introduced on behalf of these subordinate groups; they have been characterized as social rights (Marshall, 1965; Romanyshyn, 1971).[3] Supporters of unionization and social legislation sought thereby to ensure a minimum level of economic welfare and security, and to eliminate some of the more devastating effects of the free market on social groups that were in a subordinate bargaining position in the marketplace (Wilensky, 1975). In terms of the actual historical experience and of their short-run self-interest, such innovations are seen in zero-sum terms: by employers as restrictions on contractual liberty and managerial authority and by workers and their supporters as protection of labor's welfare (Dahrendorf, 1959; Friedman and Ladinsky, 1967; Gough, 1979). Viewed in terms of the long-run interests of these two classes, these reforms are seen by analysts as innovations that help to rationalize and sustain a social order organized in the employees' interests (Garner, 1977; Gough, 1979; Kolko, 1963; Miliband, 1969; O'Connor, 1973; Poulantzas, 1973, 1975; Weinstein, 1968).

These determined efforts at worker self-protection were met by staunch resistance. Even in 1979, union organizers still faced stiff opposition. Firms continue to relocate within the United States and other countries in search of a cheap and passive pool of labor or to invest huge resources to combat or prevent union organizing drives. By the same token, lobbyists proposing social legislation can expect, at best, to see such laws enacted only if their most progressive provisions are watered down (Handler, 1978;

Scheingold, 1974). Nonetheless, over the last one hundred years, both unions and social legislation have gradually become stable features of American society, and, the government's role in shaping transactions in the labor market has changed profoundly.

This study examines one aspect of the transformation in institutions for worker self-protection.[4] It explores the growth of social rights in the United States over the twentieth century. The two major questions guiding the research are: (1) what are the *patterns* in the emergence and growth of wage and hour standards laws over time? (2) how do the rise of and change in these laws relate to broader economic, social, and political change in the United States during the twentieth century? An underlying theoretical issue informs the investigation: when and under what conditions will a government committed to enforcing private property rights intervene in the employment relationship on behalf of employees to impose explicit constraints on employers?

WELFARE STATE LEGISLATION AND SOCIAL RIGHTS

Over the twentieth century, social legislation in the United States (as in other advanced industrial democracies) has proliferated. Whereas, at the turn of the century, government offered virtually no legal protection to property-less laborers armed only with their labor power, by the 1970s, legislation had been enacted to soften somewhat the harsh impact of the market on employees. Government intervention took many forms. One set of laws addressed the problems of workers. The earliest of these laws included factory acts and maximum hours legislation, followed by minimum wage and workman's compensation laws (Brandeis, 1935; Commons and Andrews, 1936; Friedman and Ladinsky, 1967; Nonet, 1969). Somewhat later came legislation protecting individuals against loss of income resulting from sickness, old age, and unemployment (Wilensky, 1975). Recently, several of the early welfare state goals have reemerged in legislation addressed to contemporary industrial problems: for example, the Occupational Safety and Health Act (OSHA), which attempts to control the physical environment of work, is in some respects analogous to the factory acts enacted in the late nineteenth and early twentieth centuries. Similarly, the equal pay acts are motivated by the perceived need to counter unfair treatment of certain categories of employees—especially women and racial and ethnic minorities—just as protective labor laws were introduced for women and children who felt exploited by employers during the early stages of industrialization (Ratner, 1980).

A second set of welfare state laws seeks to bring individuals who have rarely or never worked up to some socially constructed poverty line. While these laws providing welfare payments to the nonworking (and sometimes working) poor have been the focus of a plethora of studies (see, for example, Cnudde and McCrone, 1969; Cowart, 1969; Dawson and Robinson, 1963; Fry and Winters, 1970; Piven and Cloward, 1971; Polanyi, 1957; Sharkansky and Hofferbert, 1969), attention is directed here to work-related social legislation.

Work-related social legislation can be categorized in terms of which of two aspects of the employment process it addresses: the *normal procedures* and general conditions of a workplace or the *contingencies* that arise out of but are marginal to the way firms organize the labor process. Contingency-oriented laws, including most social security legislation such as sickness and injury insurance, unemployment insurance, and old age insurance, are activated when an individual loses—either temporarily or permanently—his or her status as an employed worker. Like welfare laws, these have been the focus of a great deal of scholarly attention (see, for example, Collier and Messick, 1975; Heclo, 1974; Rimlinger, 1971; Wilensky, 1975) and will not be examined here.

Work-related reforms include equal employment opportunity legislation, which broadens the access of certain disadvantaged groups to jobs historically denied them; factory acts and OSHA, which specify minimal standards concerning the conditions of workplaces; legislation facilitating and deterring unionization and the right to bargain collectively; and laws setting the terms of the labor contract, such as labor standards legislation. While these have received some attention from contemporary sociologists and political scientists (Lockard, 1968; Smelser, 1959), it has been extremely modest relative to the attention given other categories of welfare state legislation.[5] I examine a subset of these laws for reasons discussed below.

I separate social legislation into three policy domains—poverty laws, social security laws, and laws affecting the terms, conditions, and process underlying the labor contract—because I regard these laws as carrying different costs, benefits, and responsibilities for employers, employees, and society in general. The emergence and development of the social rights embodied in these laws are likely to vary as a consequence of these different characteristics. This is true even within the broad groupings set forth above. For this reason, each category of social legislation should be examined separately. This book focuses on one set of laws embodying one set of social rights—those establishing wage and hour standards.

WAGE AND HOUR STANDARDS LAWS

Wage and hour standards (or labor standards) legislation addresses two of the central terms of employment: how long an employee must work, and how much she or he is to be paid. Specifically, these laws establish the floor below which wages cannot fall, how long the workday is to be, the rules the employer must follow in paying his or her employee for work rendered, and the equal treatment of employees who, in their work role, perform the same task. Wage and hour standards laws constitute, therefore, explicit government intervention—at least formally—on behalf of employees into the setting of the terms and conditions of the labor contract.

Except for Karl Marx's (1906: Chapter 10) description and analysis of the development of these laws in the United Kingdom, examination of this class of laws has come primarily from labor historians, and, to a lesser extent, from legal historians and labor economists.[6] This is surprising, because wage and hour standards laws are useful and significant for sociologists and political scientists to study for at least three reasons: first, because these laws require explicit government intervention, they run directly counter to the dominant freedom-of-contract norm guiding legal relations. This makes wage and hour laws an analytically important set of reforms to investigate. Second, the division of interest groups during the almost continuous controversies surrounding the enactment and emendation of these laws facilitates, without lengthy justification, the use of a class-oriented conflict model to explain changes in the law. Finally, these laws carry two characteristics that make them of more general interest to students of reform legislation (or "policy outcomes"): their emergence and growth vary both over time and over legislative domain. Moreover, these laws predate the twentieth century and have continued right to the present. Let us elaborate on the significance of these dimensions of labor standards laws in reverse order.

GENERAL CHARACTERISTICS

Demands for government regulation of the terms of work by no means started in the late nineteenth century. When, in the late 1700s, there were serious labor shortages, skilled craftsmen and small shopowners in several New England towns and states pressured successfully for *maximum* wage rates (Cohen, 1975:396–397; Rayback, 1966:20–21). Employees some half-century later—in the 1830s and 1840s—had a considerably more difficult time gaining their demands for government regulations of the length of the working day (Ware, 1958, 1964). Legislation restricting the hours of women, children, and some men was first enacted in the late 1860s and 1870s.[7] Laws regulating how employees would be paid—with money as opposed to goods, each week or twice a month rather than at the discretion of the employer, and so on—began to be enacted in the last two decades of the nineteenth century. The first minimum wage law was passed in Massachusetts in 1912 (Brandeis, 1935:502). Until the Great Depression, most wage and hour standards laws were passed by state legislatures. The federal government enacted its first general wage and hour standards law—the Fair Labor Standards Act—in 1938 (U.S. Department of Labor, Bureau of Labor Standards, 1967:93–97).

These laws are not simply relics of our historical past; many remain the active concern of interest groups—especially labor unions and women's organizations—who exert considerable pressure on state and federal legislators. In the 1960s, for example, the civil rights movement exposed the fact that a significant number of black workers in northern and midwestern ghettos were not being paid for the work they were performing. As a result, the provisions in many wage payment laws were substantially revised and expanded in the late 1960s. Similarly, maximum hours laws that applied to women have been regarded by contemporary feminists as detrimental to the employment opportunities of women (Baer, 1978); by 1977, most of these laws had been removed from the statute books either by court decision or by legislative repeal (Babcock et al., 1975; Brown et al., 1977). Whatever standards remained were made uniform over age and sex categories. Equal pay legislation—first enacted by a significant number of states during and immediately following World War II—received a renewed push through the enactment of a federal law in 1963 and of a related equal opportunity law (Title VII of the Civil Rights Act) in 1964. Finally, increasing the scope of coverage and the statutory wage rate in minimum wage legislation has been a constant priority of the organized labor movement. Indeed, legislation that would index the minimum wage at 60 percent of the average wage in manufacturing was introduced in Congress in 1977. Not surprisingly, it is supported by organized labor and opposed by the Chamber of Commerce of the United States (Shabecoff, 1977:53, 61).

Thus, the emergence and growth of these laws span over one hundred years. Some—notably wage payment laws and maximum hours laws—were among the first welfare state legislation to be enacted. They emerged as political demands in the United States long before social security legislation. Others—such as equal pay and overtime laws—were enacted primarily between 1935 and 1975. This fact renders them extremely useful to study: tracing their development over the twentieth century offers a valuable opportunity to investigate what happens to a set of analytically related social policies beyond the early years following their enactment. Few such studies exist; none has explored this process quantitatively. Moreover, since specific laws within this category of legislation arose at different times during the twentieth century, it is possible to explore the extent to which new legislation in the same legal domain builds upon and transcends older legislation (Ratner, 1980). Finally, wage and hour standards laws were enacted by both state legislatures and Congress. Therefore, the interrelations of the political outcomes from these two levels of government can be gauged. Thus, the selection of a set of laws with these characteristics makes this study relevant to the growing body of literature on public policy outcomes (see, for example, Dye, 1966, 1978, 1979; Gray, 1979; and Hofferbert, 1966 for a compilation and synthesis of some of this literature).

THE DIMENSIONS OF POLITICAL CONTROVERSY: CLASS STRUGGLE

From the vantage point of the 1970s, minimum wage legislation seems to some an insignificant if not pernicious achievement, and maximum hours legislation is regarded as restrictive of the opportunities of women. It is important to remember that these laws were as controversial in their time as, for example, civil rights laws have been since World War II. Unlike social security legislation, these laws grew directly out of the oftentimes militant class conflict engaged in by employers and employees in the late nineteenth and early twentieth centuries. "Reduction of hours has been one of the two major demands of labor in the United States . . . the [struggle] has been . . . a constant, dogged, frequently hopeless insistence of one great part of society—labor—on the need for a shorter working day in the face of an equally determined resistance by a smaller part of employers to every suggestion for immediate change" (Cahill, 1932:11).

Statistics summarizing the eight-hour movement during the 1880s convey an impressive picture of widespread activity. Labor organized two major campaigns to achieve the eight-hour day—the first between 1884 and 1886, the second between 1888 and 1891 (Brecher, 1972; Fine, 1953). Of the mid-1880s eight-hour movement, one historian writes: "The movement centered in the major industrial cities of Chicago, New York, Cincinnati, Baltimore, and Milwaukee, with Boston, Pittsburgh, St. Louis, and Washington affected to a lesser degree. Even before May 1st, almost a quarter of a million workers throughout the country were involved in the eight-hour movement. . . . Yet the movement in fact proved even bigger than anticipated. By the second week in May, 1885, some 340,000 workers had participated, 190,000 of them by striking. . . . Nearly 200,000 workers, according to *Bradstreet's*, won shorter hours" (Brecher, 1972:39).

In the late 1880s, the American Federation of Labor (AFL) modified this earlier city-by-city strategy to place its muscle behind one national union that would strike to gain the eight-hour day. In early May 1890, the Carpenters and Joiners—the largest national union in the AFL—began the strike effort. Others followed. One hundred forty-one strikes occurred involving 280 local unions and nearly 580,000 union and nonunion men. Workers achieved their goal of the eight-hour day in only 42 of the strikes. Yet, in *every* strike employees gained some reduction in the average work-week (Fine, 1953:456).

Employees undertook political action as well—at least initially. Their efforts in the political arena met with considerably less success than their strike activity, as we shall see. Two types of laws were pursued, and state legislatures initially introduced crippling modifications into each of these proposals. Before 1900, most political action on these laws took place in New England and the North Atlantic states.

In 1842, textile manufacturing employees from the town of Lowell, Massachusetts, for example, petitioned the state legislature for a law regulating their hours. These workers made clear their strong support of hours legislation which included explicit, enforceable limits on their workweek. Men and women workers from the textile mills demonstrated for the enactment of these laws over a ten-year period with little success (Brandeis, 1935; Josephson, 1949). Rather than soften their position on enforceable legislation, these employees chose to compromise over the scope of coverage under maximum hours laws. Originally, employees had sought legislation that provided universal coverage, but their lack of power relative to employers forced them to lower their aspirations. In 1867, twenty-five years after their original demand, textile workers found acceptable maximum hours laws that restricted coverage to women and children employed by incorporated textile firms.

Massachusetts textile workers borrowed this approach of selective coverage from their English brothers and sisters: they apparently reasoned that, if they accepted a law that limited coverage to women and minors, the probability of its passage would be high. Indeed, the diffusion of factory legislation from England to Massachusetts was clear and direct: the English immigrant operatives who had settled in Fall River were among those who first presented the petition for a ten-hour day to the Massachusetts legislature (Josephson, 1949:254). Male textile employees accepting this compromise were motivated by narrow self-interest: it appeared that hours restrictions for women would become, of necessity, hours ceilings for men as well. So, "in Massachusetts as in England, the men employed in the textile industry decided to 'fight the battle from behind the women's petticoats'" (Brandeis, 1935:462).

By the turn of the century, most labor union leaders—except for those in the Far West—had abandoned the legislative route to the restriction of the workweek for men. Such legislation for women and children was, however, supported by these same union leaders and newly organized Progressive era organizations. Wage and hour standards laws became the active concern of social philanthropists, the social welfare movement, and that segment of the early feminist movement oriented to the needs of working-class women. These groups, for instance, supported the suffrage amendment because they believed that it would facilitate the enactment of protective labor laws which, among other things, restricted the length of the working day (Chafe, 1972: 18–20; Flexner, 1971:212–215; Lemons, 1973:117–119).

This review of the early political struggles surrounding the enactment of these laws is necessarily brief, and will be continued in subsequent chapters. Yet, it serves to illustrate the crucial fact that the activities of organized interest groups formed the essential backdrop to the more formal political actions of state legislatures and the Congress. Thus, while I share with Lasswell (1958) a definition of politics as being who gets what, when, and how, I part ways with most students of the policy process by broadening the view of what constitutes political influence. Along with Roberta Ash Garner (1977:248), I view political determinants as more than formal political structures, or election campaigns. Rather, I treat the political factors conditioning the development of these laws in terms of a broad interest group perspective.

Because this particular set of social rights impinges on the central terms of the labor contract, it is of concern to a distinct subset of interest groups— those who buy and sell labor power—and lends itself to a class theory of conflict (Gough, 1979:56). Marx's study of the British factory acts in the nineteenth century, for example, "demonstrated how the Ten Hours Act and other factory legislation was the result of unremitting struggle by the working class against their exploitation" (Gough, 1979:55; see also Harrington, 1976). The relation of wage and hour laws to the organization of the labor market, the distribution of power within it, and the constellation of interest groups emerging as a result of it renders this study of significance to sociologists concerned with political economy and social stratification.

REFORM AND THE THEORY OF THE STATE

Recently, a new Marxist-informed literature concerned with developing a theory of the state has emerged. (Block, 1977b; Bridges, 1974; Garner. 1977; Gold, Lo, and Wright, 1975; Miliband, 1969; Poulantzas, 1973, 1975; and Thompson, 1975 constitute a partial, but representative, list.) Previously, to the extent that a Marxist view of the actions of the state was articulated—primarily by non-Marxists—the state was defined to be the simple reflection of the interests of the capitalist class (Sweezy, 1942). Of course, social legislation would be thus defined away as a mere vehicle for the co-optation of the working class. Alternatively, false consciousness could undergird the presumably self-defeating efforts of the working class both to strengthen existing legislation and to gain new social rights.

These newer theories of the state build on several of Marx's historical writings and concede that the state, while dependent on economically grounded forces, can act autonomously of them. In other words, state policy can operate against the immediate short-run interests of the capitalist class. Indeed, it is argued, such state autonomy is essential to maintain the legitimacy of a society in which power is so unequally distributed. E. P. Thompson, for example, argues that the rule of law, itself necessary to preserve the fiction of the state's neutrality, can at times place severe restrictions on the actions of the ruling class.

> The law . . . may be seen instrumentally as mediating and reinforcing existent class relations and, ideologically, as offering to these a legitimation . . . if we say that existent class relations were mediated by the law, this is not the same thing as saying that the law was no more than those relations translated into other terms, which masked or mystified the reality. . . . For class relations were expressed, not in any way one likes, but *through the forms of law*; and the law, like other institutions which from time to time can be seen as mediating . . . existent class relations . . . has its own characteristics, its own independent history and logic of evolution (Thompson, 1975:262).

And, sometimes, in order to maintain the fundamental features of the system, political elites will make concessions to the working class. Indeed, sociologist Fred Block and others contend and I agree that pressures for political reforms initiated by subordinate interest groups have been one of the most important stimulants to the expansion of the state: "In its struggles to protect itself from the ravages of the market economy, the working class has played a key role in the steady expansion of the state's role in capitalist society" (Thompson, 1975:21–22).

Wage and hour standards laws, as one such demand of the working class, are an especially interesting set of political concessions in that they meet head-on dominant property norms that regulate the free market and contribute to the reproduction of property relations. To the extent that workers gain such rights, in other words, the legal rules reinforcing the power position of economic elites are called into question and modified. While I expect this factor to impose important restrictions on the development of labor standards laws, this study provides an opportunity to ascertain empirically just how successful employees can be in achieving legal reform in an industrial society with a capitalist political economy. Specifically, I examine the conditions under which such laws will be enacted or amended.

APPROACHES TO WELFARE STATE REFORMS

To summarize the discussion up to this point, this study examines the rise of and growth in one set of social rights embodied in a category of welfare state legislation—wage and hour standards laws—in the United States over the twentieth century. My interest in the change of social rights as a reflection of the change in the employment relationship warrants restricting attention to the growth in the *formal* provisions of legislation. In addition, I seek to paint a detailed picture of legislative change by focusing on the patterns and determinants of changes in the provisions of wage and hour standards laws. It is thus necessary to part ways with previous approaches to the study of the development of political reforms in the welfare state.

PAST APPROACHES

To date, most discussions of the development of social legislation have approached this subject from one of two explanations for the rise of the welfare state: functional-evolutionary theories and structurally based theories. Each perspective carries with it a distinctive research design. (This categorization represents a modification of Gough, 1979; Wedderburn, 1965.) The functional-evolutionary school, represented by T. H. Marshall's "Citizenship and Social Class" (1965:71–134), Karl Polanyi's *The Great Transformation* (1957), and Neil Smelser's *Social Change in the Industrial*

Revolution (1959), treats the emergence of the welfare state analytically as an inevitable outgrowth of the changes in the structure of the economy. Each author attaches the transformation of the state to a different functional need that arose out of the Industrial Revolution: to the survival of capitalism, to the smooth functioning of the market, or to the further differentiation of society growing out of the transfer of certain economic roles from the family to the marketplace. For Neil Smelser, for example, "goods and services, previously exchanged on a non-economic basis, are pulled progressively more into the market. Money now commands the movement of increasingly more goods and services; it thus begins to supplant—and sometimes undermine—the religious, political, familial, or caste sanctions which had hitherto governed economic activity" (1969:48). These "rapid, irregular, and disruptive processes" of the differentiation of economic functions required new institutions such as factory legislation to reintegrate the worker into an increasingly heterogeneous society (1969:56).

Some authors arrive at their conclusions by looking back over decades, while others examine change over several centuries to depict the broad sweep of the historical development of institutionalized rights. Detail must be averaged or left to footnotes so that the view of the larger dynamics is unobstructed. Change appears smooth and inexorable, albeit often slow.

The structural school, including Marxists and others, also acknowledges "need" as a stimulus to change, but considers political reform to be an immediate outgrowth of specific sets of economic, political, and social changes.[8] The studies that flow from this perspective tend to be historical (as, for example, Brandeis, 1935; Commons and Andrews, 1936), comparative (Heclo, 1974; Rimlinger, 1971; Stephens, 1979), or some combination thereof, and tend to describe a single case (Lockard, 1968) or present a historical overview (Baker, 1925).[9]

I regard each of the past approaches to the study of these laws as falling short of providing a systematic and comprehensive picture of the rise and growth of a set of social legislation. The analytical approach removes legislative change from the actual conditions that facilitated or constrained its development. It completely ignores both the prevalence of *discontinuity* of change and the extent to which the pattern of actual growth diverged from uniform development.

The historical overview, on the other hand, presents a plethora of facts and events which are usually not organized around a coherent conceptual framework. To be sure, it is exceedingly difficult both to compile the enormous amount of noncomparable information that is generally included in such histories *and* to cast these data into an analytic framework that will provide the basis for describing and analyzing the general patterns of growth of these laws. Information is not chosen according to some systematic criterion applied to all existing cases. Rather, the very fact that some particular material exists seems to be the basis on which it is selected. Other less available material frequently is ignored.

The case study approach shares the limitations of the historical overview studies. It offers, at best, a description of dominant and typical features of the content of several laws. In addition, the criteria for the selection of cases or examples are, more often than not, unarticulated. Finally, these three approaches share another drawback; they are difficult, if not impossible, to replicate. What should ideally be two separable stages of research—the selection of material and the organization of the data to ascertain patterns—are telescoped into one stage. An outside researcher thus would have difficulty in distinguishing the patterns isolated from the raw material on which they are based.

AN ALTERNATIVE APPROACH TO THE STUDY OF LEGISLATIVE CHANGE

The preceding discussion of the significance of labor standards laws should make it clear that this study builds from a structural approach to legislative reform. Analyzing the patterns and determinants of development in wage and hour standards laws and painting a precise picture of their growth and change necessarily involve comparisons along several dimensions: across laws, across states, and over time. To avoid overwhelming the reader with detail, a technique must be sought that summarizes the complicated provisions of a law into one or a few comprehensible measures. A precedent exists in the work of economists and economic historians, who use quantitative data sets to uncover trends and other patterns operating in the economy. For example, a wide variety of time series data such as the unemployment rate, the price level, the Gross National Product, and the supply of money and credit indicates trends and fluctuations in employment and production. Taken together, these data form the basis for an empirical generalization on the dynamics underlying the sequence of economic phenomena known as the business cycle (Auerbach, 1968). Similarly, Kuznets (1946) developed national income accounting and gross and net national product, and Easterlin (1960) created a data set measuring per capita income by region between 1840 and 1950.

The advantages of a quantitative approach to the analysis of economic phenomena suggest that it be tried in the field of social and legal studies. The construction of economic (and by analogy social) indicators to organize and distill key features of legal data has four methodological virtues: first, both comparisons at a single point in time and the examination of trends can be *systematic* rather than impressionistic. Second, discussion of qualitative features of legislation can be made on a *consistent* basis. Third, the detailed *content* of legislation can be presented in easily understandable form. Finally, the collection and organization of the data are guided by a set of articulated criteria; the procedure is, therefore, *replicable*.

Since the mid-1960s, other social scientists have focused on developing systems of social indicators to supplement those used by economists (Bauer, 1966; Hernes, 1976; Land and Felson, 1976; Land and Spilerman, 1975; Lenski, 1976; Sheldon and Moore, 1968; Wilcox et al., 1972). At the time this study was started, no research coming from the newly emerging social indicators movement used a social indicators approach to measure change in the *content* of legislation. Researchers had developed crude, additive measures of legislative content to examine the determinants of collective bargaining legislation for public employees (Kochan, 1973; Kochan and Wheeler, 1975) and the determinants of divorce cases (Stetson and Wright, 1975). Since 1975, a few other studies have been published (Berk, Brackman, and Lesser, 1977; Boli-Bennett and Meyer, 1978; Burstein, 1978). In general, then, legal statutes are a readily available data source largely ignored in sociological work (Hurst, 1971). State and federal laws have characteristics as bodies of data that make them especially useful for sociological inquiry: because they exist for extended periods, they provide the material for time series and historical analysis. Moreover, many laws are state laws and therefore suited to comparative analysis (Przeworski and Teune, 1970).

One study designed somewhat along the lines of the research proposed here does exist: William Ogburn's doctoral dissertation on the institutional concomitants of modernization as measured in the convergence across states in the provisions of child labor legislation, published in 1912. Ogburn, who initiated the study of social trends through social indicators, measured "the standard deviations of certain features of child labor laws" at several points in time (Ogburn, 1964). These measures, labeled "indices of uniformity," were then inspected over time. Differences in the provisions of the laws had in fact decreased.

The social indicators approach can be used to measure many substantive dimensions of laws, as long as the substantive dimension can be measured at many points in time. Since the growth of wage and hour laws is, viewed from one theoretical perspective, the growth of sets of social rights for employee groups, we can build social indicators on the extent and the distribution of such social rights using the coverage provisions in these laws. But, as I discuss in Chapter 2, I do more than simply code the content of laws. Rather, information culled from state and federal statute volumes is combined with decennial census data on the distribution of the labor force. The distribution of benefits embodied in these laws can thus be studied in much the same way as an economist would study the distribution of income, and legal change is treated in terms of changes in the distribution of these legal rights to employee groups. Similar sets of indicators of other provisions of these laws can also be developed. Therefore, to examine the patterns and determinants of the growth in wage and hour laws, their content is coded, and a set of time series data on several dimensions of these laws is built.

OVERVIEW OF STUDY

The development of wage and hour standards laws represents one early manifestation of the transformation of social rights in the United States over the twentieth century. A social indicators approach makes it possible to describe several dimensions of these laws. Having coded information gathered from these statutes, we can present quantitative measures which are used to construct time series data.

The distinctive features of this study are fourfold: first, I develop a quantitative method of summarizing the content of legislation. There have been no previous attempts to organize legal data in this way: as discussed in Chapter 2, I tie legal content to the actual scope of coverage, measure its distribution over a seventy-three-year period, and examine change in both state and federal legislation. Second, I use the products of this measurement to paint a quantitative and comprehensive picture of the patterns by which these laws developed. Third, I relate these patterns to specific conditions that facilitated or hindered change. Finally, the data are used to test two types of theories: those concerned with the general features of the processes of social change and those addressed to the transformation of social relationships through law. Therefore, as a study of the content of one set of legislation extending one set of social rights within one nation state, this data base will allow us to depict, account for, and further understand the concrete dynamics of social change.

ORGANIZATION OF THIS BOOK

This book is divided into four parts. Part I introduces, in Chapter 2, the methodological approach developed to study legislative change systematically. Further, I justify limiting the focus of investigation to the formal provisions of legislation, discuss the rationale behind restricting the analysis to two provisions of the law, and review the steps in the process of building a set of time series data on the scope, distribution, and strength of these social rights.

Part II explores the national patterns of development in these laws. Chapter 3 looks at the three labor standards laws enacted before the Great Depression. Chapter 4 treats the laws that were adopted during and after the Great Depression and incorporated into the major piece of federal legislation establishing labor standards—the Fair Labor Standards Act (FLSA). Despite the fact that all labor standards laws share important characteristic features, they exhibit distinctive patterns of development. In these chapters, I offer some tentative explanations of the observed variations and offer historical evidence in support of my conclusions. Chapter 5 examines the determinants of the variations in one dimension of these laws— the scope of coverage—more rigorously. I gauge how much of the variation in coverage is due to three factors: the region in which a law was passed, the demographic group of the covered employee, and the industry in which the covered employee works. Second, I measure changes in the determinants of coverage over time.

Part III moves from the national patterns of development to changes in state laws. Chapter 6 treats stability and growth of state laws in terms of three theories of legislative change: a convergence model which suggests that laws in all states will tend to become more similar over time; an imprinting model which holds that subsequent growth in legislation is a function of earlier growth; and a crisis model which regards expansion in the scope of coverage in legislation as a product of a crisis that attaches new meaning to an existing piece of legislation. In Chapter 7, I determine whether the existence of a strong state law affects the way a state's congressional delegation votes on similar federal legislation. Starting from the premise that states with strong laws operate at a competitive disadvantage to states without such laws, I develop and test a model of the interrelations of the extent of unionization in a state, the level of industrialization in a state, the quality of state minimum wage legislation, and congressional voting patterns on federal legislation.

Part IV builds upon and ties together some of the major themes implicit in earlier chapters. Chapter 8 looks at the relation between unionization and the growth in the scope of labor standards legislation. It explores the connection between these two forms of worker self-protection both cross-sectionally by industry and dynamically using time series data on all employees. Finally, it determines the extent to which the growth of union-ization and social reform legislation has been related to high unemployment, increasing industrialization, or both. Chapter 9 synthesizes findings on the patterns and correlates of legislative change. I pay particular attention to the role of social movements—most notably organized labor and women's groups—in taking advantage of or even creating crises to stimulate change in these laws. I also place considerable emphasis on the ideological (including legal) climate facilitating or inhibiting change. In addition, I note the fruit-fulness of using a social indicators approach to the study of legislative change and suggest several research projects that follow directly from this study. Finally, I address a continuing debate about the progressive or co-optive nature of reform and offer some tentative conclusions on the dynamics of social reform in the United States.

2
METHODOLOGY
Social Indicators of Legislation

This study explores quantitatively the patterns and determinants of growth in six labor laws in order to examine systematically the dynamics of change of a set of social reforms in the United States over the twentieth century. In the last chapter, I compared the methodological approach to the one economists use to analyze trends in economic indicators. In this chapter, I describe a technique for reducing the complicated provisions of legislation into time series data indicating the growth of legislation and the distribution of rights among employees. First, I define precisely the six labor standards laws and then specify which dimensions of these laws will be treated. Finally, I discuss at some length the procedure developed to translate legal provisions into time series data.

LABOR STANDARDS LAWS: DEFINITIONS

The social rights addressed in this study are those in which the wage and hour standards of employees are set explicitly through legislation. These laws form an analytically coherent subset of the larger constellation of legislation typically associated with social policy in an industrial society. Six types of laws establish wage and hour standards: wage payment and wage collection laws (WP/WC); maximum hours laws (MH); night-work laws (NW); minimum wage laws (MW); overtime laws (OT); and equal pay laws (EP).[1] Three laws regulate wages, and three regulate hours.

WAGE LAWS

The three wage laws are wage payment and wage collection, minimum wage, and equal pay laws. A *wage payment and wage collection law* speci- fies the procedures an employer is required to follow in paying an employee for work rendered. It does not specify any minimum wage level. Any wage payment and collection law can have some or all of the following requirements: that payment be in legal tender; that intervals between paydays be regular; that employers pay wages within a certain number of days after the work has been performed; that employees be informed of their payday; that, under certain conditions such as the discharge of an employee, employees receive prompt payment of their wages; that a government enforcement agency may adjust any disputes between employers and employees arising as a result of these laws; and that enforcement officers may insist on examining employer records to ensure compliance.

A *minimum wage law* specifies either an explicit wage floor or an administrative or executive procedure for establishing a wage floor.

An *equal pay law* ensures that covered workers will not be discriminated against with respect to the rate of pay or compensation because of such ascribed characteristics as age; sex; race, color, or creed; religion or national origin; physical disability; or marital status.

HOURS LAWS

A *maximum hours law* specifies a daily or weekly hours ceiling; this standard constitutes the number of hours beyond which an employee is prohibited from working.

An *overtime law*, on the other hand, establishes a daily or weekly hours threshold. An employee may work beyond this hours limit, but must be paid a premium wage—that is, more than the hourly rate of pay—when doing so.

Finally, *night-work laws* prohibit an employee from working during a certain number of specifically delimited hours in the evening, night, and early morning.

Each state could adopt some or all of these six laws. In addition, three of these legal regulations—those establishing minimum wages, overtime, and equal pay standards—have been incorporated into the Fair Labor Standards Act.

DIMENSIONS OF LEGISLATION

A complete investigation of the development of wage and hour standards legislation would analyze six dimensions of these laws:

1. *Adoption*: whether a law was enacted by a political unit;
2. *Coverage*: the portion of the population covered under a law;
3. *Standard*: the legal standard established in the law;
4. *Enforcement*: the enforcement mechanisms provided by the law;

5. *Implementation*: the degree to which the law was actually enforced; and

6. *Impact*: the impact of the law on the relationship between employers and employees in the labor market.

The first four characteristics are aspects of law on the books; they constitute the formal dimensions of legislation. The last two aspects capture features of the law in practice; they measure government commitments to and actual success in altering the relationship between employers and employees.

I restrict my attention to the formal provisions of legislation for several reasons. First, they are a better indicator for our purposes than others typically used in policy research. For our purposes data on the level of expenditures allocated to programs within a variety of policy domains, which is perhaps the most frequently encountered indicator of public policy outcomes, are less than ideal. (Aaron, 1967; Cowart, 1969; Dawson, 1967; Dawson and Robinson, 1963; Dye, 1966; Fry and Winters, 1970; Hofferbert, 1966; Pryor, 1968; Sharkansky and Hofferbert, 1969; Wilensky, 1975 are a representative group of studies using the expenditures approach.) Expenditure data, while they convey one facet of implementation, and, as a consequence, one dimension of the commitment of the state to realize its legislative goals, are one step removed from the content of any particular piece of legislation. Of course, it is hypothetically possible to disaggregate expenditures by piece of legislation; yet, at a practical level, this is not a realistic option. Because many programs are funded as part of a general allocation to an agency, department, or functional area, it is extremely difficult to determine how much funding is actually used to implement the rights embodied in one piece of legislation. Moreover, when the policy domain is one in which the state allocates rights (that is, regulative legislation) rather than goods, services, or payments (that is, distributive or redistributive legislation) (Lowi, 1969), state expenditures do not best reflect the extent of implementation.

Moreover, it is also extremely difficult to arrive at meaningful conclusions about whether the laws were actually enforced and had an impact on relationships in the labor market without a prior investigation into the scope and comprehensiveness of their formal provisions. We need to know who was covered and what kind of protection they received, for example, before we can assess whether a law accomplished its purpose. Even several early studies of the impact of these laws in a few states acknowledged the necessity of developing adequate measures of the formal dimensions of legislation in order to study its impact accurately (Beyer, 1929; Winslow, 1928). More recently, studies of the impact of minimum wage laws on employment and earnings have failed to construct such measures. Critics of such studies have pointed correctly to this methodological flaw as one important reason why research results are sometimes inconclusive and often contradictory (Goldfarb, 1974; Kaitz, 1970).

Third, historical census data at the level of detail necessary to measure impact successfully are simply not available. Consequently, any legal impact study (Lempert, 1966) would have to be limited to those few states for which such data exist. The early studies mentioned above, for instance, attempted to ascertain the employment effects on women of hours laws in several industries in two or three states (Nelson, 1921; Peterson, 1959; Obenauer and Von Der Nienburg, 1915; U.S. Department of Labor, Women's Bureau, 1921, 1938). These studies have been criticized for several reasons (Hill, 1979); one major reservation points to the difficulty of accepting findings for a set of industries in a few states as representative of the entire range of impact of these laws across states and over time. Again, an impact study on a representative sample of industries, states, and times awaits the prior investigation of the range of provisions embodied in these laws. Finally, the examination of formal dimensions of legislation constitutes a formidable task in itself. It also provides a unique opportunity to address empirically basic concerns about state activity that have previously only been treated theoretically.

In order to depict the distribution of formal social rights to employees, I further restrict the description and analysis to the first three dimensions listed above: adoption, coverage, and legal standard.

Adoption of legislation—expressed as a dummy variable (Gilbert, 1966; Goldfarb, 1974 who criticizes this approach; Moore, Newman, and Thomas, 1974; and Palomba and Palomba, 1971) or in terms of the year of enactment (Collier and Messick, 1975; Cutright, 1965; Gray, 1973; McVoy, 1940; Walker, 1969)—is a common indicator of legislation. If used as the only indicator, adoption can convey a misleading impression of legal development; it implicitly assumes both that the content of legislation at adoption is invariant across states and that growth after adoption in unimportant. Obviously, these assumptions rest on extremely shaky foundations; it is unclear what the results of studies using such indicators tell us about public policy outcomes or about the process of legislative change. An indicator of adoption does locate the activity of one state in relation to all states and does gauge the speed with which reforms initially diffuse throughout the political system. Therefore, I examine time of adoption, but add to it an analysis of two dimensions of the *content* of laws—coverage and standard.

These dimensions and their measurement are discussed in detail in the next sections of this chapter.

Finally, while I collected information on the enforcement provisions of these laws, I did not analyze these data for three reasons. First, the enforcement provisions were extremely general, and second, the enforcement mechanisms included in these laws varied little among the states. Before 1930, most wage and hour standards laws simply provided employees the right to go to court. In some states, the law allowed a government enforcement officer to seek out violations and initiate court action proactively; in other states, the employee could make a complaint that would then be taken to court by the appropriate administrative official. Some state laws even lacked a section on enforcement. After 1930, the enforcement procedures began to change: administrative agencies were now specified as the forum for resolving disputes and processing violations. With the development of modern administrative law such functions were removed from the courts. The law looked to the courts only as a last resort. This administrative procedure was quite uniform across laws. Thus, any attempt to depict provisions on enforcement would have been based on these very general procedures. Any measure developed from the laws would necessarily have been crude. Third, and perhaps most important, given the considerations just mentioned, the costs in time and money of putting this information into an analyzable form would have been prohibitive.

In summary, this study focuses on three dimensions of the formal provisions of six wage and hour standards laws: adoption, coverage, and standard. The coding of coverage and standard and the development of time series data involve an elaborate process of selecting a sample of states, collecting legal information, selecting a sample of years, creating coding rules, and constructing a set of population weights. The remainder of this chapter provides a detailed description of each step of this complicated method of distilling legal provisions into a single quantitative indicator consistent across states, over time, and, as we will see below, across subpopulations of employees.

STATE SAMPLE

The sample of states consisted of twenty-eight of the forty-eight states admitted to the United States by 1930. I selected the six states with the largest population in 1930 and one-half of the remaining states, divided by region, and drawn by means of systematic sampling procedures.[2]

Including all of the more populated states reduces the sampling error of the estimates of the regional and national indices. Yet, because it biases the state sample in the direction of including more heavily populated states, the results of the cross-state analysis on the correlates of legislative change should be approached with some caution. Note, however, that although different data transformations changed the frequency distribution of the legal indicators, they never changed the direction or strength of the results. Therefore, I am reasonably secure that this sampling procedure did not seriously distort the state-level results.

The following states were included in the sample (states with an asterisk were selected because of population size):

Northeast	South	North Central	West
Maine	Delaware	*Ohio	Montana
Vermont	Virginia	Michigan	Idaho
Rhode Island	North Carolina	*Illinois	New Mexico
*New York	Georgia	Wisconsin	Arizona
New Jersey	Kentucky	Iowa	Oregon
*Pennsylvania	Alabama	North Dakota	*California
	Arkansas	Nebraska	
	Oklahoma		
	*Texas		

COLLECTION OF INFORMATION FROM LEGAL RECORDS

After selecting the laws and the sample of states, I turned next to legal records. This information was gathered from several sources. The primary source for *state* wage and hour laws was the annual or biennial state statute books. Information collected from four additional sources served as a check on the accuracy and completeness of the survey of state statute volumes: the compiled or consolidated codes for each state;[3] the *Annual Review of State Labor Legislation* compiled by the United States Bureau of Labor Statistics; bulletins on the provisions of wage and hour laws periodically published by the Women's Bureau of the United States Department of Labor; and a single compendium: *The Growth of Labor Laws in the United States* (U.S. Department of Labor, Bureau of Labor Standards, 1967). The primary source on *federal* wage and hour laws was the *Annual Statutes at Large*. In addition, federal laws enacted prior to 1938 were consolidated in *Compilation of Labor Laws* (1941). Precise information on the changing definitions of coverage under the Fair Labor Standards Act was found in *Federal Labor Laws: A Looseleaf System Containing Laws Administered by the Wage and Hour Division with Regulations and Interpretations* (U.S. Department of Labor, Employment Standards Administration, 1974).

Extensive notes on all legislative activity pertaining to *which* employees were to be covered and *what* term or provision of the employment contract was specified were compiled from the primary sources for the twenty-eight states and the federal government. Each time we located some legislative action,[4] we recorded the year of action and the scope of or change in the provisions of the law. Through this procedure, we compiled a state-by-state and year-by-year profile of the content of each of six laws as of the year a legislative change occurred.

Once this comprehensive review of the primary sources was completed, detailed notes on state and federal legislation were taken from the secondary sources. We then compared the notes from all sources and discovered that overall less than 1 percent of the cases were inconsistent. To make sure that all inconsistent cases were dealt with similarly, I applied the following rule: if the provision of a law in question could not be located in the primary source, it was not included in the data set. Since the percentage of inconsistencies was so low, I am highly confident that these records formed a reliable base from which to generate the final time series data on the legal provisions.

SELECTION OF TIME SERIES DATA POINTS

In a cost-free world, I would have developed annual time series data. Instead, I measured coverage and legal standard at five-year intervals between 1900 and 1970 and in 1973, the most recent year of legislation it was possible to collect. In addition, for nine intermediate years the changes in these laws caused by (1) major historical crises (1918, 1937, 1938, 1943, 1947); (2) periods of heavy legislative activity (1913, 1937, 1938); and (3) the passage of major federal legislation (1937, 1938, 1961, 1966) were assessed with greater precision. Therefore, the time series data include twenty-four observations between 1900 and 1973.

I selected 1900 as the first data point because it was early enough to capture most of the growth in these laws. Although an earlier starting date would have allowed exact measurement of the growth of wage payment/wage collection and maximum hours laws in the early-adopting states, it would have meant sacrificing the precise measurement of change occurring in most states during the intermediate years. On the other hand, a later starting date would have resulted in a loss of detail on a major early period of growth of these laws between 1900 and 1920 (Baker, 1925; Brandeis, 1935; Commons and Andrews, 1936). In general, this decision proved to be reasonable.

To be sure, annual time series data would have allowed for a more refined analysis of the data, especially in Chapter 8. Since the two time series on legal provisions are cumulative, however, the contours of growth in these laws can be grasped by combining the nine intermediate data points with the more regular measurement of change at five-year intervals.[5]

CODING RULES FOR LEGAL INFORMATION

To construct a final set of time series data on coverage and standard, I reduced the somewhat complicated provisions of the law to a single quantitative measure consistent across states, across laws, and over time. This involved, as a first step, converting legal information on *which* employees were covered to an estimate of *how many* employees were covered. This was not an easy task. Laws were written, for example, with specific reference to the industrial composition of a state. Definitions of employee groups changed periodically. For instance, early hours legislation frequently referred to "laborers and workmen" engaged in "mechanical and manufacturing industries"; in current terminology, this refers to employees in mining, construction, and manufacturing enterprises (Ware, 1958, 1964). Moreover, if the text of these laws is any indication, the scope of their coverage was the object of intense political controversy, not just at the time of adoption, but throughout their history. It appears that the struggle over coverage centered around how limited and contingent a law could be made; rare indeed was the law extending coverage to all employees. The struggle over standards was likewise fraught with attempts to decrease the restrictions placed on employers. Bargaining took place over such issues as the age and sex of covered employees, the occupations or industries to be regulated, the size and location of firms subject to these government constraints, and the length of time the standards were to remain in effect. In an extremely restrictive law, for example, coverage might be limited to female minors 14 to 17 years of age in manufacturing and retail trade firms employing at least four employees. Similarly, the standard established in a minimum wage law often varied by employee and firm characteristics: for example, there was often one minimum wage for manufacturing employees and a second, lower, rate for restaurant employees. In developing estimates of coverage and standards, therefore, it was necessary to separate out employee groups by age, by sex, and by occupation or industry and develop a set of detailed rules for coding the provisions of these laws within these categories.

The coding rules addressed three general areas in which consistent decisions needed to be made: first, basic simplifying definitions—concerning laws, the year of legal activity, and the scope and disaggregation of the employee population; second, rules for coding employee coverage; and third, rules for coding the legal standard. In this section, I present a broad overview of the coding procedure and several examples illustrating the application of the rules. (See Ratner, 1977a for a complete set of coding rules.)

GENERAL SIMPLIFYING DEFINITIONS

Several definitions were introduced to simplify the coding of coverage and standard. First, concerning the laws: for the purpose of consistency, only those laws listed in the consolidated codes under the chapter entitled "Labor Law" (or its equivalent) were included. As a result, I excluded labor standards laws incorporated in the chapters compiling public health and civil service legislation; administrative or executive orders establishing wage and hour standards; and sections in state constitutions that were not separately enacted in legislation. This restriction on the range of laws actually eliminated very few regulations.

A more difficult issue concerned the treatment of federal legislation. Coverage under federal legislation could have been coded by treating it as completely separate from state laws. This would have required two coding sheets per law per state for the three labor standards acted on by Congress. Not only would this have been a costly approach, it would have ignored the important linkage between standards in the federal law and those found in state laws. What happens, for instance, when state and federal minimum wage laws cover the identical employee population? While an employee would then have access to both state and federal agencies for enforcement, the social right to protection need only be acknowledged once. I therefore chose to treat the source of the coverage and standard as secondary to the fact that protection existed and used the more stringent of the two standards for purposes of coding. When a federal law was passed, it was treated for coding purposes as if a state law had been enacted in each of the twenty-eight states. As will be seen in Chapter 4, because I knew the years of federal legislative activity in the area of wages and hours, it was fairly easy to separate out the contribution to coverage of federal and state legislation.

A second set of definitions concerns the year of legislative activity. If a law was enacted in the interval between two data points (year 1 . . . year 5), it was coded as having occurred in the last year of that interval. In addition, I considered a law to be operating from January of the year of passage and not from the statutory effective date.

Third, because of the way the scope of coverage under these laws was defined, I divided the employed population into thirty subgroups by demographic group and by industry or occupation categories. Employees were divided by sex and into two age groups: adults and minors. Minors were defined as those between 14 and 20 years of age inclusive. To separate out employees by industry and occupation, I borrowed the two-digit Standard Industrial Classification (SIC) and modified it to take into account the sex composition of a category. Specifically, since there were few male domestic service workers and virtually no female miners or construction workers, I eliminated these as employee categories (Anderson and Davidson, 1940; U.S. Department of Commerce, 1975). I also added clerical occupations as a distinct category. Prior to 1940, clerical occupations had been a separate industrial category; wage and hour laws treat them in this manner. Consequently, employees were classified in terms of nine industry/occupation categories: eight for males (adult and minor) and seven for females (adult and minor):

Female (adult and minor)	*Male (adult and minor)*
Agriculture (forestry, fishing)	Agriculture (forestry, fishing)
Manufacturing	Mining
Transportation/ communication/public utilities	Contract construction
	Manufacturing
Trade	Transportation/ communication/public utilities
Personal service	
Clerical	Trade
Domestic service	Personal service
	Clerical

Two categories of employees were excluded: (1) owners/managers; professional, executive, and administrative employees; and (2) public employees. A majority of these laws exempt from coverage salaried employees, that is, those in the first category. Minimum wage laws excluded this category almost without exception, and recent maximum hours laws also specifically exclude women in this category.

The decision to exclude public employees was made on both theoretical and practical grounds. This research examines the conditions under which government intervenes in the employment relationship on behalf of subordinate groups. The case of public employees falls outside of this type of employment relationship: it conforms more closely to one in which an employer—the government—arbitrarily sets the terms of the employment contract *for* employees. In addition, many of the laws applicable to public employees were not in the chapter on labor in the state codes. This made them difficult to locate, and consequently, I was uncertain whether I had found all the laws covering public employees. Under the circumstances, it seemed best to drop this category of employees from the sample.

The resulting thirty age-by-sex-by-industry categories formed the coding matrix for coverage and standard for each of six laws in each of the twenty-eight states. Coverage was estimated *within* each of these thirty groups for each of the twenty-four time points. Figure 2.1 presents this thirty by twenty-four coding matrix.

WITHIN-CELL RULES FOR EMPLOYEE COVERAGE

Even this thirty-category breakdown of the employee population could not fully capture the detailed specification of the scope of coverage found in these laws. Consequently, it was necessary to estimate the *extent of coverage* within a coding category or cell. Five major types of restrictions were encountered:[6] first, coverage was usually limited to a subset of employees falling within the more general demographic-occupation group category. The scope of coverage under a law could be extended to a subset of minors, as for example, all minors 14–17 years of age. Or, it could be defined in terms of very specific industry categories such as employees in restaurants and hotels, telephone operators, railroad workers, and so on. Second, many laws treated coverage in terms of firm size and restricted the purview of the laws to employees in a firm with a certain minimum number of employees. Third, coverage was often restricted to employees in workplaces located in cities or counties with a population equal to or greater than a specified number. Fourth, laws could provide for the suspension of coverage under special conditions. Fifth, wage payment/wage collection laws and equal pay laws frequently extended different rights to different groups of employees. In addition, special procedures had to be developed to code coverage under federal legislation.

Special coding rules were developed to estimate the extent of within-cell coverage for each of these types of coverage restrictions. For the first three types, the basic procedure involved matching the employee population cate-

Figure 2.1. Coding Employee
Two Sheets per

Demographic group	Industry group	1900	'05	'10	'13	'15	'18	'20
Male adults	Agriculture[a]							
	Mining							
	Contract construction							
	Manufacturing							
	T/C/PU							
	Trade							
	Personal service							
	Clerical							
Female adults	Agriculture[a]							
	Manufacturing							
	T/C/PU							
	Trade							
	Personal service							
	Clerical							
	Domestic service							
Male minors	Agriculture[a]							
	Mining							
	Contract construction							
	Manufacturing							
	T/C/PU							
	Trade							
	Personal service							
	Clerical							
Female minors	Agriculture[a]							
	Manufacturing							
	T/C/PU							
	Trade							
	Personal service							
	Clerical							
	Domestic service							

[a] Agriculture, forestry, and fishing.

Coverage and Legal Standard
Law per State.

'25	'30	'35	'37	'38	'40	'43	'45	'47	'50	'55	'60	'61	'65	'66	'70	'73

gories enumerated in the laws with data gathered from the decennial census or from the Census of Manufactures. This enabled us to gauge the portion of all employees in each of the thirty coding cells who were covered under a law. Because the distribution of employees by demographic group and by occupation or industry group changed substantially over the twentieth century, we collected census data in 1910, 1930, and 1950 when appropriate and corrected the estimates.[7] Had these compositional changes not been taken into account, changes in coverage resulting from changes in the demographic and industrial distribution of the labor force would have been obscured and estimates of coverage seriously distorted.

A somewhat different set of procedures was used to code coverage for the final two types of limitations and for federal legislation.

Coding of Restrictions on Coverage

Age-industry restrictions. For those wage and hour laws providing coverage to some subset of minors, industries, or demographic groups in selected industries, we collected information from the decennial census closest to the year the law became effective on what percentage of the applicable coding cell was covered. Separate estimates were computed for males and females; and, as indicated, estimates were revised in 1910, 1930, and 1950 for laws enacted prior or up to these years. Several shortcuts were used in making these estimates. When a law provided coverage to male minors 14 to 15 years of age regardless of industry, for example, we located an estimate of all employed male 14 to 15 year olds as a proportion of all employed male 14 to 20 year olds. Despite the fact that the proportion of male minors varied across industries, we used the resulting figure as the coverage estimate in each of the eight categories for male minors. The amount of work that would have been required to estimate 14 and 15 year olds as a percentage of all minors in each industry group separately would have far exceeded the gain in accuracy. Moreover, even when a law specified coverage for a subset of minors in several industries, we based the coverage scores on the general estimates of the age distribution of minors.

In those cases in which a law extended coverage to a subset of minors in a specific industry, such as for instance to all 14 and 15 year olds employed in laundries, we used the following two-step method to estimate coverage: we computed the ratio of covered minors to all minors in the labor force. We then multiplied this general ratio by the percentage of all employed 14 and 15 year olds engaged in the covered industry. For example, to compute this estimate for a law covering employed 14- and 15-year-old females in laundries, we found that 7 percent of all employed female minors

were either 14 or 15 and 56 percent of all employed 14- to 15-year-old females in the personal service sector worked in laundries. Multiplying these
together, we concluded that 4 percent of female personal service employees
14 to 20 years of age were covered by this law. (Of course, if this law
had been passed before 1920, this estimate would have been adjusted using
population estimates from the 1930 and 1950 censuses.)

Firm size restrictions. To compute within-cell coverage under laws introducing coverage restrictions for firm size, we collected data from the Census
of Manufactures. For laws enacted or amended between 1960 and 1973, we
gathered data directly from the census tables. As with age-industry restrictions, when the firm size restriction was general across all categories, we
calculated one estimate for the labor force as a whole and applied it uniformly across categories.

Since the distribution of employees by firm size was first tabulated in
1962, a slightly different procedure had to be developed to compute coverage
when firm size restrictions were introduced in pre-1960 legislation. Specifically, we corrected these 1962 estimates with data on the average number
of employees per manufacturing establishment, computed at ten-year intervals, so as to take into account gross changes in firm size between 1900
and 1962 and gross variations in firm size by state.[8]

The coverage estimate was calculated using the following formula:

$$\frac{X_{CD}}{X_{1960}}(A_{1960}) = B_{DP}$$

where X_{CD} = the average number of employees per manufacturing
establishment in a specified state for the decennial year
closest to the date of passage of the legal provision;

X_{1960} = the average number of employees per manufacturing
establishment in a specified state for 1960;

A_{1960} = the estimate of the percentage of employees who work in
a firm with a specified minimum number of employees
or more for 1962;

B_{DP} = the estimate of the percentage of employees working in
firms with a specified minimum number of employees
or more for the date of passage of the legal provision.

Population size restriction. It was relatively easy to locate historical data
on the portion of the population within a state that resided in a city or
county of a certain population size. It was less easy, however, to move from
this information to an estimate of the percentage of employees in an industry

working within a city or county of a certain population size. To facilitate consistent coding of these legal provisions, we assumed that firms disproportionately locate in urban areas, and that workers would therefore constitute a disproportionately greater fraction of this urban population than is reflected in data on population by city size. Consequently, we developed the following rule involving the percentage ranges used to code a final score for coverage (discussed in the section "Final Coverage Coding Score"): the coverage of employees under a law with a city size restriction was defined as the midpoint of the percentile range of the coding score one point higher than the coding score for the actual population size.

Suspension of coverage. Several laws, most notably maximum hours and night-work laws, included provisions allowing for suspension of coverage under certain conditions. These suspension clauses took one of three forms: the suspension of a law for a certain number of days per year, for a prescribed number of months per year, or for certain years. They characteristically applied to industries with peak seasons, such as fruit and vegetable canning factories or department stores, or were enacted in time of war.

These suspension clauses were treated as less complete coverage. We assumed that covered employees worked full time year-round and converted the period during which the standards were inoperative into a number of people-days or people-months per year. The percentage of the year during which these laws were inoperative was computed and subtracted from the extent of coverage within each coding cell.

Coverage differences resulting from multiple standards. As will be discussed in greater detail in "Final Coverage Coding Score," the coding procedure for the standard in two of the laws—wage payment/wage collection and equal pay—involved counting the number of procedural requirements instituted through the law. In several of the laws, some of the requirements were extended to all covered workers; others pertained only to a subgroup of employees. To compute a single measure of the extent of coverage under a law for each coding cell, we calculated an estimate of average coverage by weighting the percentage covered by the number of rules that applied to that percentage, as follows:

$$\frac{(X_A)(A) + (Y_B)(B),}{(A) + (B)} = PC$$

where PC = the average percentage of employees covered;
X_A = the percentage of employees covered under Standard A;
A = Standard A;
B = Standard B;
Y_B = the percentage of employees covered under Standard B.

Federal legislation. Coverage under the federal Fair Labor Standards Act was written in general terms to encompass employees engaged in "interstate commerce." For a definition of which employees qualified under this criterion, it was necessary to turn to the legislative history, judicial decisions, administrative rulings, and, most important, the national estimates of coverage provided by the United States Department of Labor.[9] These national estimates were used as the basis for estimating coverage at the state level.

The estimates are organized by the two-digit Standard Industrial Category; they were not disaggregated by the age or sex of the employee. This made it necessary to treat the estimates by occupation or industry as if they were identical for males and females and for adults and minors. Furthermore, separate estimates for clerical workers were not provided. Using the midpoint rule discussed in the section "Final Coverage Coding Score," we estimated that coverage for clerical workers was approximately 40 percent in 1938, 55 percent in 1961, and 70 percent in 1966, the years of the enactment of and major amendments to the FLSA. In general, since the final coding score groups extent of coverage into percentile ranges, basing estimates of coverage at the state level on national figures was not expected to raise any major problems.

Examples of Coding Coverage

A Kentucky maximum hours law covered employed females 21 and over in the following industries: laundries; bakeries; manufacturing; retail stores or mercantile establishments; hotels; restaurants; telephone and telegraph employees. Coverage was coded as follows: first, the law extended to 100 percent of adult females in manufacturing. Bakery and retail trade establishments were both grouped under trade. In 1910, 95 percent of all females in trade were employed in either retail trade or bakeries. When the distribution of the labor force within a coding cell was recalculated for 1930, the percentage of females in these occupations decreased to 90; in 1960, 72 percent of females in trade were employed in either retail trade or bakeries. Moreover, in 1910, females employed in telephone companies constituted 83 percent of all females employed in transportation, communication, and public utilities (T/C/PU); only 6 percent of all females in T/C/PU were employed in telegraph companies. Consequently, 89 percent of all females in T/C/PU were covered under the Kentucky maximum hours law. In 1930, 83 percent of all female T/C/PU employees worked in telephone or telegraph companies; in 1960, the percentage of females employed in these covered occupations dropped to 51. A similar procedure was followed for the occupations in the personal service category (that is, laundry, hotel,

and restaurant employees). In this way it was possible to estimate the
extent of coverage within a coding cell for which there was less than
complete coverage.

Between 1917 and 1921, the New York State legislature amended a maximum hours law to restrict coverage to females in factories and mercantile
firms with 6 or more employees. First, we adjusted the 1962 estimates of
firm size using data on the average size of manufacturing establishments in
1920 and 1950. In 1920, the average firm size in manufacturing was 30;
the 1960 average firm size was 39.5. In 1962, 97 percent of all employees
in manufacturing worked in firms with 8 or more employees. (Eight employees was the firm size category listed in the census that was closest to
the cutoff point established in the law.) The adjusted firm size percentage
was computed as:

$$\frac{30}{39.5} (97) = 73.6\%.$$

To adjust the percentage for mercantile establishments, we used the same
adjustment ratio as in manufacturing (that is, 30/39.5). In 1962, 74 percent
of all employees in trade worked in firms with 8 or more employees. The
adjusted firm size percentage thus equals:

$$\frac{30}{39.5} (74) = 56.2\%.$$

Since mercantile employees are a subset of female adults in trade, we further
adjusted the score for mercantile employees by multiplying 56.2 percent by
the percentage of mercantile employees in trade. In making these calculations, the 1910 estimate of mercantile employees was used to calculate
the 1918 coding score and the 1930 estimate to calculate the 1920 coding
score.

In maximum hours laws in New York and North Carolina, coverage of
mercantile establishments was suspended for thirty days each year, or approximately 10 percent of the working year. Therefore, mercantile employees
were covered under the law for 90 percent of the year. (This percentage
was of course multiplied by the percentage of all trade employees engaged
in retail trade.) Similarly, another New York State hours law allowed for
the suspension of coverage in fruit and vegetable canning industries for up
to four months. To code this, we first estimated the percentage of all
females in manufacturing engaged in the canning of fruits and vegetables.
We then multiplied that percentage by 67 percent to take into account the
period for which the law was suspended.

A 1913 Texas maximum hours law covered females employed in the following occupations and industries: manufacturing; mercantile establishments; dressmaking and millinery establishments; hotels, restaurants, and theaters; telephone or telegraph offices. The extent of coverage, however, was limited to employed females in cities with a population of 5,000 or more. In Texas in 1920, 28 percent of the population lived in cities with a population of 5,000 or more. Using the coding rule on city size restrictions, we estimated that 40 percent of employed females in any occupation or industry worked in these cities. Forty percent constitutes the midpoint of the percentile range one score above 28 percent. We also estimated that in 1910 the percentage of two-digit SIC employees who worked in the occupations and industries specified by the law was:

Legally specified occupation/industry	Two-digit SIC	Percentage covered
Manufacturing	Manufacturing	100
Mercantile Dressmaking and millinery	Trade	94
Hotels Restaurants Theaters	Personal service	35
Telephone Telegraph	T/C/PU	90

Consequently, to take the city size restriction into account, we multiplied the immediately preceding coverage estimates by 0.40. Estimates were revised in 1920 and 1950 to correct for changes in the distribution of employees within coverage coding cells.

Final Coverage Coding Score

The preceding set of coding rules was developed to treat consistently the types of restrictions in coverage prevalent in wage and hour laws. For each of the thirty coverage coding categories, we estimated what percentage of all employees were covered. Because these estimates of the employee population were based on adequate, but not precise, data on the distribution of the labor force, we decided to translate the obtained percentages into a 0 to 7 coding score indicating a percentile range of employees. The coding scores reflect the following percentile ranges:

0 = none covered, no law, or less than 1%
1 = a few: 1–9%

2 = sizable: 10–29%
3 = many low: 30–49%
4 = many high: 50–69%
5 = most: 70–89%
6 = all but a few: 90–99%
7 = all specified or greater than 99%

For each year we indicated the extent of coverage by placing the appropriate 0–7 score in each of the thirty coding cells, repeating the procedure for each of the six laws. Even with this percentage range, additional rules had to be developed to ensure consistency in coding across laws and states. First, a rule was developed to select a coding score when the extent of employee coverage fell on the borderline of two scores (that is, 10%, 30%, 50%, and so on) and when we were uncertain of the precision of the employee population estimate. In these instances, we picked the score reflecting the lower percentile group (that is, 9%, 29%, 49%, and so on). By following this rule, we decreased the possibility of inconsistent coding of difficult cases, and I feel reasonably confident that any bias in these estimates is in the direction of *slightly* underestimating (by 1 to 2 percentage points) the percentage of coverage.

Second, the detail with which coverage was specified in many of these laws made it necessary to add together several estimates of population subgroups within a coding cell. Some of these population estimates were especially imprecise—as for example firm size restrictions or certain age or industry groups. In these cases, we ascertained as precisely as possible which of these 0 to 7 percentage ranges most closely approximated the extent of covered employees. We then defined, for computational purposes, the portion covered as the midpoint of the appropriate 0 to 7 score. Since the final index of employees covered involved a summation over some subset or all of the scores in the thirty coding cells, the final scores on the portion covered remained a continuous variable ranging from 0 to 100 percent. In other words, the use of percentage ranges and of the borderline and midpoint rules made the coding of imprecise data consistent without undermining the development of interval level data.

In summary, the procedure for scoring coverage essentially involved converting the provisions of each of the six wage and hour standards laws into 0 to 7 scores for each of thirty age-by-sex-by-industry categories for twenty-four points in time. These scores, based primarily on historical census data and on a series of assumptions about how to treat suspension and multiple standards, measured the extent of employee coverage within a coding cell.

CODING RULES FOR LEGAL STANDARD

The legal standard was also coded separately for each of the thirty age-by-sex-by-industry categories used to code extent of coverage. In other words, if at least 1 percent of the employees (coding score of 1 or greater) in a coding cell was covered under a law, some indicator of the legal regulation pertaining to them was placed in an equivalent coding cell category. Unlike coverage, in which, regardless of law, a score of 0 to 7 was placed in each coding cell, the indicators of legal standard varied according to the type of standard found in the law. Some laws were measured in terms of actual numerical standards—time in hours or money in dollars—others in terms of the number of legal requirements.

Wage payment/wage collection laws. A complete WP/WC law bound the employer to follow seven conditions when paying employees for work rendered:

1. Payment in cash or legal tender;
2. Regular payday;
3. Specified maximum holdover period (between the time an employee worked and the time he or she received his or her wage);
4. Keep employees informed of time and place of payday;
5. Keep records of hours worked and wages paid;
6. Wage collection by a specified state administrative agency;
7. Prompt payment provision in case of an employer-employee dispute or an employee discharge.

We developed a cumulative index by counting the number of such requirements spelled out in a law. Consequently, any coding cell has a 0 to 7 score.

Minimum wage laws. The standard in this law was scored as the *amount* (in constant dollars) of the statutory minimum. The following formula was used to compute constant dollars:[10]

$$\frac{100(LS/MW)_A}{CPI_A} = (\text{Adj}/LS/MW)_A$$

where LS/MW = the average legal standard under the minimum wage law for a particular year;

$\quad\quad\quad CPI$ = the consumer price index price deflator for a particular year;

$\text{Adj}/LS/MW$ = the adjusted average legal standard under the minimum wage law for a particular year;

$\quad\quad\quad A$ = the particular year.

If the law provided for a wage board procedure rather than a statutory minimum, the legal standard was scored *as if* a $0.01 minimum wage had been enacted. This one-cent score indicated that the legislation provided *no* specific, uniform wage standard for the employee groups covered by the law. If the same law provided both a statutory minimum rate and a wage board procedure for the same employees, we coded *only the stipulated statutory minimum*. If two different minimum wage laws (for example, one state and one federal) provided for a wage board procedure and a statutory minimum respectively, we used a weighted average procedure described below to obtain the average minimum wage for all covered employees. In coding for minimum wage laws, *the legal standard enacted in the federal law always took precedence over the legal standard enacted in the state law.*

Maximum hours laws. We scored the standard as the *number of hours per week* beyond which an employee was prohibited from working. If a maximum hours law included both a weekly hours limit and a daily hours limit, we always scored for the weekly limit (even if the weekly hours ceiling totaled less than the product of the hours per day times the days per week limit specified in the law).

Night-work laws. A night-work law listed an hour in the early evening after which an employee was required to stop working and an hour in the early morning before which an employee could not start working. A coding score was developed by converting these time boundaries into the *number of hours* that covered workers are prohibited from working.

Overtime laws. Overtime laws established an hours limit—that is, after employees had worked a specified number of hours per week, employers were required to pay them a premium wage. The premium rate was almost always one and one-half times the regular rate. Since these laws regulated hours, the standard was coded as the *number of hours* beyond which premium pay was required.

Equal pay laws. To code the equal pay standard, we developed a cumulative index of the number of ascribed characteristics for which it was illegal for an employer to discriminate against an employee in compensation. The law identified as few as one or as many as five clusters of ascribed characteristics: sex; age; race, color, or creed; religion, national origin, ethnic origin, or ancestry; other, such as physical handicap, marital status, or draft status. The coding score ranged from 0 to 5, depending on the number of characteristics listed in a law.

Weighted Average Rule for Multiple Standards

When only one legal standard applied to all covered employees within a coding cell, the procedure for scoring the standard was straightforward. In many instances, however, standards applied to different groups of employees within the same coding cell. For example, in states that had both federal and state minimum wage and overtime laws, the state law frequently covered more employees than the federal law. The standards provided in these laws differed for covered employees within the same coding cell. Similarly, in maximum hours and night-work laws, standards established for older minors (16–18) were often less restrictive than standards established for younger minors (14 and 15). In addition, the same employees could be covered by different standards at different times of the year, for different days of the week, or even during different hours of the day.

As with coverage, it was necessary to compute an average legal standard using a weighted average procedure. The general formula for this weighted average is:

$$\frac{(X_A)(A) + (Y_B)(B)}{X_A + Y_B} = ALS$$

where ALS = average legal standard for covered employees;

X_A = the portion of employees covered under Standard A or the portion of the year, week, or day in which Standard A is in effect;

A = Standard A;

Y_B = the portion of employees covered under Standard B or the portion of the year, week, or day in which Standard B is in effect;

B = Standard B.

Three examples illustrate the use of this weighted average procedure.

Separate standards for subgroups within a coding cell. A 1968 amendment to the 1947 Michigan night-work law is representative of other hours legislation providing separate standards for minors of different ages. It revised the hours standards applicable to male and female minors 14 to 17 years of age. For industries other than manufacturing, one set of standards was established for 14 and 15 year olds and a second set for 16 and 17 year olds. Specifically, 14- and 15-year-old minors were prohibited from working between 10:30 P.M. and 6:00 A.M. or for 7.5 hours. Males and females 16 to 17 years of age were prohibited from working between 11:30 P.M. and 6:00 A.M. or for 6.5 hours. The coding score was calculated separately for males and females because of differences by sex in the age composition of employed minors. In 1960, 11 percent of all employed 14- to 20-year-old males were 14 to 15 years of age; 32 percent of all employed 14- to 20-year-old males were 16 to 17 years of age. The average legal standard for male minors covered under this law was:

$$\frac{(.11)(7.5) + (.32)(6.5)}{(.11) + (.32)} = 6.76 \text{ or } 6.8 \text{ hours.}$$

In 1960, 9 percent of all employed females 14 to 20 years of age were 14 to 15 years of age; 26 percent of all employed females 14 to 20 years of age were 16 to 17 years old. The average legal standard for covered female employees 14 to 20 years of age was:

$$\frac{(.09)(7.5) + (.26)(6.5)}{(.09) + (.26)} = 6.76 \text{ or } 6.8 \text{ hours.}$$

Thus, for all industrial categories specified in the law, the average legal standard for employed female and male minors was scored as 6.8 hours.

Separate standards under state and federal minimum wage laws. In 1913, California enacted its first minimum wage law covering all employed females as well as employed male minors between the ages of 14 and 17. It specified a wage board procedure for establishing the minimum wage rate. This minimum wage law remained unchanged until 1972, when the wage board procedure was extended to all male employees as well. Let us review the procedure for coding the standard for female adults and minors.

Beginning in 1938, the effective date of the Fair Labor Standards Act, female adults and minors could be covered by two legal standards: those covered under federal legislation were to be paid $0.25 per hour; the remaining female employees had access to the wage board procedure (that is, a minimum wage of $0.01 per hour). Since coverage under the federal law varied substantially by industry, it was necessary to compute the average legal standard for each industry category separately. The percentages of female adults and minors covered under the federal minimum wage law in 1938, with the weighted average formulas used to compute the average legal standard, which were based on these coverage estimates, are shown in Table 2.1. The minimum wage rate established under federal legislation was raised in 1940 and 1947. Therefore, the average legal standard for females in 1940 and 1947 was adjusted using these same weighted average formulas but different wage rates. In 1961 and 1966, significant changes were made in the scope of coverage under the federal law. New population weights and new wage rates were introduced into the same weighted coverage formula. The results for 1966 are shown in Table 2.2.[11] In summary, for every change in the minimum wage rate or in coverage, it was necessary to recompute the average minimum wage rate for female adults and minors using a weighted average procedure.

Two standards covering the same employees. Certain states enacted maximum hours laws in which women were allowed to work more than the

Table 2.1. Average Legal Standard for
Minimum Wage for Women, 1938

Industry	Percent covered	Weighted average formula		Average legal standard
		Federal	State	
Agriculture[a]	0	100(.01)		$0.01
Manufacturing	83	83(.25) +	17(.01)	0.21
T/C/PU	77	77(.25) +	23(.01)	0.19
Trade	18	18(.25) +	82(.01)	0.05
Personal service	5	5(.25) +	95(.01)	0.02
Clerical	40	40(.25) +	60(.01)	0.11
Domestic service	0	100(.01)		0.01

[a]Agriculture, forestry, and fishing.

Table 2.2. Average Legal Standard for
Minimum Wage for Women, 1966

Industry	Percent covered	Average legal federal standard	Weighted average formula		Average legal standard
			Federal	State	
Agriculture[a]	45	$1.00	45(1.00) +	55(.01)	$0.46
Manufacturing	97	1.40	97(1.40) +	3(.01)	1.36
T/C/PU	98	1.40	98(1.40) +	2(.01)	1.37
Trade	63	1.15	63(1.15) +	37(.01)	0.73
Personal service	67	0.98	67(0.98) +	33(.01)	0.66
Clerical	70	1.31	70(1.31) +	30(.01)	0.92
Domestic service	0	0	100(.01)		0.01

[a]Agriculture, forestry, and fishing.

maximum workweek for a certain portion of the year. A 1927 amendment
to a New York maximum hours law permitted employers in manufacturing
establishments to ask their employees to work an additional 4.5 hours per
week as long as these additional hours did not add up to more than 78
hours a year. Put somewhat differently, this stipulation permitted manufacturers to retain their employees for 4.5 hours per week for 17.3 weeks
per year. In effect, the law included two maximum hours ceilings: a 54-

hour ceiling for 17.3 weeks of the year and a 49.5-hour ceiling for the
remaining 34.7 weeks of the year. The average legal standard for females
in manufacturing was computed as follows:

$$\frac{(17.3)(54) + (34.7)(49.5)}{(52)} = 50.99 \text{ or } 51.0 \text{ hours per week.}$$

CODING RELIABILITY

To establish that the coding procedure was replicable and the scores not
the product of the arbitrary judgments of any one coder, we followed a
simple procedure for determining the extent of interjudge agreement. We
randomly selected four of the twenty-eight states. Two coders independently
scored coverage for adults for each law in one state; the coverage for minors
for each law in a second state; the standard for adults for each law in a
third state; and the standard for minors for each law in a fourth state. We
computed the percentage of columns in which the two coders agreed and
found that interjudge agreement fell safely within the bounds of 95 percent
agreement:

State	Age group	Provision	Interjudge agreement
1	Adults	Coverage	0.98
2	Minors	Coverage	1.00
3	Adults	Legal Standard	0.99
4	Minors	Legal Standard	0.95

The average interjudge agreement on the coding of legislation in all four
states was 0.98.

GENERATING EMPLOYEE POPULATION MATRICES

To generate meaningful time series data on coverage and standard, it was
necessary to generate an additional data set describing the distribution of
the labor force according to the thirty-group age-sex-industry classification
for each year coded for each state. These state-by-state employee population
data matrices were then matched with the matrices of coverage and standard
as the final step in converting information on which employees were covered
into data on *how many* employees were covered. Moreover, these labor
force data allowed us to perform various summations—across some subset

or all of the thirty employee groups, over states, and so on—and gauge coverage and standard in more general terms. In this section, I describe the process of generating these employee population matrices.

These data on the distribution of the labor force by state were estimated from industry and occupation statistics found in the eight decennial censuses between 1900 and 1970. While such data sets have been developed nationally, this constitutes the first attempt to construct a labor force matrix at the state level (Durand, 1948).[12] The difficulties in computing these population decks, while not prohibitive, were formidable. First, there were many inconsistencies in definitions and collection procedures across censuses which made it necessary to introduce correction factors. The occupations listed under the two-digit SIC of personal service, for example, shifted a great deal. Second, the current SIC categories of mining, construction, and manufacturing were combined in a single industrial category—manufacturing and mechanical industries—between 1900 and 1930. Perhaps the most troublesome modification, for our purposes, was the elimination of clerical workers as a separate industrial category in 1940. Furthermore, since the census data on the labor force were available only by decade, some procedure had to be developed to estimate the distribution of the labor force for the other sixteen years in our sample of years.

Despite these serious shortcomings in the available data base, I regarded rough approximations of the labor force as preferable to either no measure of the relative weights of different employee groups, or another, even more inadequate, measure available at more frequent intervals, such as general population figures. As with the coding of the legal data, a set of rules and definitions was developed which we applied consistently to the census data. We went to great lengths to ensure that the final data matrices on employee population were not only consistent across decades, but were also an accurate reflection of the actual distribution of employees. The procedure described below resulted in a set of rough but highly adequate labor force population weights that, when combined with the legal data matrices, afford a good picture of the extent and distribution of social rights over the twentieth century.

The procedure for building a labor force population matrix for each state encompassed four tasks: converting the census definitions to those of our thirty-group categorizations; disaggregating clerical workers from the other SICs between 1940 and 1970; introducing adjustment ratios to correct for known inconsistencies in census collection procedures in different decades; and generating labor force estimates for noncensus years in our sample.

CONSISTENCY IN CENSUS DEFINITIONS

Although each census included a table listing the distribution of the labor force by age, sex, and industry, the age and industry classifications changed substantially across decades. (See Ratner, 1977a, Appendix F, for citations and detailed elaboration of all examples of inconsistencies.) Of course, for identical categories we simply collected the data. The many differences, however, required that we develop general computational rules as well as procedures for handling special inconsistencies.

General computational rules. First, we computed the number of adults as being equal to the total number of employees minus the total number of minors. For those decades in which employees 13 years of age or less were included in the general employment statistics, we subtracted this group from the total number of employees before calculating the number of adults. Second, we calculated the employment statistics for males and females separately. Finally, all the estimates of the number of employees in the labor force were made in terms of thousands of employees. Thus, when the number of employees in any of the thirty coding cells was less than 500, we rounded down and indicated that there were 0 employees; if the number of employees in that coding cell was between 500 and 1,000, we indicated that there was 1 employee.

Correction of industry definitions. We had to correct for two general types of inconsistencies: those in which SIC categories were modified, and those in which specific occupations were reclassified into a different SIC. First, to disaggregate industrial categories, we developed a set of state-by-state ratios of our modified SIC categories to the more inclusive census classification, which could be used to allocate the labor force according to our classification. For example, for 1900 to 1930 for male adults and minors, we had to allocate the census classification of manufacturing and mechanical pursuits into three of our categories—mining, manufacturing, and contract construction. Fortunately, the 1910 census included a detailed industrial breakdown that enabled us to compute what portion of all manufacturing and mechanical employees were in mining, manufacturing, and construction. These ratios were used to allocate data from the 1900, 1920, and 1930 censuses. For example, in California in 1910, 11 percent of male adults in manufacturing and mechanical pursuits were engaged in mining; 29 percent and 60 percent of that general group were employed in contract construction and manufacturing respectively. Using these ratios to calculate labor force estimates in 1900, we found that of the 142,000 males 21 years of age and over who were engaged in manufacturing and mechanical pursuits, the number of employees in mining, contract construction, and manufacturing were as follows:

Mining: $(.11) \times 142 = 15,600$
Contract construction: $(.29) \times 142 = 41,200$
Manufacturing: $(.60) \times 142 = 85,200$

A similar procedure was used to disaggregate female employees in domestic service and personal service in the 1900 and 1910 censuses. Second, to deal with the reclassification of specific industries, we arbitrarily assigned an industry to one of the categories. For those censuses in which it was grouped in the second category, we subtracted the number of employees in the specific occupation from the total number of employees in the second category and added this figure to the total number of employees in the first category. For example, in 1940, the industry category eating and drinking places was reassigned to trade from personal service. We grouped it with personal service. For 1940 through 1970, we subtracted the number of employees in eating and drinking places from the total number of employees in trade and added the number of employees in eating and drinking places to the total number of employees in personal service.

Consistency in definitions of age. Census classifications of age groups frequently cut across our adult-minor division, and we had to regroup these age data to conform with our categories. For example, the 1950 census grouped minor employees into the following age classes: 14–15; 16–17; 18–19; and 20–24. In this case, we had to estimate how many of the employees 20 to 24 years of age were 20 years old. Since we could find no data on the probable ratio of 20 year olds to 21–24 year olds in the labor force, we assumed an equal distribution of employees. Therefore, we computed the total number of minors as being the sum of 14–15 year olds, 16–17 year olds, 18–19 year olds, and (.20) times 20–24 year olds.

ESTIMATION OF CLERICAL WORKERS, 1940–1970

Clerical workers were dropped as a separate industrial category beginning with the 1940 census. This constituted one of the most difficult problems encountered in constructing population estimates. We computed the number of clerical workers per state by first calculating for the United States as a whole the percentage of employees within each SIC who were clerical workers. We calculated separate sets of percentages for males and females for each decade between 1950 and 1970.[13] The estimates for each sex were used for both adults and minors. We removed the appropriate number of clerical employees from each SIC and added together the clerical workers from each SIC to obtain an estimate of all clerical workers. To take an example: in Alabama in 1950, 166,000 male adults and 16,000 male minors were listed in the census as being employed in manufacturing. We estimated that 4 percent of these male manufacturing employees were clerical workers. Four percent of 166,000 is (after rounding) 6,600 employees. Consequently, we revised the estimate of male adult manufacturing employees downward to 159,000; we also recorded that 6,600 employees were clerical workers. For male minors, 4 percent of 16,000 employees or 600 employees were in clerical occupations. We adjusted the number of male minors in manufacturing to 15,000 and recorded that 600 employees were clerical workers. This procedure was repeated for male adults, female adults, male minors, and female minors for each industry category. We computed the total number of clerical employees by summing these separate estimates.

When the resulting data on the number of clerical employees were inspected, we noticed that in some of the more populated states for several of the demographic groups, the number of clerical employees shifted downward between 1930 and 1940. To correct for the probable underestimation of clerical workers resulting from our estimation procedure, we assumed the 1930 ratio of clerical workers to all other nonagricultural and non–domestic service employees had remained constant between 1940 and 1970 and used it to adjust our estimates. While this probably results in a slight underestimation of clerical employees, it seemed a better approach than uniformly to impose a national ratio for 1950 to 1970 on such varied states. Finally, for a few other states, the number of clerical workers for male and female minors decreased between 1930 to 1940 from 1 to 0 (that is, from 1,000 to less than 500). For these cases, we replaced all 0's between 1940 and 1970 with a 1. While the estimation of clerical workers is somewhat imprecise, I feel reasonably confident that the estimates are sufficient for generating state population weights to be used in conjunction with the legal data.

ADJUSTING THE TREND IN LABOR FORCE DATA

Several additional problems of employment statistics that result from changing definitions of employment and changing methods of enumeration have been identified by labor economists (Durand, 1948). We were able to adjust for some of these problems; for others, we simply acknowledge their existence. Two problems of comparability are the switch from the gainful worker concept to an employed worker concept and the over-enumeration of minors in the 1900 and 1910 censuses.

Gainful workers. Between 1900 and 1930, any person was considered to be an employed or gainful worker if she or he reported an occupation. Beginning in 1940, however, a much more rigorous definition was introduced in which both occupation and employment status (that is, whether or not currently employed) were enumerated. Labor economists have estimated that the change in definition results in labor force figures for the 1900 through 1930 censuses that are "too large" relative to the 1940 census (Durand, 1948:191). To adjust for this definitional change, we corrected the 1900 through 1940 estimates by using adjustment ratios developed by John Durand. These ratios varied by demographic group but not by industry (Durand, 1948:198). One set of adjustment ratios was applied uniformly for each industry group for 1900 through 1930, and a second set of ratios was applied uniformly for each industry group for 1940.

These adjustments had the greatest impact on figures for larger states. The discrepancy between the 1930 and 1940 census figures was, however, most marked in the more populated states; the adjustment ratios, therefore, were objectively most important in these states. Furthermore, we decided against developing a more detailed set of correction factors—either by state or by industry group nationally—because to do so would have required much additional work with a questionable gain in precision. Durand has defended this procedure by remarking that "the original statistics for the period 1890–1930 are so inexact that more elaborate adjustment procedures might not be worthwhile, even if more adequate information regarding employment conditions and other pertinent circumstances in each census year were available. The census snapshots of the labor market in those years were out of focus and no amount of processing can make the pictures clear" (Durand, 1948:200).

Overenumeration of minors. Comparisons among employed 14 to 20 year olds based on the 1900 to 1930 censuses are highly unreliable. Inconsistencies are found especially in the 1900 and 1910 censuses; labor economists have concluded that in these volumes there was an overenumeration of the child labor force (Durand, 1948:193). We did not attempt to adjust the data for three reasons: first, a simple inspection of our data matrices did not reveal the serious fluctuations in the numbers of employed minors that appeared in the national estimates. Second, we found the ratios between adults and minors in different industrial categories to be relatively constant for these early decades. Third, any adjustments would have been based on arbitrary correction factors, as labor economists have not developed any formula to correct for these inconsistencies (Durand, 1948:192–194).

INTERPOLATION OF CENSUS DATA

Finally, since the data gathered directly from the census contained estimates for only eight of our twenty-four years, we decided to interpolate these data to estimate the distribution of the labor force for the fifteen time points in between the decennial censuses up until 1970. For 1973, we computed labor force estimates by adjusting for the change in the general population by region between 1900 and 1973. We applied these adjustment ratios uniformly across the age, sex, and industry categories. The final set of labor force weights, then, included census data for each decade and interpolated data for the years between decades.

The entire procedure just described—collecting decennial census data with consistent age, sex, and industry categories for each decade, adjusting the decennial census data, and interpolating the data to get between-decade estimates—resulted in a thirty by twenty-four matrix containing, for each state, the number of employees in the labor force.

CONSTRUCTION OF THE FINAL TIME SERIES DATA

Thus far, the procedure for generating three types of data matrices has been described:

1. *Coverage matrix*: for each law for each state, a score indicating the extent of coverage within each of thirty age-by-sex-by-industry-group categories of employees for twenty-four years between 1900 and 1973. The 0 to 7 scores indicating coverage were converted into the following percentages:

Score	Percent
0	0
1	5
2	20
3	40
4	60
5	80
6	95
7	100

These percentages constitute the midpoint of the percentile ranges of each of the coding scores.

2. *Legal standard matrix*: for each law for each state, a score indicating the average legal standard for each of thirty age-by-sex-by-industry categories of employees for twenty-four years between 1900 and 1973.

3. *Labor force matrix*: for each state, the number of employees in each of thirty age-by-sex-by-industry categories for twenty-four years between 1900 and 1973.

Thus, the raw material out of which the final indicators were formed included, for each state, twelve 720-cell matrices describing the scope of the six laws and one 720-cell matrix of labor force data.

The final time series data were created first by matching a matrix of legal data with a matrix of labor force data to obtain the number of covered employees (NC) and the total legal standard (TLS) for covered employees. Second, at the state level, we summed NC or TLS over some subsets or all of the thirty age-by-sex-by-industry groups and divided the product by the appropriate labor force data to arrive at time series data on the portion of employees covered under a law and the average legal standard for covered employees. In addition, we computed regional and national estimates of portion covered and average legal standard in the same way, introducing the state sampling weights. (We never performed summations over time or over laws.) The general computational formulas were:

$$\sum_{i=1}^{i=n} \frac{(NC_1 + NC_2 + NC_3 + \ldots + NC_n)}{(LF_1 + LF_2 + LF_3 + \ldots + LF_n)} = PC_n; \text{ and}$$

$$\sum_{i=1}^{i=n} \frac{(LS_1 + LS_2 + LS_3 + \ldots + LS_n)}{(LF_1 + LF_2 + LF_3 + \ldots + LF_n)} = ALS_n;$$

where NC_i = number of employees covered in a particular age-by-sex-by-industry group;

LS_i = total legal standard for a particular age-by-sex-by-industry group;

LF_i = total number of employees in a particular age-by-sex-by-industry group;

i = 1 to n for each of the n age-by-sex-by-industry groups and each of the states summed over;

n = the appropriate employee population subgroup computed from the summation procedure, such as demographic group at the state, regional, or national level, the indus-

try group at the regional or national level, and all employees at the state, regional, or national level;

PC_n = portion of employees covered in terms of the appropriate employee population subgroup;

ALS_n = average legal standard in terms of the appropriate employee population subgroup.

Table 2.3 lists the summations performed by geographic level and employee population. The resulting 277 time series on the percentage of
employees covered and on the average legal standard for covered employees constitute the final data set used to analyze the rise of and growth
in wage and hour standards laws in the United States in the twentieth
century.

Table 2.3. Summations for Generating Time Series Data
on Legal Provisions for Six Wage and Hour Standards Laws

Geographic level	Summation across 30-cell employee category	Percentage of employees	Average legal standard for covered employees
State	Total—across all categories	×	×
	By demographic group[a]	×	
Region	Total	×	×
	By demographic group	×	
	By industry group[b]	×	
National	Total	×	×
	By demographic group	×	×
	By industry group	×	
	For each industry group— by demographic group	×	

NOTE: × indicates that time series data were computed for that category.
[a]Male adult, female adult, male minor, female minor.
[b]Agriculture, forestry, and fishing; mining; contract construction; manufacturing;
transportation, communication, and public utilities; trade; personal service; clerical;
domestic service.

SUMMARY AND CONCLUSIONS

In this chapter, the dimensions of wage and hour standards laws explored in this study and the procedure used to construct the dependent variables—the time series data indicating the scope of coverage and the extent of protection—have been described. Social indicators were developed to facilitate the systematic comparison of these laws and the presentation of somewhat complicated material. Since we are dealing with an enormous amount of legal data—six laws in twenty-eight states over a seventy-three-year period, this latter characteristic of a social indicators approach was especially important.

Most of this chapter reviewed the procedure for constructing the time series data. The six laws that established explicit labor standards were defined, and the rationale behind the selection of a sample of states and a sample of time observations was discussed. State and federal statute books, state and federal compiled codes, and other government documents were combed to locate all laws and amendments to these laws. Since we were able to locate at least two independent sources on this legal material, I am reasonably confident that the records that form the basis of the time series data encompass all legal changes in wage and hour standards laws.

Starting with the nearest sampling year *after* a law had been adopted, we coded the contents of the laws to indicate, first, the extent of coverage within each of thirty coding cells categorized by age, sex, and industry group, and, second, the legal standard embodied in the laws. Detailed rules were developed to ensure consistent coding of the legal data. The objective was to distill the somewhat complicated legal provisions specifying who is to be covered and what the legal standard is into a single quantitative indicator. We tested for the reliability of our coding procedure and found that the extent of interjudge agreement fell safely within the bounds of 95 percent agreement.

Next, we developed estimates of the distribution of the labor force by the age-by-sex-by-industry classification for the twenty-four years between 1900 and 1973. These labor force data served as *population weights* to be matched with the coded legal data. The estimation of the composition and distribution of the labor force required that we reorganize the census classification of employees to make it consistent over time and with our categorization, correct for inconsistencies in census collection procedures, and interpolate estimates on the distribution of the labor force for the years in our sample between the decennial censuses.

Finally, we created the time series data from three data matrices—the coverage matrix, the legal standard matrix, and the labor force matrix. The two basic indices constructed for each law were: (1) the percentage of all employees covered; and (2) the average legal standard for covered employees. The two sets of time series data were generated nationally, for the entire employee population as well as by demographic group and industry group; by region for all employees and by demographic group; and by state for all employees and by demographic group. These time series data form the basis for the analysis of legal change in the United States over the twentieth century, to which we now turn.

II

NATIONAL PATTERNS OF LEGISLATIVE CHANGE

3

EARLY LABOR STANDARDS
LEGISLATION
Women and Children First

From the vantage point of the 1970s, most American workers regard such social rights as the right to organize into unions, to be compensated for job-related injuries, to receive a minimum retirement income, to receive unemployment compensation, and to enjoy minimum terms and protections in the employment contract as stable, government-backed features of the society in which they live (Heclo, 1974; Wilensky, 1975). Yet, these and other welfare state programs are not ancient markings on our social map. Furthermore, if one looks beyond the mere existence of these programs to the actual rights and benefits embodied in them, one still finds much room for improvement. In short, the system of social rights in the so-called welfare state has been emerging over the twentieth century through a gradual process as legislation is adopted, amended, and interpreted in the courts.

In the three chapters of this section, the pattern by which labor legislation grew over the twentieth century is examined in detail. The six wage and hour standards laws neatly divide into two categories—early labor laws and modern labor laws. Early labor legislation includes wage payment and wage collection laws, maximum hours laws, and night-work laws. These laws grew out of state legislative action that began in the late nineteenth century and continued in the twentieth century; there was almost no federal legislation in this area.[1] Modern labor legislation includes minimum wage laws, overtime laws, and equal pay laws. These laws began to receive widespread acceptance at the state level during or subsequent to the Great Depression. These types of standards are also embodied in the Fair Labor Standards Act. This chapter looks at the patterns of adoption and growth in the early labor standards laws. The next chapter treats the patterns of change in modern labor standards laws, comparing them to the early laws as well. In Chapter 5, I assess systematically three determinants of growth under labor standards laws to ascertain their contribution to coverage.

BACKGROUND

Historical accounts differ over which years constituted the major period of legislative activity on the three early labor laws. Lawrence Friedman, for example, in his *History of American Law* (1973:492), identifies the decades between the close of the Civil War and 1900 as a period during which "an impressive web of legislation" accumulated. (See also Yellowitz, 1977.) Several other historians of labor legislation, however, isolate the first two decades of the twentieth century as the period during which the greatest legislative gains were made. John R. Commons and John B. Andrews, in *Principles of Labor Legislation* (1936:97), for instance, consider 1900 to 1930 to be the years of greatest reform, especially in the area of hours of labor for children. Elizabeth Brandeis, author of the definitive historical account of early labor legislation (1935), narrows even further—to between 1909 and 1917—the years when the greatest legislative strides were made. She remarks of hours legislation that while "the whole period 1909–1917 was a time of great activity, within that period the years 1911 and 1913 brought bumper crops of new hours laws and amendments to old ones. Thirty-nine states passed some of their legislation in this nine-year period, 24 of them took important action in this respect in 1911 or 1913" (Brandeis, 1935:474).

Except in Brandeis's work, "legislative gains" are defined narrowly as the adoption of new laws, with little attention paid to the content of the laws or their subsequent revision. As noted in Chapter 1, to the extent that content is mentioned, it is treated in terms of how many laws were amended, which occupational groups were covered, and what the modal, rather than the average, legal standard was. I use, instead, the indicators of adoption, coverage, and standard both to assess the competing statements about the key period of development and to provide a more complete picture of the pattern of growth in these laws. Several preliminary remarks about the three indices precede an examination of the trends.

DATA

In this analysis, we relied on three indicators of these laws: a national index of the portion of employees covered aggregated from the twenty-eight state indices, using state sampling weights; a national index of the average legal standard for covered employees, modified as described below; and a cumulative index of state adoption. While most studies measure adoption in terms of the effective date of the first law enacted in a legal domain (Walker, 1969), I define adoption somewhat differently; I consider a state to have adopted a law when a minimum of 1 percent of employees in that state is covered under a law for at least six years. (For MH, the coverage cutoff point was revised upward to remove the effect of a minor piece of federal legislation establishing maximum hours for a small group of construction workers.) This approach is preferable for two reasons: first, since the index of employee coverage does not register less than 1 percent coverage, this definition facilitates comparison between indices. Second, since the definition explicitly excludes from consideration laws that are empty of formal rights, it ensures that included laws have more in common than their titles. Following from this approach, when a law covered less than 1 percent of employees for six years (or for MH, 5 percent), it was considered to have been repealed. Since the cumulative index of state adoption also was based on the twenty-eight-state sample, sampling weights were introduced to generate an estimate of adoption for all states.

Finally, to compare the average legal standard across laws, we developed a measure of a maximum legal standard (or, a reasonable measure of "complete protection") and expressed the average standard as a percentage of the maximum standard. This transformed indicator of the standard provides a clearer reading of whether a change in the law resulted in its being strengthened or weakened and of how much change occurred. For WP/WC, the modified index of legal standard (MLS) indicates what portion of the seven possible procedures are provided in the law. For MH, we assumed, as a general rule, that the lower the hours ceiling, the stronger the legal standard. We estimated MLS as the deviation from complete lack of protection, defined to be an hours ceiling of eighty-four hours per week. For NW, MLS indicates what portion of twelve hours (of the evening, night, and early morning) covered workers are prohibited from working. Since these maximum or complete legal standards are somewhat arbitrary, but reasonable, benchmarks, the actual percentage listed is less meaningful than the change in direction of the standard.

INITIAL FINDINGS: PATTERNS OF ADOPTION AND
THE DISTRIBUTION OF RIGHTS

Table 3.1, which displays the cumulative percentage of state adoption and the percentage of employees covered for each of the three laws at ten-year intervals, reveals several patterns of interest.

Table 3.1. State Adoption and Employee Coverage
under Early Labor Legislation, 1900–1970
(in percent)

Year	State adoption			Employee coverage		
	WP/WC	MH	NW	WP/WC	MH	NW
1900	29	26	14	19	4	1
1910	53	58	50	27	7	3
1920	92	76	60	45	12	4
1930	92	84	58	48	12	4
1940	92	88	61	56	15	5
1950	92	92	86	62	18	5
1960	96	92	83	67	19	4
1970	96	62	92	76	15	4

ADOPTION

First, the pattern of adoption of laws by state is strikingly uniform across
the three early labor laws. A substantial minority of states had adopted
WP/WC (29%) and MH (26%) by 1900. While state adoption of NW
legislation lagged behind the other two laws, a roughly equal number of
states had adopted all three labor laws by 1910. In the decade 1910–1920,
more states passed WP/WC laws than MH and NW laws. By 1920, just
over 15 percent more of the states had adopted a WP/WC law than had
adopted either of the laws limiting hours: over 90 percent of the states had
adopted a WP/WC law, 76 percent an MH law, and 60 percent an NW
law. In general, however, the adoption of all early laws "took off" between
1900 and 1920.

After 1920, state adoption of course tapered off very rapidly. By 1940,
88 percent of the states had adopted an MH law, and over 90 percent of
the states had done so by 1950. Indeed, except for a spurt of adoption of
NW laws following World War II, state adoption of early labor laws tapered
off by 1950. The period of 1900–1920 is characterized by the extensive
acceptance of these new legal rights within a relatively short time span.
Adoption finally ceases some thirty years later with more than 85 percent
of the states having passed some law in each of these areas.

These data on state adoption support Brandeis's position, although I find the period 1900–1910 to be nearly as active as the decade she singles out. Commons and Andrews cast their net too widely. State adoption appears to be a much more intense process than they suggest. Furthermore, while Friedman is correct in concluding that "an impressive web of" laws was passed before 1900, he appears to confuse the first, trend-setting legislative activity with the enactment of these laws in the majority of states. This is not unusual among historians who dwell on the innovative without realizing that the fact of being an early adopter relative to other states renders a state atypical.

COVERAGE

The patterns of growth in employee coverage differ markedly from those in state adoption. For all three laws, coverage applies to only a small portion of the employee population. Second, the pattern of growth of coverage over time varies a great deal among these laws.

WP/WC laws covered 19 percent of the employee population by 1900; this represents a significant minority of that population, especially in comparison to the other two early laws. The right to WP/WC was continuously broadened over the entire seventy-year period, although coverage grew most rapidly during the period of greatest state adoption. During the decade 1910–1920, coverage increased by almost 20 percent. After state adoption began to level off, coverage continued to expand by approximately 5 percent per decade. Despite the fact that WP/WC laws were extended to more employees than any other early law, the percentage of employees included in the provisions of this law did not reach 50 until 1940. The extension of the rights embodied in WP/WC laws continues today, although at a snail's pace, with 76 percent of employees covered in 1970.

The data suggest a significantly different path of growth in coverage under MH and NW laws. At the peak of coverage, MH laws barely reached the level of coverage attained for WP/WC legislation in 1900. As was the case for WP/WC, coverage was expanded most rapidly during the period of state adoption. For MH, coverage grew from 4 percent of employees to 12 percent between 1900 and 1920, with slightly greater growth between 1910 and 1920. The portion covered by NW remained trivial, increasing from 1 percent to 4 percent in these same twenty years. Subsequent to the period of state adoption, coverage under MH expanded gradually until 1960, when coverage began to decline—a decline treated more fully in Chapter 6. At no time, however, was the right to a limited workweek extended to more than one-fifth of all employees. In the case of NW legislation, the lack

Table 3.2. Employee Coverage under
Early Labor Legislation, 1900–1970

Year	Total covered population (in thousands)		
	WP/WC	MH	NW
1900	5,031	1,147	388
1910	9,086	2,351	885
1920	16,475	4,427	1,448
1930	20,534	5,231	1,780
1940	22,932	6,301	2,055
1950	31,062	9,174	2,390
1960	35,242	10,210	2,328
1970	47,167	9,433	2,462

of growth is even more extreme, with the scope of coverage never extending above 5 percent of employees.

Of course, even a small percentage of a large base can represent a substantial absolute number. Thus, even the most restricted of these rights—NW—protected over 1 million employees by 1920 (Table 3.2). At the other extreme, the right to coverage under WP/WC applied to more than 47 million employees.

In summary, for each law, the portion of employees covered changed most rapidly during the same decades that first adoption by state legislatures was greatest. Coverage under WP/WC and MH continued to expand after state adoption had subsided, although the *pace* of expansion was greater for WP/WC than for MH. At one extreme, the rights embodied in WP/WC came, after seventy years, to be allocated to slightly more than three-quarters of all employees—only 20 percent fewer than the percentage of states that adopted this law. By contrast, 96 percent of employees remained *excluded* from coverage under NW. But, since 4 percent of employees translates into almost 2.5 million employees, the potential effect of even limited coverage is cast into relief.

PROCESS OF CHANGE: ADOPTION AND COVERAGE

The preceding findings suggest that there is a gap between the percentage of legislatures that have adopted each of these laws and the percentage of citizens to whom these rights are extended. For NW, the difference in the cumulative percentages of these two dimensions reaches 88. Even for WP/WC, however, where the discrepancy decreases over time, the difference at one time approached 50 percent. We can measure the process of growth and the gap between adoption and coverage more precisely by fitting a curve to these data. For each law, the twenty-four time points on state adoption and on the national aggregate coverage were fit separately, using the method of least squares to each of three functional forms: a logistic curve, a decaying exponential equation, and a linear function. (The raw data used in this analysis are listed in Table A.1 of the appendix.) Each equation corresponds to a different process of growth. In all three functional forms, time was the independent variable. The S-shaped logistic curve is

$$Y = \frac{K}{1 + 10^{(a - bt)}}$$

where Y = cumulative percentage of states that have adopted labor standards laws or of employees covered;

K = the asymptote or the point at which adoption subsides or at which the scope of employee coverage stops expanding;

b = rate of adoption or coverage;

t = time; and

a = the point of inflection or the year at which an increasing rate of change becomes a decreasing rate of change.

This equation expresses the following process of growth: the laws initially are accepted by a few trail-blazing states or extended to a small subset of employees. Subsequently, adoption or coverage snowballs, subsides, and reaches an equilibrium. By contrast, the decaying exponential curve, $1 - (Y/N) = e^{(-bt)}$ (where N = the number of states or the number of employees, and Y, b, and t are defined as in the logistic equation), describes a different process of growth. In this case, acceptance or coverage accumulates at a decreasing rate of change; thus, there is more adoption or coverage relative to the first process when the laws are initially being considered. However, as state adoption or employee coverage continues, fewer states adopt a law or fewer additional employees are covered each year. As with the logistic curve, adoption or coverage gradually levels off and reaches an equilibrium. Finally, the linear function, $Y = bt + a$, indicates that adoption or coverage never takes off or reaches an equilibrium. Rather, the initial rate of change in adoption or coverage remains constant throughout the period of growth. (Of course, since we are dealing with finite populations, for the rate of change to remain constant over a seventy-year period, the slope must be quite shallow.)

We used the R^2 statistic to choose between these equations. The higher the R^2, the better the fit between what actually happened and the process of change described by the mathematical function. If a more parsimonious function—such as a linear equation—describes the process of change almost as well as the more complicated logistic or decaying exponential expression, convention dictates that the linear equation be selected as the best fit. In other words, a growth curve, such as a logistic function, must explain significantly more about the process than a simple linear function does. Significance is assessed in terms of the F-ratio of the difference between the R^2s of the two curves being compared. If the obtained F is greater than the criterion F-value, it is reasonable to conclude that the higher-order curve better describes the change that occurred.

Table 3.3 lists, for each law, the R^2 and related statistics of the fit for the time series on state adoption and aggregate employee coverage for each of the three functional forms. Figure 3.1 on WP/WC, Figure 3.2 on MH, and Figure 3.3 on NW display the two curves best representing the process of state adoption and the spread of employee coverage. The actual points to which these curves were fitted are also plotted in these figures. Before turning to a discussion of the substantive results, it is worth noting that the outcomes of several statistical tests indicate that our findings are statistically reliable. First, F-tests were conducted to determine if the findings were significant; all the regression equations are significant at the .05 level (Table

Table 3.3. Goodness-of-Fit and Level of Significance of Logistic,
Decaying Exponential, and Linear Equations
Fit to Early Wage and Hour Standards Legislation, 1900–1973

Law	Dimension	Linear R^2	F	Decaying exponential R^2	F	Logistic R^2	F	F linear to logistic
WP/WC	Adoption	.58	30.1*	.92	258.4*	.97	336.9*	273.0*
	Coverage	.97	811.4*	.98	1132.4*	.97	396.1*	.5
MH	Adoption	.63	38.2*	.92	241.1*	.97	354.7*	246.3*
	Coverage[a]	.90	180.6*	.90	189.9*	.89	75.1*	Linear > logistic
NW	Adoption	.58	30.8*	.91	219.4*	.98	533.6*	432.6*
	Coverage	.29	9.1*	.30	9.3*	.75	32.2*	39.5*

*Significant at the .05 level.
[a]1900–1966.

Figure 3.1. Actual Points and Best Fitting Curve
Indicating Growth of State Adoption and Employee Coverage for WP/WC, 1900–1973.

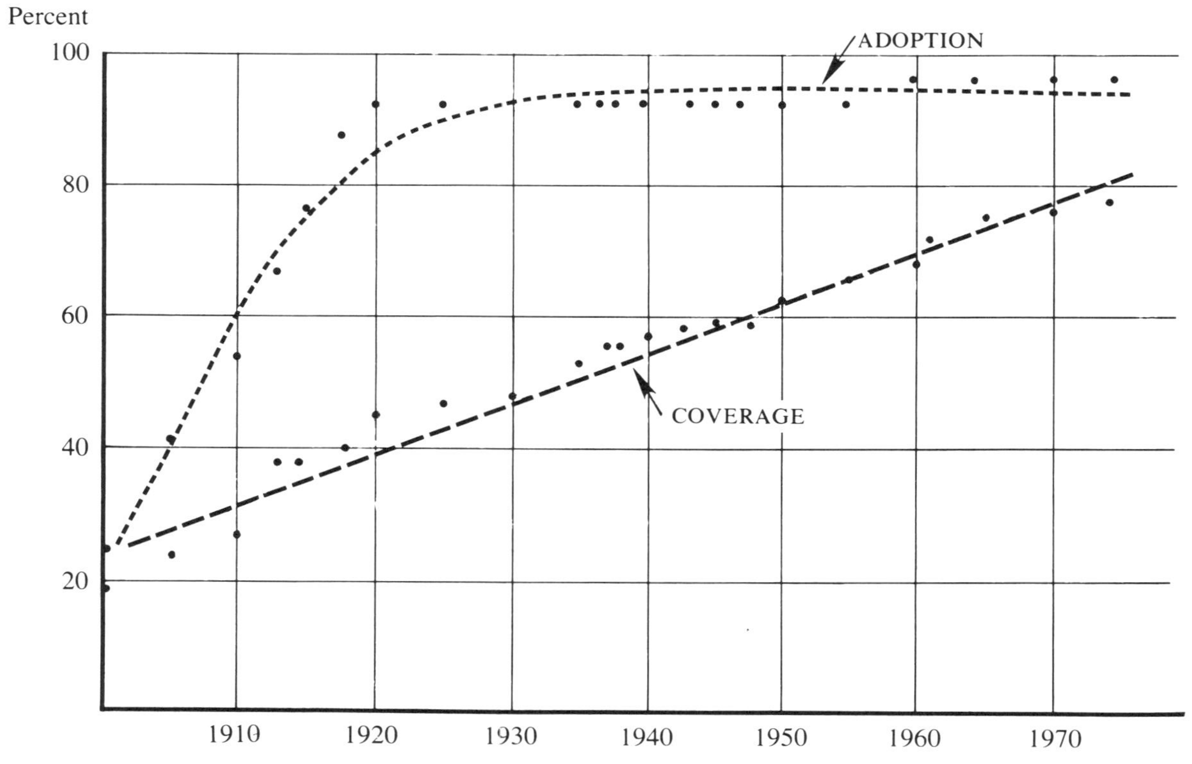

Figure 3.2. Actual Points and Best Fitting Curve
Indicating Growth of State Adoption and Employee Coverage for MH, 1900–1973.

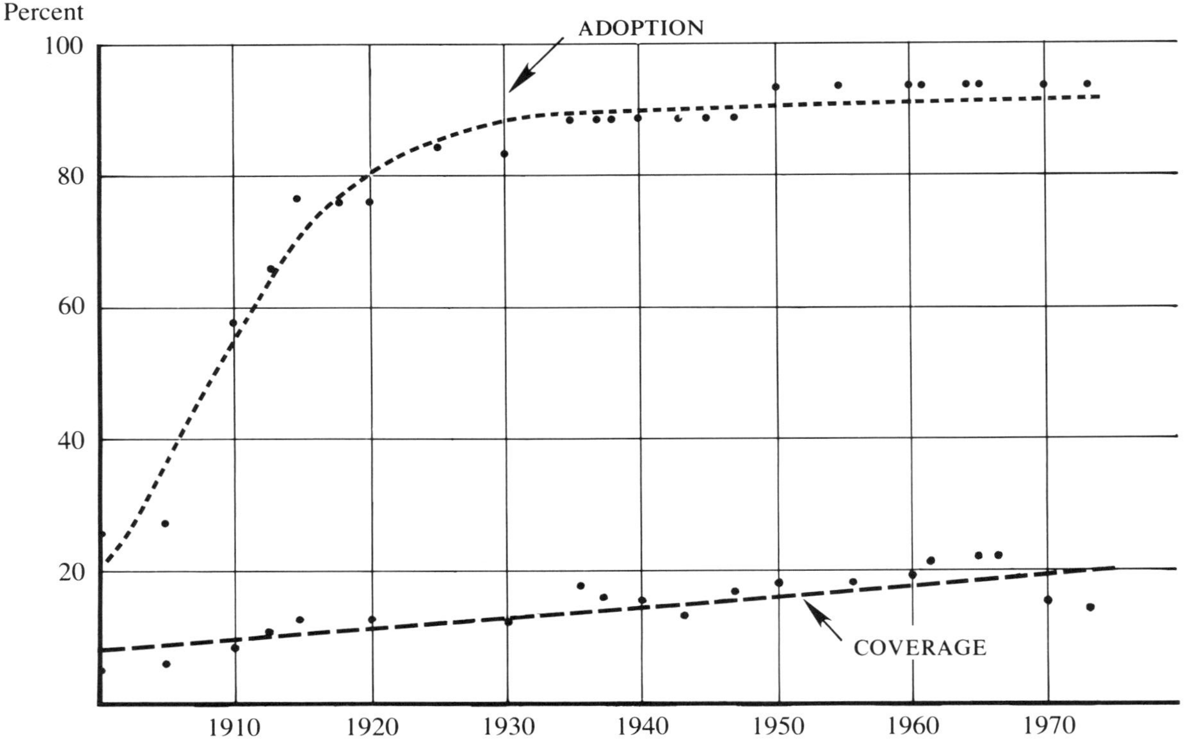

Figure 3.3. Actual Points and Best Fitting Curve
Indicating Growth of State Adoption and Employee Coverage for NW, 1900–1973.

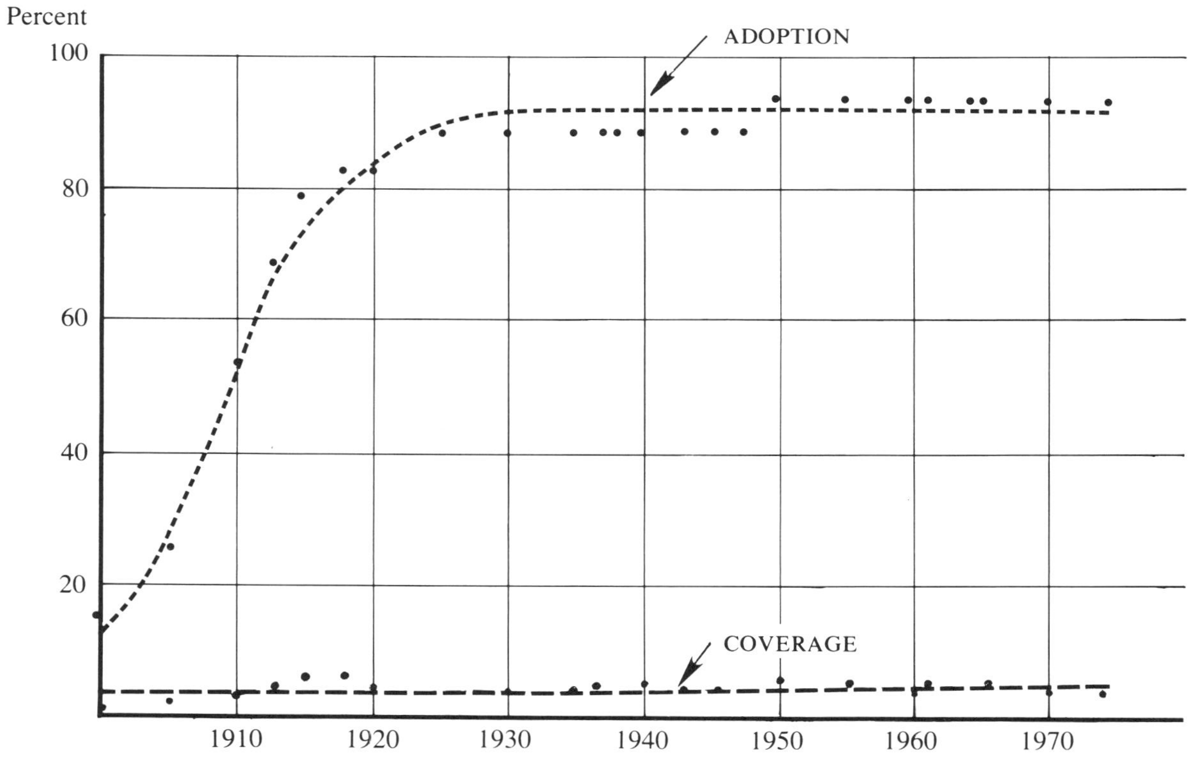

3.3). This standard procedure is particularly important because goodness of fit statistics can be misleading when there are few observations and hence few degrees of freedom. Second, for the two functions fitted to the two indices of each law, the estimated parameters had the expected sign, suggesting that our equations were properly specified.

Using the criteria described above to assess the fit of the functions to adoption and coverage of early wage and hour standards laws, we find that, first, both the logistic and the decaying exponential functions fit the *adoption* data for each law quite well, and distinctly better than the linear curve. In addition, for each law, the fit of the logistic function is slightly better than that of the decaying exponential function. Thus, while these findings do not make a strong argument in favor of one growth process over the other, they do seem to suggest that the logistic curve captures the legislative adoption process somewhat better than the decaying exponential curve. It adds some support to the argument that state legislative bodies were cognizant of the legislative decisions made in other states, and that legislators may well have been in communication with each other prior to the establishment of the Council of State Governments—a formal channel of communication among states financed largely by the states (Gray, 1973). Furthermore, the parameters of the logistic functions fitted to the cumulative state adoption data (Table 3.4) confirm several findings pointed to above: that a large majority of states adopted each of these legal innovations (with a K or asymptote of 94.3 for WP/WC, 90.1 for MH, and 89.4 for NW); that the majority of states adopted their first laws within the first twenty years of the twentieth century; and that the process of state adoption was quite uniform across these laws. (Note, for example, that the Bs or the

Table 3.4. Parameters of Logistic Functions Fit to Time Series Data
on State Adoption and Parameters of Linear Functions
Fit to Time Series Data on Employee Coverage
for Early Labor Legislation, 1900–1973

	State adoption				Employee coverage	
Law	B	A	K	Year of inflection	B	A
WP/WC	−.07	.47	94.3	1907	.76	24.59
MH	−.07	.51	90.1	1907	.19	7.06
NW	−.10	.80	89.4	1908	.03	3.20

rates of adoption are similar across laws, as are the years of inflection—
1907 for WP/WC and MH and 1908 for NW. This latter summary measure
indicates the year during which the rate of adoption shifted from an increasing rate of change to a decreasing one.)

Concerning the process of employee coverage for WP/WC, all three
functions—the linear, the decaying exponential, and the logistic—fitted
to employee coverage have an R^2 of .97 or better. Therefore, the most
parsimonious function, the linear equation, is chosen as best describing
the process of growth. For MH, the R^2 for the linear equation for employee coverage is higher than the R^2 for the logistic equation. Finally,
for NW, the fact that the R^2 for the logistic curve fits better than the
R^2 for the linear curve may be an artifact of the trivial employee coverage
under this law. The logistic curve describing the data on employee coverage under NW reaches an equilibrium at 4.2 percent of the general
employee population. Such a growth curve is, at best, a contradiction in
terms! Consequently, for early labor legislation, neither the logistic curve
nor the decaying exponential curve characterizes the spread of the rights
in these laws to the employee population better than a simple linear function.
The growth in employee coverage seems to occur at a constant rate.

Thus the process underlying the growth in employee coverage appears
to be fundamentally different from the process underlying state adoption.
The adoption process is characterized by a period of extremely rapid
growth—best described by a logistic curve—which does not occur for
employee coverage—best described by a simple linear function. Moreover,
while earlier I stressed the differences among laws in the level of employee
coverage, here we find that the process by which employee coverage grows
is the same across laws. Finally, the discrepancy between the widespread
adoption of these laws by states and the limited scope of employee coverage
is graphically clear, revealed not only in the area between the two curves,
but also in the distinctive curves that best capture their growth.

LEGAL STANDARD

The observed differences in the scope of coverage across these laws are
consistent with the findings on changes in legislative standards (Table 3.5).
First, WP/WC standards grow gradually over the seventy-year period: in
1900, the average WP/WC law was likely to require an employer to follow
one-third of the possible procedures. By 1970, the number of rules to which
employees were subject had nearly doubled.

By contrast, the legal standard under MH remained stable over time;

Table 3.5. Average Standard for Covered Employees (as a Percentage of Maximum Coverage) under Early Labor Legislation, 1900–1970

Year	WP/WC[a]	MH[b]	NW[c]
1900	33.4	29.4	75.0
1910	33.2	31.2	81.7
1920	43.3	32.5	75.0
1930	48.4	33.2	72.5
1940	54.7	38.9	69.2
1950	56.3	39.4	65.8
1960	57.7	39.5	66.7
1970	65.6	38.7	68.3

[a]Maximum coverage = 7 provisions.
[b]Maximum coverage = 1.00 minus the maximum hour standard divided by 84 hours per week.
[c]Maximum coverage = 12 hours per night.

only during a crisis do we find a shift taking place. In 1900, the average weekly maximum was approximately 29 percent lower than with no protection. This standard remained at nearly the same level until the Great Depression. Indeed, the single strengthening of the hours standard by over 15 percent between 1930 and 1940 was greater than all of the change in the hours ceiling during the previous thirty years. This shift was to be the final strengthening of the legal standard in this law; between 1960 and 1970, the MH legal standard was weakened slightly. This was the same decade during which the scope of coverage under MH declined.

The failure of MH standards to keep up with changes in the actual average workweek can be observed through direct comparison (Table 3.6). In 1900, the average workweek for manufacturing employees and the average legal standard were virtually identical. By 1910, the legal standard was the same as the actual workweek in 1905. By 1920, the average standard allowed for five and one-half more hours per week than manufacturing employees worked on average. During the decades of greatest state adoption, then, the legal standard failed to keep pace with changes in the normal hours of work. As indicated above, the Great Depression stimulated a major modification in these MH standards that brought them more in line with the average workweek.[2]

Finally, NW standards present yet a third pattern of growth. For this law, the standard was strengthened during the period when most states

Table 3.6. Average Weekly Hours for Manufacturing Employees and Average Legal Standard under Maximum Hours Laws, 1900–1925

Year	Average weekly hours	Average legal standard
1900	59.0	59.3
1905	57.7	
1910	56.6	57.8
1915	55.0	
1920	51.0	56.7
1925	50.3	

SOURCE: U.S. Department of Commerce, 1975, Series D-589.

were adopting these laws; subsequent to this, it declined slightly. As of 1910, covered employees were prohibited from working for 82 percent of the night. The standard then began to weaken. By 1950, it was possible for employees to work for almost two hours more of the evening, night, and early morning than in 1910.

Thus, change in the standards provided in early labor laws is law specific: WP/WC standards grew slowly but continuously throughout the twentieth century with the least change occurring when adoption and coverage grew most rapidly. For MH, the standards were strengthened between 1900 and 1910 and again between 1930 and 1940, after which no change was exhibited. The NW standard was strongest when growth in adoption and coverage was greatest; it subsequently weakened, leveling off in 1940 at a standard that prohibits work for a period of eight hours each night.

This apparent dissimilarity in these laws may result from a common feature. When we examine changes in coverage and standard within each law, it appears that, when initial state adoption subsides, the strengthening of the legal standard seems to be a function of an expansion in coverage. If the scope of coverage does not grow, the standards of those who are covered decline. Compare coverage and standard in WP/WC and NW— the two extreme cases. Coverage in WP/WC grew steadily over the twentieth century; the legal standard was likewise strengthened. By contrast, coverage under NW is limited to an extremely small segment of workers. Although already covered employees were able to strengthen the standards under which they were covered during the period of state adoption, the standards weakened immediately thereafter. Maximum hours laws are an intermediate case in which a slight but insubstantial increase is coupled with a stable legal standard. It took a major crisis, however, to change the standard provided in the law.

These findings underline the importance of looking at the growth of legislation both systematically and for several dimensions. Had state adoption been the only indicator of the distribution of these social rights within American society, for example, we would have arrived at a very different picture of the extent of rights actually accorded to employees. We would have concluded inaccurately that, by 1920, these social rights were regulating the hours and mode of payment of employees. We also would have concluded, again inaccurately, that, by 1920, the growth in these laws was complete. Yet, in no way can mere adoption of legislation give a complete picture of the extent to which the formal relations between employers and employees are affected by these laws. When we take all three dimensions into account, the development of these laws becomes somewhat more complicated: although state adoption is uniform across these three laws, and the process underlying growth in coverage is also similar across laws, the level of coverage and changes in the legal standard are law specific.

Indeed, these findings raise several questions never before asked: first, what accounts for the marked discrepancy between state adoption and the scope of employee coverage? Second, why do these laws diverge so in the extent of coverage and the level of standards provided? Third, to what might we attribute the observed relationship at the national level between coverage and legal standard within each law? The remainder of this chapter addresses these questions. While any explanation offered at this point is tentative, an analysis of certain features of early labor laws in terms of historical evidence suggests the beginnings of an answer.

ADOPTION-COVERAGE DISCREPANCY

THE STRUCTURAL BIAS OF LEGAL NORMS

Karl Polanyi (1957:216) has argued that a society in the throes of industrialization must "resolve" a conflict over alternative ways to organize the relations between political and economic institutions: either as a self-regulating market "in which workers [are] put under the threat of starvation if they [fail] to comply with the rules of wage labor" or as a system in which the "powerful protective reactions" of state intervention in the marketplace are deemed legitimate. The observed differences between the percentages of state adoption and employee coverage suggest that American society compromised between these two extremes: it passed legislation but severely restricted (in some cases, to an insignificant minority) the population to whom the benefits accrued. Why was this compromise necessary and on what was the scope of coverage based?

If we view these laws, first, in relation to the legal principles dominating transactions in the labor market in the early twentieth century, and second, as an outgrowth of the general conflict between employers and employees over the definitions of the rules of work in an industrial society, the discrepancy between coverage and adoption becomes comprehensible. Indeed, the bias created by legal norms serves as a power resource to employers at the same time that the differential power of employers maintains the bias in the legal norms.

As was discussed in Chapter 1, during the nineteenth century, the classical notion of freedom of contract or the right to unconstrained property transactions was the dominant legal norm governing contract law as it pertained to the labor market. Judicial action in this area was of such significance that the legal historian Lawrence Friedman has described the doctrine of laissez-faire as "one of the sovereign notions of the 19th century" (1973: 464). While it has long been believed that liberty of contract guided most nineteenth-century judicial and legislative decisions, more recent research holds that the uniform application of laissez-faire principles was more myth than reality. "Certainly," Friedman says, "during much of the century, there was a great deal of public sympathy for business, productivity, growth. Particularly, the first half of the century was a period of promotion of enterprise, of the release of creative energy; government, reflecting its powerful constituencies, wanted business and the economy to grow; where this required subsidy or intervention, no overriding theory held government back" (1973:157; see also Hurst, 1956; Kolko, 1963). The freedom of contract doctrine only selectively deflected government involvement in economic decisions; but nowhere was resistance to government involvement stronger than in the area of labor law, and nowhere was resistance more consistently expressed than in the decisions handed down by state and federal courts in the late nineteenth and early twentieth centuries. Court decisions are an especially important indicator of the lack of sympathy for workers in their fights for government protection. Although court decisions varied from state to state, wage and hour laws were repeatedly struck down because judges believed that labor and capital bargained as equals and, therefore, that labor did not need state protection (Fine, 1953; Keller, 1977; Paul, 1969).

In a classic article criticizing the excessive reliance of the courts on the "liberty of contract" notion, Roscoe Pound summarized the dominant judicial position: "Legislation designed to give laborers some measure of practical independence, which, if allowed to operate, would put them in a position of reasonable equality with their masters, is said by the courts, because it infringes on a theoretical equality, to be insulting to their manhood and degrading, to put them under guardianship, to create a class of statutory laborers, and to stamp them as imbeciles" (1909:463). Prior to the twentieth century, judges were indifferent to the sex of a worker and applied the doctrine of freedom of contract uniformly to women and men. According to Commons and Andrews, "opinions opposed to legal restriction [of women] emphasized the interference with woman's freedom to contract to work each day as long as she pleases, implying that employer and employee stand on an equal footing in determining working conditions, and that an employee works long hours of her own free will. Such a restriction of freedom of contract, they hold, deprives a woman worker without due process of law of the valuable property right of disposing of her own labor as she sees fit" (1936:112). In the period 1887–1910, the United States Supreme Court alone handed down 558 decisions on a wide variety of issues using the due process and equal protection clauses of the Fourteenth Amendment (Keller, 1977:369). But this legal rationale must be assessed in terms of the interests it served. In the area of labor law, perhaps more clearly than in other areas, as we will see, choosing "liberty" over "protection" meant, for the most part, choosing the employers' liberty over the employees' protection.[3]

Court resistance to labor standards legislation began to break down in 1898 when, in *Holden* v. *Hardy*, the Supreme Court reversed many precedents to conclude that "intervention by the State was justified on . . . [the] grounds . . . [of] gross inequality in bargaining power between the parties to the labor contract" (Brandeis, 1935:668). The decision highlights both the legal bias and the differential power resources available to employers and employees. In the words of the court, "the proprietors of these establishments and their operators do not stand upon an equality, their interests are, to a certain extent, conflicting. The former naturally desire to obtain as much labor as possible from their employees, while the latter are often induced by fear of discharge to conform to the regulations. . . . In other words, the proprietors lay down the rules and the laborers are practically constrained to obey them" (as quoted in Brandeis, 1935:669).

While court decisions upholding liberty of contract did not decisively prevent the passage of laws in this area, until the early twentieth century they delayed considerably their extensive adoption. But court decisions continued until 1914 to uphold the fiction that certain groups of employees—

namely male adults—were the equals—at least formally—of employers in their bargaining over the labor contract. Consequently, while decisions such as *Holden* v. *Hardy* paved the way for the widespread passage of these laws, the nature of the arguments that needed to be made for *Holden* v. *Hardy* to hold meant, in reality, that the scope of coverage of these laws was strictly limited. In the famous *Lochner* v. *New York* case (198 U.S. 45.75, 1905), for example, bakery workers could not convince the Court that they were engaged in dangerous work; hence, they lost their right to a legally established ten-hour day. Seen in this light, the norm of equal legal status was a power resource for employers whose contractual rights were encroached upon by wage and hour legislation. As such, freedom of contract served to justify, structure, and therefore reinforce authority relations that already existed in the marketplace.

To throw into relief the relation between legal norms and the power position of contending parties, consider a society in which security of employment and wages, and not freedom of contract, is the dominant legal norm. In that situation, employers might find that, to improve their operations as well as their profits, some aspects of the employment relationship would better be freely bargained for rather than given by social convention and legal prescription. The employers would then have to appeal to courts and legislatures to gain a measure assuring the legality of contracts made by free bargaining. They would have to demonstrate that their enterprise or industry was "extraordinary" and that, for example, free contractual interaction would yield *more* stable employment than traditional and legal sanctions.

By contrast, the norm of freedom of contract placed the burden of proof on employees. Workers needed to demonstrate that they worked in extraordinary situations   that is, a situation in which equal status was demonstrably more fiction than fact—in order to qualify for government protection. John R. Commons argued in 1924 that there was a parallel between the situation facing the first employees seeking these kinds of government protection and European merchants and manufacturers attempting to loosen the hold on the marketplace of restrictive guild rules. His position captures the basic thrust of the argument being made here:

> Just as the prerogative courts of the Sixteenth and Seventeenth Centuries could not comprehend and yield to the demand for liberty and power on the part of small merchants and manufacturers outside the guilds, so the courts do not comprehend and yield to the demand for new definitions of liberty and power on the part of the aggressive

laborers. History repeats itself, and the Supreme Court takes over the protection of the liberty and power of business, just as the prerogative courts protected the privileges of the monarch and his party. . . . The reasons and precedents are on the side of business, and the liberty and power demanded by labor is as contrary to precedent as the liberty and power demanded by business was contrary to the precedents of feudalism. . . . The prerogative today is the prerogative of business. . . . Apparently, a "new equity" is needed—an equity that will protect the job as the older equity protected the business (1968:307).

Thus, a class conflict in the economic marketplace takes the form of a conflict over *legal* rights accorded to employers and employees when it is resolved within the existing political channels of a society. The laissez-faire doctrine creates a structural bias in favor of employers (Bachrach and Baratz, 1970; Lowi, 1969; Schattschneider, 1960). The limited extension of social rights can thus in part be attributed to the subordinate power position of employees relative to employers. I turn to this factor next.

THE RESOLUTION OF SOCIAL CONFLICT

Of course, the contention that the gap between adoption and coverage represents a compromise solution is plausible only if it can be demonstrated that employees sought universal coverage and that employers opposed them. The connection between legal doctrines and class conflict can be substantiated. Historical accounts of key legislative decisions suggest that organized groups perceived themselves as having much to win or lose by these political outcomes. Here is Lawrence Friedman's somewhat dramatic summary: "Labor problems multiplied because economic interests conflicted, in a game of life that *both sides were convinced was zero-sum*. . . . Each group had to scramble for its share; what accrued to one was subtracted from another. This attitude . . . profoundly affected every aspect of the living legal system" (1973:483, italics added). Employers put the existing legal bias to good use in their campaigns to overturn early labor laws. For example, in the late 1860s, manufacturers in Massachusetts "attacked . . . proposed [hours] legislation with the prevailing laissez-faire arguments. They advised workers to 'keep clear of governmental care, . . . stick to individual effort, make your services so necessary to the public that they cannot be dispensed with and you will have no need of . . . governmental aid'" (Brandeis, 1935: 462–463).

It was pointed out in Chapter 1 that manufacturing workers in Massachusetts battled for some fifteen years to obtain a ten-hour law with universal coverage provisions. Only when coverage was limited to women, minors, and children was a law passed.

The Massachusetts maximum hours law covering only female and minor employees set a precedent for this category of legislation. This formed the crucial political compromise, one that would never have been made had employees had sufficient power to achieve their original demands. A legally limited working day had been on the agenda of employees since the mid-nineteenth century. But, partially as a result of the early battles, the focus of trade unions and employee organizations shifted in the 1880s and 1890s from the right to government-imposed terms to the labor contract to the right to a collectively bargained contract—at least for adult males. The revision downward of the initial demands in the Massachusetts fight for a government-defined workweek was the consequence of a realistic assessment of the small likelihood that these rights would be universally extended through legislation.[4] The "voluntaristic" philosophy of the AFL at this time was characterized by a general distrust of government and a skepticism about what could be accomplished through political reform (Vale, 1971:29; Yellowitz, 1977). A delegate from the International Typographical Union to the 1884 convention of the AFL made the following remark: "A united demand for a shorter working day, backed by thorough organization will prove vastly more effective than the enactment of a thousand laws depending for enforcement upon the pleasure of aspiring politicians or sycophantic department officials" (Brandeis, 1935:555). At the time it represented a minority opinion, but it soon became the majority position.

With labor's change in approach to the reform of the labor market, subsequent efforts to obtain laws regulating the hours of work were built upon these first crucial political lessons. State-commissioned histories of labor laws are replete with stories of battles within state legislative chambers over which industries or occupations would be required to abide by hours legislation (Breckner, 1929; Downey, 1910; Eaves, 1910; Newman, 1943; Ryan, 1932; Whitin, 1908). Yet, restrictions in coverage to women and minors were accepted without question except by the eight-hours movement, organized on the West Coast between 1911 and 1914 (Ratner, 1980). When the Supreme Court finally legitimated this basis of coverage in its 1908 *Muller* v. *Oregon* decision, it became a permanent feature of almost all laws establishing daily or weekly hours ceilings.

For an understanding of why rights denied to men were offered to women and minors, we must turn again to the use of legal norms by organized interest groups. At the same time that the leaders of the trade union movement were turning away from these types of political reforms, women's groups like the Women's Trade Union League (WTUL) and the National Consumers League (NCL) were placing MH and NW laws at the center of their political agenda. The membership of these organizations, along with their many sympathizers, constituted the critical mass of popular support necessary to win the passage of these laws. Women's groups developed a set of arguments that were persuasive precisely because they differentiated between men and women, and therefore were consistent with conventional thinking about the division of labor between the sexes. The WTUL and the NCL approach focused on a few key differences between men and women, including physical and emotional differences. The groups argued that these differences justified special protection for women. The fact that women held a subordinate position in society because of their position within the family was used as a power resource, however misguided from the perspective of the 1970s, to gain for them legal rights denied to their male counterparts in the labor market (Beyer, 1929; Boone, 1942; Chafe, 1972; Collins, 1972; Davidson, 1939; Flexner, 1971; Martin, 1976). The legitimacy of these rights for minors was based as well upon their legal status as wards of the state. Commons and Andrews (1936:99) explain that "as a minor is legally incapable of entering into a free contract, such laws cannot be said to abridge without 'due process of law' his freedom to dispose of his labor."

This approach reached its most glowing and frequently cited moment in the 113-page brief Louis D. Brandeis filed on behalf of the NCL in the landmark *Muller* v. *Oregon* case (208 U.S. 412, 1908). In spite of the fact that the evidence presented about employed women would not stand up to current scientific standards, it proved sufficient to convince the Supreme Court Justices of the legitimacy of special protection for women. The court unanimously upheld the Oregon maximum hours law; the opinion is worth quoting at length:

> Even if all restrictions on political, personal, and contractual rights were taken away, and [women] . . . stood, so far as statutes are concerned, upon an absolutely equal plane with [men] . . . it would still be true that she will rest upon and look to him for protection; that her physical structure and a proper discharge of her maternal functions—having in view not merely her own health, but the well-being of the race—justify legislation to protect her from the greed as well as the passion of man. The limitations which this statute places upon her contractual powers, upon her right to agree with her employers as to the time she shall labor, are imposed not only for her

benefit, but also largely for the benefit of all. . . . The two sexes differ in structure of the body, in the amount of physical strength, in the capacity for long-continued labor, the influences of vigorous health upon the future well-being of the race, the self-reliance which enables one to assert full rights, and in the capacity to maintain the struggle for subsistence. This difference justifies a difference in legislation (as quoted in Baer, 1978:421–423).

These arguments fortified NCL lobbyists in state legislatures, as well as WTUL delegates to AFL conventions who were seeking general trade union endorsement of labor laws for women, as for example the WTUL delegate who argued to her union brothers that these laws would serve as "[a]nother weapon in the hands of the trade union women to protect not only themselves and their children but the great mass of unorganized women to whom has not yet come the social visions which will redeem the world" (Beyer, 1929:10–11).[5]

Thus, at the same time that the vast majority of unions lost interest in legislative reform of the labor contract, women's groups deepened their commitment to the enactment of such reforms. The original compromise on the scope of coverage under the Massachusetts maximum hours law in the 1860s had firmly taken root in the first few decades of the twentieth century. Because of repeated failure, trade unions abandoned MH and NW legislation, and the constellation of forces in favor of these laws changed markedly over the forty-year period between this Massachusetts compromise and the *Muller* decision. Not surprisingly, employers continued to oppose this legislation throughout this period. Yet, it was precisely this shift in the composition of group support that led to the pervasive association of maximum hours legislation with the inferior position of women in their role as workers in the labor market.

The preceding discussion indicates that, if we disaggregate coverage by demographic group, the observed discrepancy between adoption and coverage should disappear for women and minors—at least for MH and NW. On the other hand, for WP/WC, no historical evidence exists that employees compromised over the scope of coverage. Rather, it appears, for reasons discussed below, that the need of employees for these kinds of protections was fairly easy to document. Table 3.7, which lists employee coverage by demographic group for each early labor law, suggests that the revision of employee demands did account for some of the adoption-coverage discrepancy observed for MH and NW. It also accounts for some of the difference in coverage across laws, a topic I discuss in the next section.

Table 3.7. Employee Coverage under Early Labor Legislation
by Demographic Group, 1900–1970
(in percent)

Year	Wage payment/ Wage collection					Maximum hour					Night work				
	MA	FA	AM	MM	FM	MA	FA	AM	MM	FM	MA	FA	AM	MM	FM
1900	19	23	18	21	16	1	16	10	6	22	0	6	4	3	10
1910	28	24	26	27	26	3	17	15	10	24	0	6	10	8	15
1920	46	42	42	43	42	5	39	23	10	46	0	13	15	11	25
1930	49	45	45	46	44	5	38	21	10	43	0	13	16	11	27
1940	57	54	49	54	47	5	49	27	15	50	0	16	21	17	28
1950	63	60	57	61	55	4	56	38	25	55	0	11	27	25	31
1960	68	63	64	63	65	4	52	37	27	59	0	7	29	29	30
1970	77	74	76	75	76	4	31	35	29	43	0	2	30	31	27

While the variation in coverage across demographic groups for WP/WC laws is trivial, the differences in coverage for MH and NW when demographic group is controlled are substantial: male adults are never covered by night-work regulations and rarely covered by restrictions on their weekly hours.[6] By contrast, female minors are the most extensively covered demographic group under MH and NW.

When we compare coverage by demographic group with state adoption (Table 3.1), however, discrepancies remain even for female adults and all minors under MH and NW. Women workers covered under MH laws were barely a majority in 1960, the peak year. NW never extended to even one-fifth of employed women; for minors, the portion covered increased over the twentieth century to 30 percent by 1970.

This residual gap between state adoption and employee coverage controlling for demographic group describes, in one respect, what labor and other groups had to relinquish to win passage of this legislation. Moreover, although these national time series data obscure the prevailing power distributions between labor and management as they operated in any particular case (such as the Massachusetts example described above), they do represent some overall proxy for the superior power of employer groups (Coleman, 1974). The power position of employers rested both on the favorable bias in legal norms and on the actual pressure they exerted on legislatures. The complicated decisions of legislators on early wage and hour standards laws are cast into relief: faced with the conflicting demands made by groups with differential power, the legislators enacted a law and limited its application, thereby rendering everyone a victor, although not in equal measure.

Furthermore, after 1920 the decrease in the gap between adoption and coverage over time may be accounted for by a fundamental difference in the nature of the decisions reflected in the two dimensions of legislation. The decision to adopt a law is an all-or-nothing decision—once a law has been enacted, it matters little whether 51 percent or 100 percent of the legislators voted favorably. But, once a law has been enacted, deciding whom to cover can be reconsidered as often as is wanted. Coverage can be introduced in stages and clearly was. Whether introducing coverage in stages made these reforms more palatable or reduced the number of employers opposing their adoption or both is unclear. And, once a set of social rights has been extended to some employees, it serves as a power resource for uncovered workers. Whatever the reason, the conflict in the labor market over sets of incompatible rights available to employers and employees did not need to be resolved once and for all. I examine this more fully in Chapter 5.

VARIATIONS IN EMPLOYEE COVERAGE AMONG EARLY LAWS

One aspect of differences in coverage across laws was addressed in the last section: the scope of coverage demanded by employees varied across laws. For WP/WC, coverage appears to be independent of the demographic group of employees; for MH and NW, demands were limited to women or minors or both. But, even when coverage is disaggregated by demographic group, the variation remains substantial. With a few exceptions, employee coverage within each demographic group moves from more extensive to less extensive from WP/WC to MH to NW.

One explanation for this residual difference hinges on an understanding of the variations in the types of legal standards enacted. First, the standards in early labor laws vary in the degree to which they constrain the discretion of the employer to organize the work process. Second, standards in these laws divide into those that enumerate specific terms of an employment contract (for example, an employer shall not hire a worker for more than sixty hours of work per week) and those that specify more general (and often procedural) features of an employment contract (such as the mode of payment). Each early labor law varies along these two dimensions.

Wage payment/wage collection laws call for state intervention to uphold the contract obligations of the employer. These laws are therefore more consistent with the freedom-of-contract doctrine than the other early laws. If an employee fulfills his or her contract obligation to work, the employer must fulfill his or her contract obligation to pay for work rendered. The state intervenes to see that the terms of the labor contract are fulfilled by establishing the conditions of wage payment. It leaves employer discretion completely intact. As long as an employer pays a worker for her or his time on the job, she or he is free to control how or when that work is accomplished.

On the other hand, both MH and NW involve very different constraints on employers. First, these laws deny to the parties in the labor market the right to negotiate certain terms of the contract. While employees may work less than the prescribed weekly hours or during any part of the day if night work is prohibited, the parties must negotiate within the limits set by the law. Even MH and NW, however, vary in the extent to which discretion is constrained. If all employees in a firm are prohibited from working at night, it is impossible for an employer to violate the provisions of the law successfully. In this case, any workplace operating at night, however defined, would be in clear violation of the law. Weekly hours ceilings are much easier for employers to ignore. If a firm is operating under multiple shifts and intimidates its workforce from making complaints, MH becomes quite easy to violate. The preceding distinctions among these laws are summarized in Figure 3.4.

On the basis of this analysis of the types of legal standards found in early labor laws, the variations in coverage across laws are rendered more comprehensible: the resistance by employers to legislation would be greatest for NW, somewhat less strong for MH, and weakest for WP/WC. But, this

Figure 3.4. Variations in the Restriction of Employer Autonomy
under Early Labor Laws.

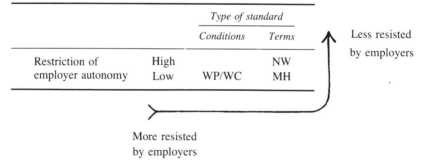

		Type of standard			
		Conditions	Terms		Less resisted
Restriction of	High		NW		by employers
employer autonomy	Low	WP/WC	MH		

More resisted
by employers

discussion also uncovers a general reason for employer resistance to state legislation. Employers repeatedly argued in legislative chambers during hearings that the cost to them of meeting the requirements of wage and hour legislation would either put them out of business or place them at a competitive disadvantage to firms in states without such laws. When possible, they threatened to move their operations out of a state if a law was enacted. In addition to being motivated by this narrow economic interest, which is examined more carefully in Chapter 7, employers apparently also valued the right to run their firms as they saw fit. Certainly this strong preference is a clear enough motivation in campaigns against unionization: in many instances, employers improve wages and hours to undermine union organizing drives. Perhaps an even more fundamental factor accounting for general resistance is the change in the employment relationship brought about as a result of these reforms. Wage and hour standards laws change the relations between employers and employees in three important ways: first, they introduce limits (however weak) on employer autonomy; second, they institute some procedure for government to determine the extent of employer compliance with the regulations; and, third, they create a situation in which employees see themselves as having a government-backed right to demand from the employer certain minimum terms. Consequently, these laws undermine one of the major ideological pillars legitimizing a capitalist economy—that, since employers have taken the "risk" of ownership, they can run their enterprises as they see fit and treat labor in the way most conducive to the maximization of profits.[7]

THE CONNECTION BETWEEN COVERAGE AND STANDARD IN EARLY LABOR LEGISLATION

Finally, the data suggest that there is a definite relation between coverage and standard within a law. Specifically, more extensive coverage provisions accompany legal standards that become stronger over time. Conversely, very restricted coverage, as in NW, results in a weakening of standards included in the initial piece of legislation subsequent to the period of state adoption. To make sense of this pattern requires that we assume that laws are most visible when they are first being considered and that the greatest gains in coverage occur during the period of initial state adoption. While the overall process of growth in coverage is linear, the findings (Table 3.1) suggest that the rate of growth in coverage at the national level is somewhat greater when states are first adopting legislation. But, both the rate of growth and the level of coverage varied substantially across laws, with WP/WC covering the most workers and NW laws covering the fewest workers. From this, I further infer that a critical lower threshold of covered population is necessary to maintain even the meager standards instituted in initial legislation. This critical mass must constitute a large enough group of interested parties to continue interest in these laws beyond the period of initial adoption.

In the case of WP/WC, the pool of employees was apparently of sufficient size, not only to maintain standards, but also to strengthen them as coverage expanded. Coverage under NW, on the other hand, fell considerably below this threshold—and so the standard became weaker over time. MH constitutes an intermediate case; the number of employees covered seems to have been sufficient initially to maintain established standards. Yet, a comparison of MH standards to the actual workweek leads us to conclude that the standards enacted during the major period of state adoption were fast becoming obsolete for large numbers of covered employees. Only a crisis as fundamental as the Great Depression shifted this standard to bring it more in line with the number of hours employees actually worked.[8]

SUMMARY AND CONCLUSIONS

The period between 1870 and 1920 is considered the crucible in which the parameters of American industrial capitalism were forged. In this new environment, a class-based struggle for legislation setting wage and hour standards took root. The uniform pattern of enactment—between 1900 and 1920—of the initial forms of this legislation signaled that the legitimate domain of governmental action now encompassed a new arena. By the same token, a precedent was set for further action in this area of legislation.

Had we, however, looked only at the adoption of legislation, the analysis would have missed much of the complicated history of these laws. For early labor laws, great limitations were placed on the extent of coverage. While the fundamental legal right governing transactions in the labor market—that is, freedom of contract—delayed but did not block adoption of legislation, it provided the legitimating basis for extending or denying coverage. There were two general reasons why those who sold their labor were accorded a set of rights that met this legal norm head-on. In both cases, the entering wedge to coverage was the undeniable conclusion that the assumed equality between those who bargained did not in fact exist. First, for WP/WC, workers' subordinate bargaining position could not be questioned when they were denied pay for the work they had performed. This constituted a clear violation of their contract, one that warranted legal intervention to ensure that the terms of the contract were being carried out. Second, for MH and NW, since women and children were not granted the property rights assumed to exist for male adults, they were denied the legal equality that was the underpinning of the freedom-of-contract doctrine. Labor standards compensated for this legal deficiency.

This legal and ideological tension between the maintenance of civil rights and the extension of social rights can also be viewed as a conflict between employers and employees. If there had been no legal change, and the doctrine of freedom of contract had barred completely the adoption of these early wage and hour standards laws, the legal environment would have remained totally advantageous to employers. Even if all other power resources were distributed equally between employers and employees, this distribution of legal rights, especially in a situation of labor surplus, put employers in a secure position of dominance. The burden of proof to remedy the inequality of bargaining in the labor market rested with employees. The extent to which there was a structural bias resisting the redistribution of legal rights is suggested by the discrepancy in the aggregate between the extent of state adoption and the level of employee coverage. When demographic group of employee is controlled for, this discrepancy is reduced somewhat but is certainly not eliminated.

Several striking differences in the patterns of growth in these laws suggest additional factors that facilitate or hinder their passage. Variations in the content of these three early laws suggest that growth in employee coverage and strengthening of standards go hand in hand. Moreover, for the standards to remain stable or be strengthened over time, it appears that a critical mass of employees must be covered under a law. Finally, coverage is affected by the consequences that the social right will have on the discretion of the employer in structuring his or her enterprise. The more a legal right threatens that discretion, the more limited is the scope of coverage.

4

MODERN LABOR STANDARDS
LEGISLATION

The Socialization of Conflict

In this chapter, the development of modern labor legislation is examined. Minimum wage laws, overtime laws, and equal pay laws are grouped as modern labor laws because their widespread adoption occurred several decades after most states had adopted early labor laws. Moreover, modern labor laws are characterized by the involvement of the federal government in a legal area previously the exclusive domain of state governments. MW, OT, and EP standards are encompassed in the Fair Labor Standards Act, enacted in 1938 and amended frequently thereafter. The growth and change in these laws are compared with the patterns observed for early labor laws. Specifically, the contribution federal legislation made to the distribution of these social rights is assessed. The comparison of the growth of early and modern labor laws is based on the legal indicators described in the last chapter, with one exception.

DATA

As was the case for early labor laws, we generated national indicators of employee coverage and average legal standard from state indicators using sampling weights as described in Chapter 2. We converted the legal standard for each law into a percentage of complete legal protection. For MW, complete legal protection was defined as the hourly wage rate necessary to earn in 1968 dollars a government-defined "modest but adequate income" for a family of four.[1] The legal standard was then calculated as a percentage of this modest but adequate income. Because of assumptions made in the calculation of both the average MW rate and complete protection, this indicator better reflects the change than the level of protection. For OT, the indicator is computed as a percentage of complete *lack* of legal protection which is defined, as in MH, as an eighty-four-hour weekly limit. In other words, if an employee was required to work eighty-four hours before a premium wage had to be paid, a law was regarded as having provided no legal protection. The legal OT standard is calculated as the average standard found in the law, divided by eighty-four, subtracted from 1.00.[2] For EP, since a complete law allows employees with five sets of characteristics to seek government protection, the legal standard is computed as the average legal standard in the law divided by five.

We did not develop an indicator of cumulative state adoption for modern labor laws. Since a federal law was coded as if twenty-eight states had adopted a law, it would have proven difficult once the FLSA was passed to determine when a state adopted a law covering at least 1 percent of employees. Instead, as explained below, coverage is disaggregated not only by demographic group but also by level of government. But first the general patterns of growth in coverage and standard are examined.

COVERAGE AND STANDARD: GENERAL PATTERNS OF GROWTH

The pattern of growth in employee coverage under modern labor laws is quite uniform across laws (Table 4.1). In the period 1900–1930 few employees were accorded these rights, confirming the assumption underlying the categorization of these laws. A small group of employees obtained the legal right to premium pay, but most coverage under OT appears to result from a special class of pre-1900 legislation. Between 1860 and 1910, several states, especially in the Northeast or North Central regions, enacted what

Table 4.1. Employee Coverage under Modern Labor
Legislation, 1900–1970
(in percent)

Year	MW	OT	EP
1900	0	7	0
1910	0	9	0
1920	2	12	0
1930	3	12	0
1940	43	38	0
1950	48	43	23
1960	58	46	43
1970	90	71	78

came to be called normal day's work or legal day's work laws. Most employees were paid by the day rather than the hour in the nineteenth century, and workdays expanded or contracted as was necessary to the employer. Normal day's work laws established a fixed number of hours constituting a workday and required that additional compensation be paid for additional hours of work. They pertained to laborers in manufacturing and mechanical industries, as well as a host of (typically male) industries such as mining and railroads (Ware, 1964).[3] Until 1940, however, coverage was extended to a small minority—12 percent—of employees.

For MW, coverage hovered around 3 percent until the 1930s when it took off. For EP, coverage remained at less than 1 percent of employees until 1950. Only Montana and Michigan adopted laws before 1940. But by 1950 more employees were covered by EP than were covered by MH after sixty years of growth. Furthermore, growth between 1950 and 1970 was greater for EP than for any of the other labor standards laws.

Between 1940 and 1970 the growth in coverage under modern labor laws appears to be steady, continuous, and extensive. By 1970, each law reached at least 70 percent of all employees, and MW standards applied to 90 percent of employees.

Translated into numbers (Table 4.2), the rights embodied in each of these laws were available to over 10 million employees by 1950. Some twenty years later, approximately 55 million employees were covered under MW, almost 49 million under EP, and about 44 million under OT. Consequently, while there were some variations in the scope of coverage in these laws, coverage under modern labor standards laws was more uniform than coverage under early labor laws. And these rights were available to an

Table 4.2. Employee Coverage under Modern Labor
Legislation, 1900–1970
(in thousands)

Year	MW	OT	EP
1900	0	1,896	0
1910	14	3,006	0
1920	909	4,314	152
1930	1,183	5,041	154
1940	17,585	15,438	184
1950	24,121	21,558	11,715
1960	30,659	24,464	22,639
1970	55,566	44,067	48,537

extraordinarily large number of people who sold their labor in the market-place.

There is another, even more striking uniformity in the pattern by which these laws developed. Coverage under all modern labor laws seems to take off during the final stages of a major societal crisis: the Great Depression for MW and OT and World War II for EP. For each law, while coverage was small for OT and almost nonexistent for MW and EP prior to the crisis, it grew between 20 and 40 percent during the decade of the crisis: between 1930 and 1940, coverage under MW grew 40 percent and under OT grew 26 percent. This is discussed again in the section on the FLSA, as well as in Chapters 6 and 8.

Compared to early labor laws, coverage under modern labor laws grew rapidly. It took WP/WC—the most extensively distributed of the early labor laws—seventy years to reach the same level of coverage as was attained for MW and OT in thirty to thirty-five years and EP in twenty to twenty-five years. MH and NW laws never reached the level of coverage attained for MW and OT between 1930 and 1940. All three of the modern labor laws reached the same or a greater level of coverage much more rapidly than the early labor laws.

Turning next to standards, we observe in Table 4.3 that each law moves

Table 4.3. Average Legal Standard as a Percentage of
Complete Legal Protection under Modern Labor Legislation, 1900–1970

Year	MW[a]	OT[b]	EP[c]
1900	0	30.6	0
1910	0	30.6	0
1920	1	32.1	0
1930	1	36.4	0
1940	24	51.0	0
1950	34	51.1	35.8
1960	39	51.1	50.8
1970	52	51.9	59.4

[a]Minimum wage standard as a percentage of the hourly wage necessary to earn a minimum but adequate income for a family of four (estimated at 40 hours per week for 52 weeks a year, in 1968 dollars).

[b]The number of hours per week beyond which employers are obligated to pay employees more than the normal rate of pay: 0% means that the hours threshold is 84 hours.

[c]The average percentage of provisions included in the law. A complete law has five provisions.

from weaker to stronger standards as expressed as a percentage of complete protection. Like employee coverage, standards under MW and EP were established on the heels of a crisis. Once these standards were in place, they moved toward providing greater protection. In the case of OT laws, the crisis provided the push necessary to strengthen the provisions substantially. Interestingly, OT standards were improved during the same decade that MH standards were strengthened.

The legal standard as a percentage of complete protection peaks at approximately the same levels for each of the modern labor laws—at around 50 to 60 percent of complete protection. This is quite a bit lower than the level of protection attained under WP/WC and NW. There are other differences between the level of standards in early and modern labor laws, especially between the two hours laws. OT standards became considerably stronger than MH standards, even though both were strengthened during the same decade. Until 1930, the standards for OT and MH were both about 30 percent of complete protection. But between 1930 and 1940, the number of hours a week constituting an OT standard was reduced decidedly more than the average workweek under MH. Indeed, the average workweek under OT was reduced to forty to forty-five hours, which made it much closer to the actual average workweek of manufacturing employees than was the case for MH.

Furthermore, the continued strengthening of the average legal standard for WP/WC and MH seemed clearly related to the growth of employee coverage. To determine whether this pattern obtained for modern labor laws, we calculated the five-year changes in coverage and legal standard between 1900 and 1970 for MW and OT and between 1940 and 1970 for EP and computed a Pearson product moment correlation relating employee coverage to legal standard for each law. The results of this analysis (Table 4.4) indicate that, for MW and OT, there is a very close fit between the growth in employee coverage and the growth in legal standard ($r = .71$ for MW and .84 for OT). On the other hand, change in coverage and legal standard for EP is inversely related ($r = -.56$), suggesting a trade-off between coverage and standard. In other words, new characteristics for which it is illegal to pay unequal wages are introduced in the law, but extended to a smaller group of employees, thereby decreasing the average coverage. When coverage and standard by demographic group are disaggregated and the five-year changes in the two legal provisions within each law are correlated separately by demographic group, the results are almost identical to those found for the entire United States employee population. With the exception of EP, legal standards under modern labor laws were strengthened

Table 4.4. Pearson Product Moment Correlation of Five-Year Change in Coverage and Legal Standard under Modern Labor Legislation for All Employees and by Demographic Group, 1900–1970

Demographic group	MW	OT	EP[a]
All demographic groups	.71	.84	− .56
Male adults[b]	.60	.88	− .33
Female adults	.51	.69	− .71
Male minors	.66	.72	− .41
Female minors	.43	.66	− .53
All minors	.65	.68	− .54

[a]Computed on 1940–1970 data because of small number of employees covered prior to 1940.

[b]Computed on 1935–1970 data because of small number of employees covered prior to 1935.

more frequently than was the case for early labor laws, no doubt because of the more extensive distribution of social rights to employees. This is yet another indication that the pattern of growth of coverage and standard under modern labor laws is more uniform than was found to be the case for early labor laws.

COVERAGE AND STANDARD:
PATTERNS OF GROWTH BY DEMOGRAPHIC GROUP

Recall that, when the data for early labor laws were disaggregated by demographic group, we uncovered enormous variations in coverage: virtually no men were covered under MH and NW. On the other hand, a large minority of female minors were covered under these laws, probably because they were considered to be the most marginal employee group by virtue of their combined female and child status. By contrast, there were no differences in coverage by demographic group under WP/WC. How does this compare with modern labor laws? Table 4.5 lists the percentage of employees covered under MW, OT, and EP by demographic group, and Table 4.6 presents the average legal standard for covered employees as a percentage of complete protection for each law by demographic group.

Before 1940 variations in coverage under modern labor laws by demo-

Table 4.5. Employee Coverage under Modern Labor Legislation
by Demographic Group, 1900–1970
(in percent)

Year	Minimum wage					Overtime					Equal pay				
	MA	FA	AM	MM	FM	MA	FA	AM	MM	FM	MA	FA	AM	MM	FM
1900	0	0	0	0	0	7	8	7	6	9	0	0	0	0	0
1910	0	0	0	0	0	10	8	7	8	7	0	0	0	0	0
1920	0	10	7	6	8	13	8	9	9	9	0	2	1	0	2
1930	0	12	7	6	8	14	6	8	9	7	0	2	1	0	2
1940	39	57	47	42	55	40	30	30	30	30	0	2	1	0	2
1950	42	66	57	51	67	46	36	35	36	35	19	38	23	14	38
1960	53	69	63	60	69	51	37	36	39	33	42	46	36	33	41
1970	89	91	88	88	89	73	69	67	66	67	78	75	87	87	87

Table 4.6. Average Stipulation for Covered Employees as a
Percentage of Complete Legal Protection for Modern Labor Legislation
by Demographic Group, 1900–1970

Year	Minimum wage					Overtime					Equal pay				
	MA	FA	AM	MM	FM	MA	FA	AM	MM	FM	MA	FA	AM	MM	FM
1900	0	0	0	0	0	30.4	32.0	30.6	29.8	32.0	0	0	0	0	0
1915	33	1	0	0	1	30.2	32.0	30.5	29.4	32.4	0	0	0	0	0
1918	22	1	0	0	0	32.5	31.8	31.1	30.6	32.0	0	0	0	0	0
1920	12	1	0	0	1	32.4	31.8	30.8	30.4	31.9	0	20	20	0	20
1930	13	0	0	0	0	32.7	32.1	31.3	31.1	31.1	0	20	20	0	20
1937	15	0	0	0	0	32.5	32.3	47.0	51.3	31.1	0	20	20	0	20
1938	24	13	15	17	14	46.4	47.1	46.5	46.5	46.5	0	20	20	0	20
1940	29	15	18	19	16	50.8	51.5	51.1	51.1	51.2	0	20	20	0	20
1950	42	23	25	28	22	51.0	51.7	51.3	51.1	51.5	39	30	35	40	31
1960	45	29	30	33	27	51.0	51.4	51.2	51.1	51.3	52	49	49	50	48
1961	50	38	39	41	36	50.7	51.0	50.6	50.7	50.6	52	49	49	50	48
1965	51	41	41	43	39	51.1	51.3	51.1	51.1	51.1	47	46	41	41	41
1966	53	47	47	48	45	51.2	51.1	51.0	51.0	51.0	46	45	40	40	40
1970	54	49	49	50	47	51.8	52.0	52.0	51.9	52.0	62	62	41	41	42

graphic groups are surprisingly similar to those observed for MH and NW; for MW, no male adults were provided a government-backed wage floor until the decade following the enactment of the FLSA. OT laws in which a slightly higher percentage of male adults than other groups were covered prior to 1940 must be assessed in relation to MH. During the period of adoption of early labor laws, normal day's work laws were regarded as a more flexible alternative to setting of hours standards than MH and NW. After all, men subject to the provisions of this law could work for however long they contracted. They simply had to be paid accordingly. Early OT legislation appears to have encompassed an hours standard regarded as acceptable for male adult employees.

Beginning in 1940, coverage and legal standard became strikingly uniform across demographic groups. In addition, variations across demographic groups declined over time: by 1970, for MW, for example, the maximum and minimum coverage for demographic groups differed by only 3 percentage points: 91 percent for female adults versus 88 percent for male minors. The most extreme variation in coverage was found for EP: varying from 87 percent for all minors to 75 percent for female adults. The variation in legal standard across demographic groups was likewise modest and also decreased over time as would be suggested by the correlations in Table 4.4.

Prior to 1940, coverage and legal standard varied by demographic group in a similar way for modern labor standards legislation and for early labor standards laws. Yet, beginning in 1940, modern labor laws departed from their earlier counterparts. The timing of these new patterns suggests an obvious factor accounting for this change in modern laws: the introduction of federal legislation in a legal domain that had previously been the exclusive concern of state legislatures. In the next section, I explore directly the extent to which the extensive distribution of social rights under modern labor laws and their uniform distribution across laws and across demographic groups are the consequence of the adoption of and amendments to the FLSA.

COVERAGE UNDER MODERN LABOR LAWS:
THE CONTRIBUTION OF FEDERAL LEGISLATION

In order to examine the federal contribution to the distribution of social rights, the national time series data on employee coverage were disaggregated by level of government. The calculation of the estimates of the portion of total coverage contributed by state and federal legislation was complicated somewhat by two features of the coding procedure: first, the fact that the enactment of federal legislation was coded as if twenty-eight states had passed a law; and second, the necessity, due to cost constraints, of limiting the sample to twenty-four years within the seventy-three-year time frame.

DISAGGREGATION PROCEDURE

Taking these limitations into account, we disaggregated the data as follows: additional data on coverage were introduced at key intermediate years when the FLSA or minor federal legislation was enacted or amended. Since we generated estimates for the year before federal legislation was enacted as well as the year of enactment, we were able to gauge more precisely the change in coverage attributable to federal legislation. These intermediate years included 1915, 1918, 1937, 1938, 1961, 1965, and 1966. (Unfortunately, we were unable to include in our time series data three years during which equal pay legislation was adopted or amended: 1962, the year before the federal equal pay law was passed; 1963, the year this law was passed; and 1967, the year the law was amended to prohibit age discrimination. Because of these missing years, the procedure for disaggregating coverage by level of government will result in attributing some of the employees who were actually covered by state equal pay legislation to the federal equal pay law.)

The procedure used to disaggregate coverage was based on a simplifying assumption: when no federal legislation was enacted during an interval (as in 1905–1910 or 1940–1950), we assigned all the additional coverage occurring in that interval to state legislation. When federal legislation was enacted, all of the increase in coverage in that interval was assigned to federal legislation. Specifically, for MW standards, the federal contribution to coverage occurred between 1937 and 1938, 1960 and 1961, and 1965 and 1966. OT was also enacted in these years; in addition, an early labor law extending OT standards to railroad workers was passed between 1915 and 1918. For equal pay legislation, changes in coverage between 1961 and 1965, and between 1966 and 1970, were assigned to the federal category. For each law, all other changes in the extent of coverage were treated as having been contributed through state legislative activity.[4] We disaggregated employee coverage both for the entire United States employee population (Table 4.7) and by demographic group (Table 4.8 for MW, Table 4.9 for OT, and Table 4.10 for EP).

Table 4.7. Cumulative Percentage
of Employees Covered by Modern Labor Legislation
Disaggregated by State and Federal Statutes, 1900–1970

Year	Minimum wage		Overtime		Equal pay	
	State	Federal	State	Federal	State	Federal
1900	0	0	7	0	0	0
1915	3	0	9	0	0	0
1918	3	0	9	3	0	0
1920	2	0	9	3	0	0
1930	3	0	9	3	0	0
1937	11	0	8	3	0	0
1938	11	32[a]	8	30[a]	0	0
1940	11	32	8	30	0	0
1950	16	32	13	30	23	0
1960	26	32	16	30	43	0
1961	26	44	16	38	44[b]	0
1965	30	44	17	38	44	33
1966	30	56	17	52	44	42
1970	34	56	19	52	44	34
Cumulative contribution	34	56	19	52	44	34

[a]The fact that the estimate for the federal contribution to employee coverage remains constant indicates that no significant changes in the coverage provisions of the Fair Labor Standards Act occurred between 1938 and 1961.

[b]The fact that the estimate of the state contribution to coverage under equal pay legislation remains constant is to some extent an artifact of the simplifying assumption used to assign coverage to state or federal legislation. Since federal equal pay laws were enacted in 1963 and 1967, all the change in coverage under equal pay laws between 1961 and 1970 was attributed to these federal laws.

FINDINGS

A number of interesting findings emerge, all of which point to the importance of federal legislation in dramatically increasing the distribution of social rights. First, while MW and OT differ somewhat from EP, it is clear that the additional employee coverage resulting from the first federal law establishing each set of rights included as many *additional* employees as had been covered up to that point under all state legislation. Subsequent congressional amendments to the FLSA revising MW and OT standards

Table 4.8. Cumulative Percentage
of Employees Covered by Minimum Wage Legislation by Demographic Group
Disaggregated by State and Federal Statutes, 1900–1970

Year	Male adults State	Male adults Federal	Female adults State	Female adults Federal	All minors State	All minors Federal	Male minors State	Male minors Federal	Female minors State	Female minors Federal
1900	0	0	0	0	0	0	0	0	0	0
1915	0	0	10	0	8	0	8	0	9	0
1918	0	0	11	0	8	0	8	0	9	0
1920	0	0	10	0	7	0	6	0	8	0
1930	0	0	12	0	7	0	6	0	8	0
1937	0	0	43	0	31	0	26	0	42	0
1938	0	39	43	14	31	17	26	18	42	13
1940	0	39	43	14	30	17	24	18	42	13
1950	3	39	52	14	40	17	33	18	54	13
1960	14	39	55	14	46	17	42	18	56	13
1961	14	54	55	20	46	25	42	26	56	19
1965	18	54	60	20	51	25	47	26	61	19
1966	18	68	60	27	51	34	47	38	61	24
1970	21	68	64	27	54	34	50	38	65	24
Cumulative contribution	21	68	64	27	54	34	50	38	65	24
Total coverage, 1970		89		91		88		88		89

maintained a ratio of federal-state contribution to employee coverage of approximately two to one. Therefore, the extensive employee coverage under modern labor laws witnessed in Tables 4.7–4.10 is primarily the result of federal legislative action.

By contrast, when we look only at the contribution to coverage from state laws, we find that it conforms more closely to the extent of coverage observed for early labor laws: by 1970, state legislatures extended the right to a wage floor to only 34 percent of all employees and the right to premium pay to a mere 19 percent of employees beyond what federal legislation had established. Consider that in 1970 employee coverage under OT by state legislation approximated that for MH legislation. Only in the case of EP

Table 4.9. Cumulative Percentage
of Employees Covered by Overtime Legislation by Demographic Group
Disaggregated by State and Federal Statutes, 1900–1970

Year	Male adults		Female adults		All minors		Male minors		Female minors	
	State	Federal	State	Federal	State	Federal	State	Federal	State	Federal
1900	7	0	8	0	7	0	6	0	9	0
1915	10	0	8	0	8	0	7	0	8	0
1918	10	3	8	0	8	1	7	2	8	1
1920	10	3	8	0	8	1	7	2	8	1
1930	11	3	6	0	7	1	7	2	6	1
1937	10	3	7	0	9	1	10	2	6	1
1938	10	31	7	23	9	22	10	21	6	26
1940	9	31	7	23	8	22	9	21	4	26
1950	15	31	13	23	13	22	15	21	9	26
1960	20	31	14	23	14	22	18	21	7	26
1961	20	39	14	32	14	31	18	29	7	35
1965	21	39	16	32	15	31	19	29	9	35
1966	21	50	16	50	15	49	19	44	9	55
1970	23	50	19	50	18	49	22	44	12	55
Cumulative contribution	23	50	19	50	18	49	22	44	12	55
Total coverage, 1970	73		69		67		66		67	

do we find state legislation contributing disproportionately more than federal legislation to total employee coverage. Had wage and hour standards legislation remained the exclusive domain of state governments, they might well have fared little better than their earlier legal counterparts.

Second, if we look at the rate of growth of coverage in state laws as a function of federal legislation, we find very little relation between the growth of federal legislation and the subsequent growth of state laws. We can observe this directly in Figures 4.1 and 4.2, which present the least squares regression lines fit to the data on employee coverage for each period of state adoption for MW and OT respectively. The parameters of these linear functions are indicated in Table 4.11. While coverage at the state

Table 4.10. Cumulative Percentage
of Employees Covered by Equal Pay Legislation by Demographic Group
Disaggregated by State and Federal Statutes, 1900–1970

Year	Male adults		Female adults		All minors		Male minors		Female minors	
	State	Federal	State	Federal	State	Federal	State	Federal	State	Federal
1900	0	0	0	0	0	0	0	0	0	0
1915	0	0	0	0	0	0	0	0	0	0
1918	0	0	0	0	0	0	0	0	0	0
1920	0	0	2	0	1	0	0	0	2	0
1930	0	0	2	0	1	0	0	0	2	0
1937	0	0	2	0	1	0	0	0	2	0
1938	0	0	2	0	1	0	0	0	2	0
1940	0	0	2	0	1	0	0	0	2	0
1950	19	0	38	0	23	0	14	0	38	0
1960	42	0	46	0	36	0	33	0	41	0
1961	43	0	47	0	37	0	34	0	42	0
1965	43	35	47	29	37	35	34	36	42	33
1966	43	44	47	37	37	46	34	49	42	42
1970	43	35	47	28	37	50	34	53	42	45
Cumulative contribution	43	35	47	28	37	50	34	53	42	45
Total coverage, 1970	78		75		87		87		87	

level appears to grow at a slightly increasing rate over time, the betas for the lines fit to the four periods of state activity on MW and OT reveal no significant differences in the rate of growth.[5] Not only did state activity on these laws remain quite meager over time, it also appears to have been remarkably unresponsive to federal legislative action. To the extent that state responded to legislative action, state MW and OT laws at best included coverage provisions identical to those found in the FLSA. Therefore, the pattern of growth for MW and OT laws displayed in the figures is characterized by long stretches of modest growth in coverage resulting from state legislation, followed by a rapid increase in coverage resulting from federal legislation.

Figure 4.1. Least Squares Regression Lines Fit to Coverage
under State Minimum Wage Legislation, 1900–1973.

Breaks in line indicate change in level of coverage resulting from federal legislation.

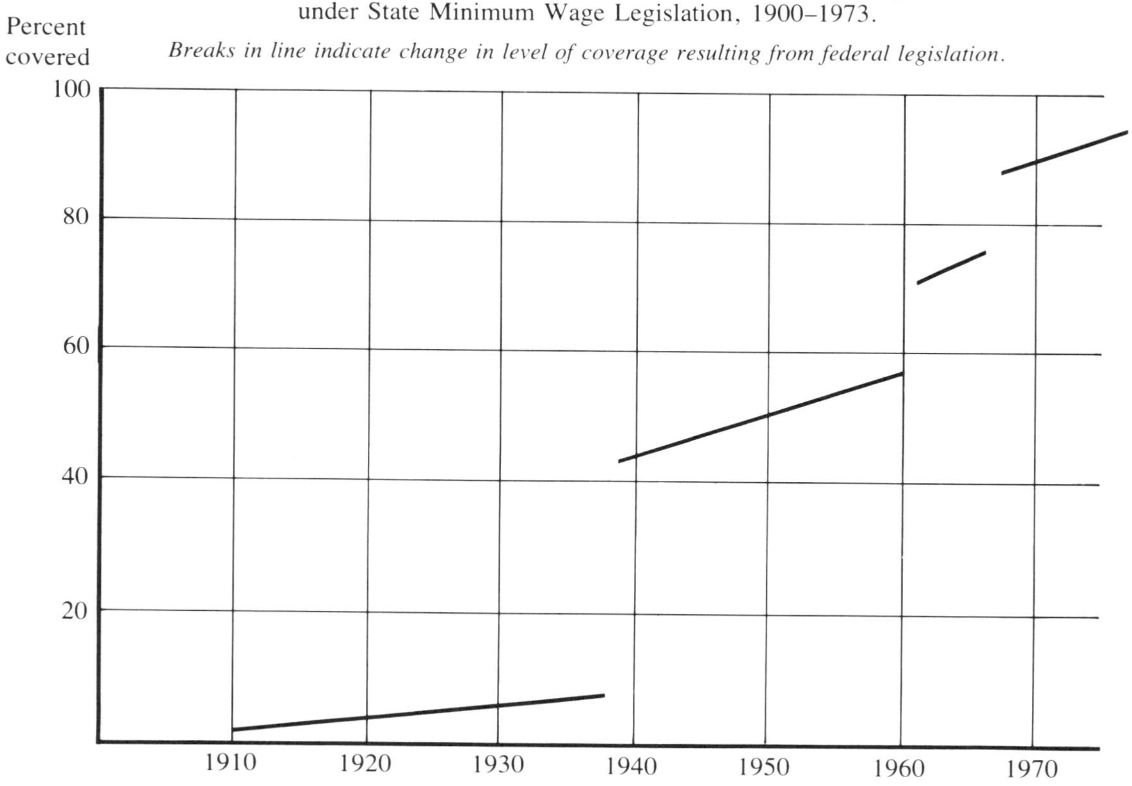

Figure 4.2. Least Squares Regression Lines Fit to Coverage
under State Overtime Legislation, 1900–1973.

Breaks in line indicate change in level of coverage resulting from federal legislation.

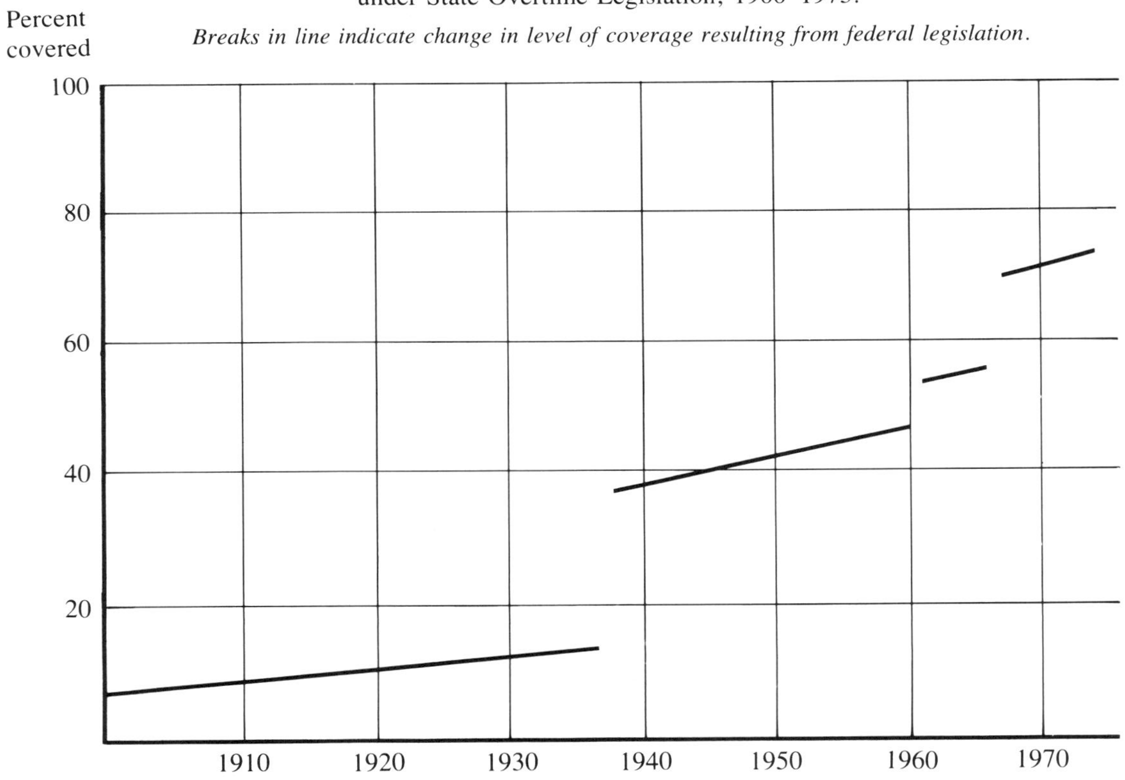

Table 4.11. Parameters and Goodness of Fit for
Least Squares Regression Lines Fit to Percentage of Employees Covered
under State Minimum Wage and Overtime Legislation, 1900–1973

Law	1900–1937			1938–1960			1961–1965			1966–1973		
	B	A	R^2	B	A	R^2	B	A	R^2	B	A	R^2
Minimum wage coverage	.24	−1.35	.73	.65	17.28	.93	1.00	9.00	1.0	.86	29.08	.99
Overtime coverage	.12	7.90	.62	.41	21.88	.97	.25	38.75	1.0	.57	31.46	.99

Third, when the contribution of federal legislation to the greater uniformity in coverage under these laws, as well as the uniformity in coverage
by demographic group, is examined, employer discretion again turns out
to be an important factor. Recall that for early labor laws there were striking
variations in the extent of coverage: it was most extensive for WP/WC and
extremely limited for NW. One factor believed to account for the differences
in coverage across these laws was the extent to which employers' discretion
to organize the work setting was restricted by the legal standard: the more
the rights in these laws restricted employer discretion, the more limited
the scope of legal coverage. In other words, the more a law implied the
possible reorganization of production, the more it would be resisted by
employers. Moreover, I argued that labor standards specifying the conditions
to be followed were more flexible than labor standards setting the actual
terms of contract and hence met with less employer resistance. Consequently,
the scope of coverage under laws with more flexible standards would be
greater than it would be for the less flexible laws.

Of the modern labor laws, OT standards require the most radical reorganization of work arrangements, regardless of the occupational category.
In OT, the employer is allowed to work the labor force as many hours per
week as she or he wants as long as employees are paid premium pay for
hours worked beyond the government-specified workweek. OT regulations,
on the other hand, are more sophisticated than early hours standards laws.
Although MH and NW constrain work arrangements to a greater extent than
OT, the requirement that premium pay go directly to employees is effectively
an additional enforcement mechanism: if the employee does not report a
violation, it is the employee who loses. Therefore, it is in the economic
interest of employees to report violations. Indeed, OT laws were designed
by Secretary of Labor Frances Perkins precisely to provide more flexibility
to the employer and greater enforceability than was achieved under early
hours standards laws. Hence, OT standards impinge upon an employer's
discretion to the extent that retaining employees beyond a certain number
of hours is not cost free.

Both EP and MW regulate the wage bargain. Neither curtails the autonomy of all employers over the organization of production in the workplace,
except in extreme cases where employers choose to substitute capital for
labor because of increased labor costs. But this is where the similarity
between EP and MW ends. EP specifies a set of conditions that must be
followed: it prohibits the employer from paying employees who do the same
work differently because of their age, sex, color, religion, or other ascribed
characteristics. It does not tell an employer what the rate of pay should

be. MW, on the other hand, establishes a specific term that must be met. This standard constrains owners, especially in low-wage, labor intensive industries. It impinges on employers by changing their production costs; however, it applies to a smaller range of employers than OT does. Perhaps even more important is the fact that MW involves government directly in determining one of the most important items in the employment contract. The liberty of contract of the laborer rests, after all, on the freedom to sell labor to the buyer who offers the highest wage. Perhaps more to the point, the liberty of contract of the employer rests on his or her freedom to buy labor at the lowest possible wage. Establishing a wage floor constitutes a more direct intervention in the labor contract than the establishment of procedural guidelines in EP. In this respect, EP laws impinge upon the autonomy of the employer to a lesser extent than MW laws. The matrix in Figure 4.3 presents a rough summary of this discussion.

The data in Table 4.7 indicate that, at the state level, the extent of coverage under modern labor laws varied: specifically, state-level coverage was most extensive for EP and least extensive for OT. Therefore, the variation in coverage observed for state-initiated legislation is plausibly explained by the employer-autonomy argument. More than one-half of all employees covered under EP reap these benefits from state legislation. On the other hand, the greatest resistance at the state level appears to be to OT laws. In this case, a mere 13 percent of the employee population received state protection against excessive working hours in the postdepression era. In fact, by 1970, fewer employees were covered under all state OT laws than were protected as a result of the enactment of the FLSA in 1938. As

Figure 4.3. Variations in the Restriction of Employer Autonomy under Modern Labor Laws.

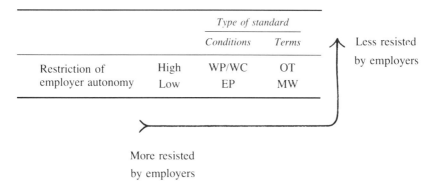

		Type of standard		
		Conditions	Terms	
Restriction of	High	WP/WC	OT	Less resisted by employers
employer autonomy	Low	EP	MW	

More resisted
by employers

predicted, MW falls between EP and OT. Almost one-third of all covered employees received MW rights through state laws. Yet these rights were extended after, not before, the enactment of the FLSA. (The linkage between state and federal MW laws is explored in Chapter 7.) At the state level, then, the variation in coverage across legislation appears to persist. Federal legislation becomes a force counteracting the tendency for coverage under state laws to vary by, among other things, the threat to employer discretion posed by the standards.

Finally, the parallel fate of early and modern wage and hour standards legislation at the hands of state legislators is further demonstrated in the data on coverage by demographic group. Women and minors, who were regarded as the legal inferiors of male adults, were disproportionately covered under early labor laws, especially MH and NW. Moreover, the more the standard curtailed employer discretion, the lower the extent of coverage. The same holds for modern labor laws. Approximately 40 percent of female adults and female minors were covered by pre-FLSA state MW legislation, with slightly more than one-quarter of male minors receiving these rights (Table 4.8). No male adults were covered under pre-FLSA MW, and very few gained these rights through state legislation between 1940 and 1970. Even more striking is the finding that, subsequent to the adoption of the FLSA, the federal law disproportionately contributed to the coverage of male adults. Indeed, the relative contributions to coverage of male adults from state and federal legislation are almost the reverse of those for female adults and minors with, by 1970, 68 percent of all male adult employees subject to legislation initially passed by Congress and 64 percent of all female adult employees covered by state legislation.

At the other extreme is EP legislation (Table 4.10). Although at first legislation seemed to benefit women workers to a greater extent than men, the coverage across demographic groups became quite uniform within twenty years. In 1950, for example, an almost 20 percent difference in coverage existed between male and female adults; by 1960, the gap between the two groups had been reduced to 4 percent.

Coverage under state OT laws constitutes the one exception to this general pattern. There were only slight differences in coverage across demographic groups over most of the seventy-year period (Table 4.9). As indicated, OT laws should be treated as both an early and a modern counterpart of MH. Normal day's work laws were treated as early hours standards for men. The fact that coverage is uniform across demographic groups should not obscure the fact that, left in the hands of state legislatures, coverage under OT would have remained extremely small.

STATE AND FEDERAL CONTRIBUTION TO THE
GROWTH OF SOCIAL RIGHTS: CONCLUSIONS

The contribution of state legislation to coverage under modern labor laws follows several patterns similar to those observed for early labor standards legislation. Coverage under state labor legislation throughout the twentieth century remains a function of both the stringency of standards to which employers are subject and the perceived contract rights of employees based on their demographic characteristics. In both these respects, the introduction of federal legislation compensates for the limited scope and basis of coverage under state legislation. First, federal legislation particularly benefits male adults, who were excluded from coverage under most of the early labor laws. Second, federal legislation contributes more to coverage than state legislation for those laws curtailing employer autonomy. The legal rights extended through the FLSA are distributed to employees previously excluded from these forms of government protection. Consequently, the introduction of federal legislation is especially advantageous to subordinate power groups.

These findings about modern labor laws confirm some hypotheses put forward by E. E. Schattschneider in *The Semisovereign People* (1960). Schattschneider hypothesized that in a polity guaranteeing to all individuals formal democratic rights—including (by the end of the 1930s) the right to organize—the greater the "socialization" of a conflict between groups with unequal power resources, the greater the benefit to those in a subordinate power position. To nationalize a conflict is to further socialize it in Schattschneider's view. Broadening a conflict to involve Congress in an issue heretofore the exclusive domain of state legislatures provides subordinate groups with access to decision makers whose actions will affect more employees than any single action by a state legislative body possibly could. Socializing a conflict also means that a large number of "neutral" citizens will become aware of the situation faced by employees. Since the rules of the game are structured so as to place subordinate groups at a disadvantage to other groups, they are more likely to bring an issue into the political arena in the first place. Once in that arena, they can do best at the level of government that affects the greatest number of employees. Federal legislation contributes to overcoming the structural bias against employees in the labor market by expanding the distribution of their social rights, and in so doing, changes the rules of the game (Bachrach and Baratz, 1970).

Moreover, increasing the scope of the conflict provides subordinate groups with an additional power resource necessary to transform the basis upon which social rights are extended. Indeed, the extensive and uniformly distributed coverage under modern labor standards laws reflects a profound transformation of the legal basis upon which coverage is extended. Until the late 1930s, labor standards legislation was regarded as a set of legal rights available to those who were seen as operating outside the legal boundaries of a laissez-faire system by virtue of some characteristic. Beginning in the 1930s, the right to the government resource of a legislative standard became the precondition to the realization of equal legal status of the employee and employer—the legal pillar upon which freedom of contract rests. Starting as stop-gap legislation under extraordinary conditions, wage and hour standards laws became an ordinary right accorded to those who must sell their labor. Over the twentieth century, the status of workers became the primary basis of coverage under these government reforms.

Furthermore, the transformation of the legal basis of coverage signaled a change in the role of law in the labor market. When women and children entered the industrial labor market, it became necessary to introduce new legislation to regulate social relationships that fell outside the existing legal framework. In this sense, law was a tool to create new social relationships through contractual means. The more universal coverage of modern labor legislation, however, suggests that law is introduced to compensate workers for the political inequalities that underlie all social relationships in the labor market. MW, OT, and EP laws are modern, then, not only because they include legislation more recently adopted, but also because the basis for coverage reflects more closely the legal realities operating in modern industrial society. The early labor laws that emerged in the new industrial society tenuously rested upon the legal assumptions of the old laissez-faire state. With modern labor laws, the new industrial state has been created out of the old industrial society.

THE POLITICS LINKING SOCIAL CHANGE AND SOCIAL REFORM

Thus far, our attention has been focused on the development of modern labor legislation. We have seen that congressional action on a set of laws which had previously been the exclusive domain of state governments transformed the basis of coverage under these laws. We have also observed that coverage under all of these laws took off on the heels of a major societal crisis: for MW and OT, the Great Depression and, for EP, World War II. The discussion turns now to the history underlying the enactment of the laws and the strengthening of the coverage provisions, specifically why the federal government intervened in this legal domain when it did.

It is clear from the differences in the pattern of development for MW and OT on the one hand, and EP on the other, that it would be wrong to assume that a simple equation can be made between social crisis conditions and the enactment of federal laws benefiting subordinate power groups. First, such an explanation fails to account for the fact that, following the Great Depression, MW and OT were enacted by Congress, whereas, following World War II, equal pay legislation was enacted on a state-by-state basis. It also obscures the fact that the federal government's previous response to political demands by subordinate groups had been to suppress the groups. Finally, a simple formula brackets all the steps that link the emergence of a crisis and the subsequent adoption of a piece of legislation without considering the general conditions under which progressive social policy is likely to be passed and sustained over time.

The economic crisis of the 1930s was of such major proportions that only federal programs could begin to solve the pressing social problems it created. It constituted, however, a different type of crisis from World War II. Modern wars are characterized by government-directed economic "superorganization" as well as by a significant (and visible) influx of women and racial minorities into the work force. In these crises class conflict is subordinated to larger nationalist sentiments. Depressions, on the other hand, are periods of massive dislocation and social disorganization which lower the bargaining position, and therefore the status, of all workers. They therefore crystallize class differences. Finally, the nature of the political demands for the enactment and improvement of these laws, as well as the nature of organized collective action and the perceived voter support of these groups, further influenced the development of these laws.

THE FAIR LABOR STANDARDS ACT

THE FISCAL CRISIS OF THE STATES

The backdrop for New Deal legislation, of which the MW and OT standards of the FLSA were one component, was the most severe economic depression in United States history (Grey and Peterson, 1974:428). Not only was it the longest depression, it was also the most staggering in terms of the number of employees who were thrown out of work: by 1933, approximately one-third of all workers were unemployed (Piven and Cloward, 1971:49). Those who continued to work suffered major cuts in wages: "In September 1931, United States Steel surrendered with the announcement that wages would be reduced 10 percent; despite A.F.L. protests the announcement started an avalanche of wage reductions. . . . A second wholesale round of cuts was imposed in the spring of 1932; a third round began in the fall of 1932" (Rayback, 1966:314). Obviously, a crisis of this magnitude created political demands for programs to alleviate the distress. One labor historian has written of this period that "when labor recovered from the initial shock of the depression, its first impulse was to turn to the government for aid" (Rayback, 1966:315). During the early period of the Great Depression, the calls for action by state legislatures fell on deaf ears. State governments themselves faced a set of double binds exacerbated by this economic crisis. They proved incapable of responding to these demands for at least two reasons identified in an informative study, *The New Deal and the States* (Patterson, 1969:24–25): first, the economy had become one of national rather than local markets. By the 1920s, "many reforms remained within the potential of the states, but many more did not: only Congress could . . . establish nationwide labor standards . . . and control the increasingly inter-state character of commerce." Second, and more important, the great crash of 1929 rendered the states insolvent. Summarizing this situation, Patterson says: "The Depression staggered state and local officials, and it was years before they recovered from the blow. Already deep in debt from the deficit spending of the 1920's, they now faced sharply rising welfare costs at a time when tax revenues were falling with equal speed. The economic crisis, de-scending so quickly and unexpectedly, paralyzed the state governments. The resulting chaos (in state public policy) between 1929 and 1933 exposed the limits of the states in an increasingly centralized age" (Patterson, 1969:26).

If there was to be a political response to this national crisis, it would have to be a national one. Yet, the historical record of federal response to such political demands did not leave much room for optimism. Federal activity prior to the New Deal was always directed at suppressing labor action and restoring order and was generally a response to the requests of employers. To cite several examples: in 1877, in reaction to the recession of 1873, the railroad workers organized what is now called the Railway Strike of 1877, which has been described as "the most violent and significant labor upheaval of the nineteenth century." Federal troops were sent in by President Grant as a last resort to quell this labor militance. The govern-ment troops successfully broke the efforts of the strikers (Rayback, 1966: 133–134). Again, the depression of 1893 formed the background for further labor unrest in the Pullman strike. The response by government was some-what more complex. In 1894, the Pullman Palace Car Company workers walked off the job in reaction to, among other issues, a wage cut of 22 percent. That labor action was supported by a general boycott on the part of the American Railway Union headed by Eugene Debs. Fortunately for the railroad managers, United States Attorney General Richard Olney was a former railroad lawyer and sympathetic to their interests. Viewing a railway as a public highway, he saw federal intervention as justified protection against the restraint of trade. A highly misleading telegram concerning the extent of labor militance from some of Olney's proemployer subordinates convinced President Cleveland that a federal response was justified. Within two weeks, approximately "fourteen thousand state and federal soldiers patrolled the streets and railroad right of way." A subsequent commission report on the strike confirmed that it was the appearance of federal troops that had provoked labor violence. It also spurred the collapse of the strike (Rayback, 1966:200–204).

As late as 1932, President Hoover turned his back on citizens—largely unemployed workers—who marched on Washington for food and jobs. "Where he did not turn his back, in December 1931, participants in the first two . . . national hunger marches on Washington were met on the ramps leading to the Capitol by police armed with rifles and riot guns (backed up by machine-gun nests concealed in the stonework above)" (Piven and Cloward, 1971:64–65). Indeed, the New Deal reforms, which include wage and hour standards laws, have been called by E. E. Schattschneider "the greatest reversal of public policy in American history" (1960:86).

Two questions emerge: what reversed the federal response to labor's political demands? What led to the continued extension of these rights after the Great Depression had passed into history?

By 1920 the market in commodities had shifted from the local to the national level. What brought about the New Deal programs was a unique realignment of American politics that grew out of the Great Depression. A combination of factors was involved: the landslide elections of 1932 and, perhaps more important, 1936, which, building on the electoral strength of the working class, accorded Roosevelt a substantial electoral majority; the persistence (despite the setbacks of the 1920s) of an organized labor movement that represented, by the end of World War I, a significant minority of the total work force; and, finally, the existence of institutionalized channels of communication between representatives of organized labor and government bureaucrats, which allowed for an immediate give and take on appropriate government solutions of the crisis. While the electoral majorities of 1932, 1934, and 1936 facilitated the adoption of the FLSA, even against the opposition of organized labor, the support by organized labor of the FLSA after its enactment facilitated the continued improvement in the law.

MINIMUM WAGE AND OVERTIME LEGISLATION

The battle for the FLSA was first fought in the halls of the Department of Labor. Frances Perkins, secretary of labor under Roosevelt, wanted to enact a statutory minimum wage to bolster the purchasing power of employees. Organized labor opposed such a measure for two reasons: a wage law would undermine existing union contracts and would quickly turn a wage floor into a wage ceiling (Brandeis, 1972:203–204; Forsythe, 1939:467). They proposed, instead, a bill establishing a mandatory thirty-hour workweek without loss of pay (Brandeis, 1972:201). Such a measure was introduced by Senator, soon to be Supreme Court Justice, Hugo Black; it passed in the Senate, but Roosevelt's lack of support led to its defeat in the House (Brandeis, 1972:203–204).

Realizing the importance of hours standards to organized labor, Perkins set out to achieve a compromise: a law that included both a minimum wage standard and a flexible hours standard—that is, a standard requiring additional pay at a higher hourly rate for work beyond forty hours a week.[6] Organized labor's ambivalent backing of these laws was more than compensated for by the overwhelming support of the New Deal electoral coalition. In 1936, the FLSA was a major campaign issue for both parties. The Republicans proposed state legislation, while the Democrats pledged national legislation. President Roosevelt personally spoke in support of the law on many occasions (Rayback, 1966:358). The reelection of Roosevelt constituted the biggest landslide victory ever enjoyed by a candidate: "A rise of nearly 6 [million] above the polling figures of 1932 had carried every state for Roosevelt save New Hampshire and Vermont, and all cities of 100,000 inhabitants or more; 5 out of 6 new voters had given him their ballots . . . in almost every major city of the United States the Republican-Democrat voting division broke along a horizontal economic line. . . . An entire economic class had given Roosevelt a majority of more than 3 to 1 in the House and more than 4 to 1 in the Senate" (Vale, 1971:62–63).

This electoral victory was the resource Roosevelt and Perkins needed. When what has come to be called the self-reconstructed Supreme Court reversed its opposition to government-enacted minimum wage standards, Perkins was waiting in the wings.[7] The Fair Labor Standards Act was introduced in Congress in mid-1937, and, upon further compromise with representatives of the labor movement (which resulted in the removal of regional wage differentials and of provisions for wage board procedures in addition to the flat but flexible wage and hour standards), it was adopted (Brandeis,

1972; Forsythe, 1939). Thus, the transformation of the basis upon which employees were accorded the right to government protection under the FLSA rested on nothing less than a national class conflict, as expressed in the 1936 election.[8]

Once the FLSA was implemented, organized labor found its fears to be groundless. In turn, once the labor movement (and especially the AFL) had reversed its early opposition to the FLSA, the survival and extension of this reform rested on secure foundations. Even if most union members were earning well above the minimum wage, the overtime provisions requiring one and one-half times the rate of pay for work done beyond a forty-hour week benefited all workers regardless of their rate of pay. Indeed, since the higher the hourly rate of pay, the higher the hourly rate of overtime benefit, trade unionists (among the highest paid workers) differentially benefited from the overtime provisions of this law. (Other reasons for union support are discussed in Chapter 8.) Within a few years of the adoption of the FLSA, the extension of its coverage and the improvement of its standards became a routine part of the political agenda of organized labor. In its legislative history of the FLSA, the Bureau of National Affairs repeatedly cites organized labor as the major group pressuring for continual improvements in this law. For example, of the 1949 amendments, the bureau writes: "In 1949, Congress undertook the first general overhauling of the Act since it went on the statute books in 1938. Like the original Act, the 1949 amendments represented a compromise. While the minimum wage was raised from 40 to 75 cents an hour, the coverage of the Act was narrowed. Pressure for restoring this lost coverage began building up within organized labor immediately" (Bureau of National Affairs, 1961:i). Recounting the history of the 1966 amendments, the bureau writes: "In a special message on labor legislation, President Johnson proposed that the Act be amended (1) to extend its protection to an additional 4½ million workers and (2) to restrict excessive overtime work through the payment of doubletime. . . . The proposals fell short of the goals of the AFL-CIO, which wanted a broader extension of coverage and increase in the minimum wage for employees already covered by the Act" (Bureau of National Affairs, 1967:39). The Great Depression, a national crisis that divided the nation along economic lines, stimulated concern over the level of wages. An electoral mandate to act proved the sufficient condition for stimulating a federal response. Once the crisis had passed and the concern with wages and hours had retreated from public consciousness, organized group support was necessary to sustain the gains that the crisis and electoral returns had made possible. But, the AFL-CIO not only sustained these gains, they fought successfully to extend them to as yet uncovered workers.

The importance of the labor movement to the survival and further development of the FLSA can be seen by contrasting it to welfare legislation, such as Aid to Families with Dependent Children (AFDC). In their path-breaking study, *Regulating the Poor*, Frances Fox Piven and Richard Cloward describe a cyclical pattern for AFDC, in which amendments strengthening the provisions of welfare laws are instituted during an economic crisis and rescinded after the crisis subsides. Insofar as the original adoption of AFDC is concerned, the essential difference between it and the FLSA is the different casts in the two dramas. The underlying process was essentially the same in both cases. Piven and Cloward attribute the passage of federal welfare programs to political factors: political unrest among the unemployed and the electoral realignment of 1932. In fact, because AFDC was unencumbered by conservative Supreme Court precedents, programs for the unemployed were established during Roosevelt's first year in office.

Yet, the subsequent histories of welfare legislation and labor standards legislation diverged sharply. Change in welfare legislation, according to Piven and Cloward, involved the expansion and contraction of coverage and benefits, which occurred as a function of the political visibility of unorganized and unemployed workers. By contrast, modern labor standards legislation continuously improved as coverage was expanded and standards strengthened.

Perhaps the differences in the fate of the two reforms in the mid-twentieth century can be accounted for by the absence of stable, institutionalized groups to support welfare reforms. As Piven and Cloward amply document, groups who at various times during the twentieth century protested their unemployed status dissipated quickly when economic conditions began to improve. But organized labor had come a long way since the mid- and late nineteenth century when, like the organizations of the unemployed, its survival depended on the peaks and troughs of the business cycle. By the Great Depression, the labor movement had become a stable federation of organizations, and the national leadership of the AFL was perceived as the legitimate representative of a certain segment of the working class. Finally, organized labor had direct access to the executive and legislative branches of government and no longer had need for militant demonstrations to gain visibility (Piven and Cloward, 1971:Chapter 2). In this way are the nature of group support and the outcome of public policy integrally linked.

EQUAL PAY LEGISLATION

In certain respects the evolution of equal pay coverage diverged sharply from that of MW or OT. By isolating the differences, it becomes possible to reveal several important factors necessary to achieve federal action on social legislation in general. First, the crisis stimulating interest in equal pay legislation was substantially different from the one that led to the adoption of the FLSA. Second, the constellation of social forces supporting federal EP legislation was different from those supporting MW and OT. For EP, the labor movement was the primary, and in many states, the sole proponent of these laws; it took almost twenty years for labor to amass the electoral support necessary to legitimize nationally its political demands. In the meanwhile, it turned to state legislatures: until 1963, the adoption of state equal pay laws was the result of extensive lobbying by representatives of labor unions—especially the industrial unions organized in the 1930s. Finally, despite the fact that EP was established in state legislation, existing federal labor standards legislation covering male adults set a precedent for laws with universal coverage provisions, regardless of the level of government: in 1950, for example, 36 percent of the states had adopted some piece of legislation aimed at correcting wage discrimination. Approximately 36 percent were subject to the provisions of these laws. Again, in 1960, 54 percent of the states distributed these social rights to about 51 percent of all employees. Employee coverage did not quickly fall behind the cumulative percentage of state adoption for equal pay legislation as it did for all early wage and hour standards laws.

During World War II, the combined needs of the military and of industry for war production created an unprecedented demand for new workers.

During the course of the war some 11,000,000 men and women dropped their peacetime pursuits to enter the armed services. At least 60 percent either were employed in industry and allied enterprises or would have become industrial workers under normal circumstances. The manpower needs of the fighting front thus created a very large gap in the nation's labor supply. In addition the need for war material increased the demand for industrial workers to hitherto unheard-of numbers. In 1938, nonagricultural enterprises used the services of 27,000,000 persons; by war's end the total of nonagricultural employees reached 38,000,000. This additional working force was recruited from many elements: the formerly unemployed, the normally unemployable, farmers, oldsters, women—of which there were 6,000,000 employed—and children who were ordinarily barred from industry (Rayback, 1966:375).

Because women and blacks had previously been a source of cheap labor, trade unions and other employee representatives made great efforts to ensure that the wage scale that had been established for white adult males would not be undercut by those who filled their positions.

To deter the deterioration of pay scales, temporary federal regulations established the right to equal pay for equal work. This policy initially emerged out of a dispute between the General Motors Corporation and the United Auto Workers brought to the War Board. In its decision, the board required these parties to include a provision guaranteeing equal pay in their next contract (Baker, 1964:414). The decision became Executive Order 16 which "authorized employers voluntarily to raise women's wage to those of men 'for work of comparable quantity or quality on the same or similar operations' without applying to the board for advance permissions" (Baker, 1964:414). It was to be effective for the duration of the war.[9] Moreover, several states, including New Jersey, Illinois, and New York, enacted either a fair employment practices act, which prohibited wage discrimination, or an equal pay law.

It was assumed that women workers would leave the labor market when the war was over. At the very least, women and black workers were expected to step out of the skilled positions they had occupied during the war and assume semiskilled or unskilled production work if they chose to remain in the labor market. Contrary to expectations, a large portion of these employees remained in the labor market (Chafe, 1972:Chapter 8). The economic conditions of this postwar period—in which there was an ample labor supply relative to demand—spurred the labor movement to secure equal pay legislation so that workers would not divide among themselves and drive down the wage rate. Theresa Wolfson, a prominent observer of the labor movement, summarized labor's reasoning in an article she wrote during the Second World War: "Even though some members of trade unions balked at the entrance of women into their industry, they recognize that . . . wage differentials represent a serious bone of conflict in a possible postwar era of unemployment. Not out of altruism but out of pure self-preservation, many unions have insisted on the 'equal pay for equal work' doctrine; for where an employer can get his work done by a labor force which costs less, he is less likely to concern himself with sex, race, or religion of that labor supply" (1943:50). Another observer, writing somewhat later, remarked that "the timing, phrasing, and interpretation of the orders and laws have made clear, irrespective of the justice to women that may be involved, that they are designed to protect men, to prevent degradation of the wage structure at a time when it is necessary to maintain the morale of the worker" (Brady, 1947:54).

At the same time that the labor movement was pressing for equal pay legislation at the state level in industrial states, it was also pressing for identical federal standards. In addition to equal pay legislation, pressure to pass a federal fair employment practices act came in 1941 from "a threatened march on Washington, organized by the Negro Brotherhood of Sleeping Car Porters" (Vale, 1971:122). Neither proposal came to a vote in Congress. In 1945, the equal pay bill was approved in the committees of both houses, but never came to a vote (Baker, 1964:415). In 1947, President Truman proposed that the FLSA be amended to prohibit discrimination in employment, including wage discrimination on the basis of sex. Although the law was strongly supported by the CIO, it made little headway (Rayback, 1966:405).

These legislative defeats reflected the changing tide of public opinion toward organized labor following World War II. The labor movement was suffering from a crisis of legitimacy in which the public was outraged by what it perceived to be labor's excessive power. The public felt that labor, having engaged in large-scale strikes in 1945–1946, was to blame for the current economic problems (Rayback, 1966:394–395). So, instead of passing equal pay laws, Congress enacted, for example, the antiunion Taft-Hartley Act in 1947. This antiunion bias was compounded by an apathetic electorate. The mid-term elections of 1946 were a great setback for labor. In spite of the attempt by the CIO's Political Action Committee to get out the vote, "barely 38 percent of the electorate balloted. . . . Only 73 out of the PAC's 318 endorsees were returned to the House, only 5 out of 21 to the Senate" (Vale, 1971:101). These elections ushered in what one author has called "government by default" (Vale, 1971:89).

Consequently, the absence of political support for both labor and labor's political agenda delayed federal legislation for some twenty years. An electoral base, which had been the crucial underpinning of the enactment of the FLSA, was conspicuously absent on the issue of equal pay. It was not until 1960 that labor could demonstrate its capacity to deliver the critical votes to a winning presidential candidate. Not surprisingly, the following year the wage and hour provisions of the FLSA were extensively revised. Two years later, the equal pay amendment to the FLSA was passed. Until the Kennedy and Johnson administrations, labor had been forced to follow a more narrow political route: it had to win equal pay legislation in highly unionized states because in those states it could demonstrate its capacity to reward or punish state legislators on the basis of their positions on the laws it favored.

In summary, crisis conditions are not automatically translated into the enactment of social reform legislation by Congress. Political factors form a crucial mediating link. Those groups that desire the adoption of federal legislation—be they government bureaucrats in the case of MW and OT, or labor lobbyists for EP—must demonstrate, at the very least, that the support of the general electorate is solidly behind their political demands. The history of the enactment of these laws, therefore, identifies the centrality of electoral outcomes to the successful enactment or emendation of federal legislation designed to benefit subordinate groups. Electoral outcomes cannot bring about change by themselves, however. Rather, voting outcomes must be used by organized groups to prove that widespread support for their political demands exists.

SUMMARY AND CONCLUSIONS

By contrast with early labor legislation, the coverage and the legal standard in modern labor laws were uniform across laws and across demographic groups. Furthermore, the distribution of legal rights was far more extensive under modern labor laws than was true for the earlier laws. Once the relative contributions to coverage made by federal and by state legislation were separated out, it was strikingly apparent that these observed gains in the distribution of legal rights to subordinate groups could be accounted for by the differential contribution of the provisions of federal legislation. Moreover, the contribution to coverage by federal legislation varied both by demographic group and by the characteristics of the law in relation to its restraint on employer discretion. Federal legislation significantly benefited male adults who had been excluded from coverage under most state wage and hour standards laws. Also, the more restrictive the standards were with respect to the curtailment of employer autonomy, the greater the federal contribution to coverage.

Viewed symbolically, with the introduction of federal legislation, the right to the government resource of a legislative standard became a precondition to the realization of equal legal status—the legal pillar upon which freedom of contract rested. In the case of these laws, the legal rights simultaneously transformed the concrete application of freedom of contract and reestablished it as the primary norm guiding economic relations. Consequently, the status of being a worker became the primary basis of coverage under government labor standards in the second third of the twentieth century.

Perhaps the greatest uniformity of the three modern labor laws is that their development took off on the heels of a major societal crisis: for MW and OT, the Great Depression; for EP, World War II. The pattern of enactment of these laws, however, is intricately tied to the nature of the crisis as it affects social relations in general, and the economic relations in the labor market in particular. The impact of the crisis on social relations affects, in turn, the political response to legislative demands. When groups committed to legislation helping those in a subordinate power position can legitimize the groups' demands through voting returns, it is more likely that Congress will act favorably on the issue at hand. If groups cannot display such support at the national level, they must resort to political action at the state level where the scope of the outcome is more restricted in the short run. In this respect, elections—which have been called "the expression of the democratic class struggle" by Seymour Martin Lipset (1960)—form the crucial political factor shaping the limits and possibilities of social reform at the federal level of government in twentieth-century America.

5

THE SOCIAL MEANING OF
INDUSTRIALIZATION

Histories of labor standards laws, especially of the subset known as protective labor laws, single out the demographic group of the employee as the predominant factor accounting for the observed variations in coverage across employee groups. Demographic group served as the basis for the formulation of coverage, at least for MH and NW, where legal protection for women and minors not accorded conventional contract rights was perceived as appropriate and legitimate. During the 1930s, however, the Great Depression transformed notions of the power relations in the labor market. This experience permanently altered the basis upon which government standards were distributed: in particular the sex and age of the employee came to be seen as secondary to the more fundamental fact that all employees selling their labor in the free market bargained from a position subordinate to that of employers.

Moreover, these histories of labor standards laws more often than not arrived at their conclusions concerning the distribution of coverage through a simple reading of the provisions of legislation, which they then related to the more indirect evidence provided in Supreme Court decisions. The data generated here, however, in which these legal provisions are tied to the actual distribution of the labor force in a state, provide a more direct measure of the actual distribution of coverage. It is likely that a variety of factors accounted for the distribution of coverage to employee groups. It is also possible that such determinants of coverage changed over time. Since we estimated coverage over the twentieth century, we can systematically analyze how, if at all, the determinants of coverage changed over time. In this chapter, the earlier analysis of the national patterns of change in these laws is extended by probing further into the observed variations in coverage. Whereas, in earlier chapters, I described and discussed the distribution of coverage by demographic group and by level of government, in this chapter I assess how much of the actual distribution of employee coverage under these laws can be accounted for by the following three characteristics of employees: their demographic group, their industry group, and their region.

THREE FACTORS: A BACKGROUND

In Chapter 3, the legal and social basis for extending certain social rights to women and minors that were denied to male adults was discussed at considerable length. It is likely that coverage under these laws varies as well, however, by industry and by region. For example, the general consensus is that labor standards laws are a concomitant of an industrial society, and it seems likely that agricultural employees will be excluded from coverage under these laws—at least when the laws are first enacted. Similarly, if the states in one region are, in general, less sympathetic to the civil and social rights of subordinate groups than the states in another region, it is likely that the region in which a law is passed may explain the variations in coverage across some of these laws.

Even more specific industrial, regional, or demographic group differences than those captured in the preceding examples may cause the variations of coverage. A state in one region, for instance, may have as high a percentage of employees in manufacturing as a state in another region; yet, most workers in one state may work in labor-intensive industries, such as textiles, while a second state's industrial economy may hinge largely on steel and iron. States with labor-intensive industries are likely to have a higher percentage of females in the work force. Therefore, as suggested above, it may be that although the coverage provisions are written in terms of the sex of the employee, the actual distribution of social rights is more a function of industry than of demographic group. Second, states vary with respect to the number of women and children employed in nonagricultural and non-domestic service occupations. For example, in 1900 the number of women and minors in manufacturing pursuits was high in the Southeast and North-east and almost nonexistent in some states such as California. Again, is the actual variation in coverage attributable to region or to demographic group?

Moreover, coverage may change over time because of changes in general conceptions concerning which occupations should be included as part of the industrial labor force. For example, in Western societies, mining is defined by economists to be part of the secondary, or industrial, sector of the economy. The same occupation in non-Western countries is included as part of the primary, or nonindustrial, sector (Clark, 1940:337). In addition, basic perceptions of work relationships in the tertiary, or service, sector have been modified as the percentage of employees in these occupations has increased. All these specific factors affect the social meaning of industrialization, which is, in part, indicated by the distribution of government-backed rights to employees.

INDUSTRY

If the process of "industrialization refers to the actual course of transition from the preceding agricultural or commercial society toward the industrial society," then such changes should initially touch the lives of a minority of workers: those employed in the industrial sector (Hays, 1957:Chapters 1–3; Kerr et al., 1964:14). We might find, then, that the right to protection was gradually extended to employees according to which occupations were subjectively defined as a part of the industrial sector. Commons and Andrews, for instance, observed such a pattern for coverage under maximum hours legislation: "The number of employments covered . . . in America appears to depend largely on what occupations public opinion considers dangerous to the health . . . the exclusion of farm work and domestic service from regulation is at least in part due to the belief that they in no way endanger health. The earlier laws . . . applied mainly to manufacturing establishments. . . . In the same way, as the field of employment broadened, the dangers of excessive hours and injury to health were discovered in one occupation after another, and the need for extending protective legislation became correspondingly apparent, until practically every form of industrial employment has been covered" (1936:103–104). In other words, they suggest that coverage spread from work settings that were industrial in the narrow sense—such as manufacturing or mining—to other occupations in which the social organization of work came to parallel closely the one associated with manufacturing. Concretely, the right to coverage under these laws spread first to workers in the industrial sector, and then to workers in the service (or postindustrial) sector. Indeed, in a fully developed society, work relationships in agriculture finally mirror those prevalent in the rest of society, and agricultural employees are understood to need legal protections associated with an industrial society.

In several states, wage and hour standards laws initially extended coverage to employees in a few industries. These laws were amended several times to provide coverage to employees in other—usually tertiary—industries. In Delaware, for instance, a 1913 maximum hours law covered females in manufacturing and mercantile establishments, in laundries, in bakeries, and in telephone or telegraph companies. In 1917, the law was amended to extend coverage to females in hotels, restaurants, places of amusement, and offices. This pattern is found in wage payment/wage collection laws as well. A WP/WC enacted in Maine in 1887 extended coverage to all employees in manufacturing, mining, and mercantile establishments, as well as to employees in railroad, telephone, telegraph, and public utility companies when these companies or establishments had ten or more employees. In 1911, an amendment to this law dropped the firm size limitation and covered construction workers as well. Further amendments to the coverage provision were passed in 1915, 1935, 1941, 1957, and 1973. (Other examples are given in Chapter 2.)

Even if the coverage provisions had never been amended, significant changes in the distribution of the labor force could have affected variations in coverage by industry over time. For example, in 1900, most females in the two-digit SIC of transportation, communication, and public utilities worked in telephone companies. By 1950, only one-half to two-thirds of female employees in this SIC worked in telephone establishments. Similarly, the distribution of the female labor force across SICs has changed over time—especially with the growth of clerical and service occupations.

Thus, if the distribution of coverage under labor legislation depends on an initially narrow but ever-expanding concept of industrial work, we should expect to find that variation in coverage by industry exists and that it is strongest in the early twentieth century and decreases over time.

REGION

Employee coverage should also vary as a function of the differing importance regions attached to the distribution of these legal rights. In the early 1920s, for example, the child labor amendment to the United States Constitution was blocked by staunch opposition in the southern states (Davidson, 1939). Southern states also resisted the enactment of equal pay laws because of their connection to antidiscrimination legislation (Lockard, 1968).

Region serves as a proxy for differences among states along several dimensions. In part, it captures an array of unique historical experiences which result in "patterns of orientation to political action" (Elazar, 1966: 79). Not surprisingly, then, region is frequently used by political scientists to gauge these basic differences: "Because neighboring states in the various regions of America have experienced in-migrations, economic crises and political trauma at similar points in history, they may have acquired regional patterns in political attitudes, forms or processes" (Sharkansky, 1968:42–43).

In part, region captures the economic interests common to neighboring states (Elazar, 1966:112). For instance, economic historians indicate that differences in regional patterns of industrialization contributed greatly to the rapid economic growth of the late nineteenth and early twentieth centuries. The Northeast was the early manufacturing center of the country, its dominance facilitated by its large population and a national transportation system that distributed goods to all parts of the United States. In general, the western states initially tended to specialize in the extractive industries; raw materials, vital for manufacturing, were transported to the East Coast (Grey and Peterson, 1974; Perloff and Dodds, 1963). The formulation of coverage provisions in wage and hour standards laws is likely to be sensitive to these cultural and historical forces as well as to these economic differences. Moreover, since the regional differences in economic development have declined over the twentieth century, employee coverage is likely to converge across regions during that period (Kerr et al., 1964).

DEMOGRAPHIC GROUP

Another important determinant of coverage transcended these state and regional boundaries, however: the near universal acceptance by legislative and judicial decision makers of freedom of contract as the dominant legal norm shaping relations in the labor market (Fine, 1976; Paul, 1969). Because freedom of contract is antithetical to the right of employees to government protection, proponents of wage and hour laws faced an uphill battle in their attempts to enact laws with universal coverage provisions. For male adults, Lochner v. New York (1905) established a prohibitive burden of proof such that most efforts to obtain legal protection proved futile. Only men in underground mining and smelting were able to gather a sufficient amount of convincing evidence. The compromise solution came in 1908 with the landmark Muller v. Oregon decision, which modified the application of the freedom-of-contract assumption so that women and minors alone were entitled to reap the benefits of government protection. The Muller decision damped whatever impetus existed to extend these laws to all workers. It was only in 1938, with the Supreme Court decision in West Coast Hotel v. Parrish and with a government committed to labor law reform, that a sex-and-age-neutral federal wage and hour law was enacted. But, even with this breakthrough, it appears that many state minimum wage laws and equal pay laws continued to be restricted to women and minors through the late 1950s and early 1960s.

Despite these early decisions and the half-century of debate surrounding this legislation, it remains unclear whether, in fact, the employee's demographic group was the most important determinant of variation in coverage. For example, a maximum hours law could extend coverage to females within a specified group of industries and occupations. Coverage under this law would appear to be structured in terms of the demographic group of the employee, but the actual distribution of the female labor force in the state in question might be such that the industry of the employee was an equally or more important determinant of coverage.

There are sufficient reasons to expect that each of these factors will account for some of the variation in employee coverage under wage and hour standards laws. In addition, one general hypothesis emerges from the preceding discussion: employee coverage will become more uniform over time. In other words, variations in coverage attributable to demographic group, industry group, and region will decline over the twentieth century.

METHODOLOGY

For this analysis, national estimates were selected of the number of employees covered for each wage and hour law and of the total number of employees. These national estimates were further subdivided by industry group, by region, and by demographic group for each law (see Chapter 2).

For the three early labor laws, for which at least 5 percent of all employees were covered by 1920, variations in coverage were analyzed at five points in time—1900, 1920, 1940, 1960, and 1970. Minimum wage and overtime laws reached this level of coverage in the 1930s. Consequently, we analyzed these data only for 1940, 1960, and 1970. For the same reason, data on equal pay were analyzed only for 1960 and 1970. (The raw data are listed in the Appendix.)

The extent of variation in coverage determined by industry, by demographic group, and by region, is calculated using Cramer's V-statistic. It measures the strength of the relationship between two or more nominal scales with any number of categories (Blalock, 1960; Loether and McTavish, 1974).[1] Since we are interested in comparing the strength of the relationship across factors with a different number of categories—nine for industry and four for both region and demographic group—it is extremely important to select a measure that remains unaffected by the number of categories of a variable. As is the case for most measures of association, the V-statistic varies between 0.00 and 1.00.

RESULTS

The results in Table 5.1 suggest several interesting patterns. While all three factors are determinants of variations in coverage, industry group

Table 5.1. Variation in Coverage Attributable to Industry,
Region, or Demographic Group, 1900–1970

Law	Dimension	1900	1920	1940	1960	1970
WP/WC	Industry	.387	.384	.374	.304	.183
	Region	.447	.338	.376	.382	.338
	Demographic group	.045	.036	.052	.048	.031
MH	Industry	.369	.330	.275	.205	.155
	Region	.195	.137	.090	.086	.055
	Demographic group	.303	.423	.502	.549	.389
NW	Industry	.275	.221	.185	.114	.093
	Region	.137	.183	.261	.140	.118
	Demographic group	.222	.354	.377	.411	.475
MW	Industry			.651	.544	.499
	Region			.225	.248	.142
	Demographic group			.146	.145	.032
OT	Industry			.738	.710	.581
	Region			.167	.097	.152
	Demographic group			.093	.136	.054
EP	Industry				.199	.253
	Region				.647	.260
	Demographic group				.059	.084

NOTE: Variation is measured by means of Cramer's V-statistic.

consistently accounts for more of this variation when the laws are first enacted. (Equal pay laws provide the only exception.) The relationship between coverage and industry is especially strong for minimum wage and overtime laws. Coverage proves to be as much a function of industry group as of demographic group for maximum hours and night-work legislation.

Moreover, for all laws except equal pay, variations in coverage attributable to industry group clearly decline over time. By 1970, for the three early labor standards laws, such variations almost disappear. For minimum wage and overtime laws, while industry continues to influence strongly whether an employee will be covered, the V-statistic for 1970 is quite a bit lower than the V for 1940. In fact, by 1970, industry is no longer the strongest determinant in coverage for four of the six labor laws.

The variations in coverage attributable to region and demographic group tend to be law specific. Region seems to be a major factor shaping whether an employee will be covered under wage payment/wage collection laws and equal pay laws; demographic group appears to account for coverage under maximum hours and night-work laws. In general, the region in which an employee works becomes a less significant determinant of coverage over time—although the pattern is somewhat less consistent than the one found for industry. By contrast, the importance of the demographic group in explaining variations in coverage is mixed. It is strengthened over time for maximum hours laws and night-work legislation. It remains quite insignificant for all of the modern labor standards laws. But, by 1970, the decline in industry as the primary determinant of coverage results in region or demographic group emerging as the major determinant, especially for the three early laws.

The general pattern of change in variations in coverage attributable to each of these three factors becomes crystal clear when the Spearman r between the V-statistic and time is computed separately for early and modern labor standards legislation (Table 5.2). Coverage of employees becomes more uniform over the twentieth century across industry groups and over regions. Variations attributable to demographic group increase, particularly for early labor standards laws.

Table 5.2. Changes in Variation in Coverage
Attributable to Industry, Region, or Demographic Group, 1900–1970

Law	Industry	Region	Demographic group
Average: early labor laws	− 1.00	− .70	.70
Average: modern labor laws	− 1.00	− .50	.20

NOTE: Spearman's rank-order correlation is used to measure change.

THE SOCIAL BASES OF VARIATIONS IN COVERAGE

The preceding analysis indicates that employee coverage converges over the twentieth century across industry categories and over regions, but diverges by demographic group. In this section, these tendencies are explored in somewhat greater detail.

DEMOGRAPHIC GROUP

Contrary to the assertions of historians such as Baker (1925), political scientists such as Baer (1978), and legal scholars such as Babcock et al. (1975) and Davidson, Ginsburg, and Kay (1974), and the famous *Muller* v. *Oregon* decision notwithstanding, demographic group was not the primary factor accounting for the distribution of legal protection under maximum hours and night-work laws. Rather, whether employees were covered was based more on where they worked than on whether they were men or women.

Demographic group became the most salient determinant by 1940, however. If we examine the percentage of employees covered under each labor standards law by demographic group (Table 5.3), we observe that the major change in coverage under maximum hours and night-work laws occurred between 1940 and 1960 when the extent of coverage for male minors increased from 15 to 27 percent and from 17 to 29 percent respectively.

Whether the special attention given to male minors can accurately be called protection is open to serious question. After World War II these laws were used as additional tools to manipulate the allocation of jobs in a situation in which there were too many employees contending for too few jobs. Previous discussions of this aspect of maximum hours and night-work laws have made much of the impact of this situation on women workers. Less attention has been paid to male minors. While the overt motive for enacting these laws was to keep teenage males in school, the laws also made it less desirable for employers to hire (cheaper) male minors instead of (more expensive) male adults.

The reincorporation of male adults into the labor market after World War II was a particularly pressing problem. Women and male minors had replaced them during the war; most hours legislation had been suspended or significantly modified to facilitate the efficient use of this "marginal" labor force (Ratner, 1980). After the war, hours legislation was restored and, at least as it was extended to male minors, strengthened. Employers, who would have had to restructure their production schedules to conform to these hours standards, simply replaced women and minors with male adults. The law justified their actions.

REGION

A considerable literature on state politics has been built upon the premise that differences in regions result in differences in political institutions and

Table 5.3. Employee Coverage by Demographic Group, 1900–1970
(in percent)

Law	Year	Male adult	Female adult	Male minor	Female minor
WP/WC	1900	.19	.23	.16	.21
	1920	.46	.42	.42	.43
	1940	.57	.54	.47	.54
	1960	.68	.63	.65	.63
	1970	.77	.74	.76	.75
MH	1900	.01	.16	.06	.22
	1920	.05	.39	.10	.46
	1940	.05	.49	.15	.50
	1960	.04	.52	.27	.53
	1970	.04	.31	.29	.43
NW	1900	.00	.06	.03	.10
	1920	.00	.13	.11	.25
	1940	.00	.16	.17	.28
	1960	.00	.07	.29	.30
	1970	.00	.02	.31	.27
MW	1940	.39	.57	.42	.55
	1960	.53	.69	.60	.69
	1970	.89	.91	.88	.89
OT	1940	.40	.30	.30	.30
	1960	.51	.37	.39	.33
	1970	.73	.69	.66	.67
EP	1960	.42	.46	.33	.41
	1970	.78	.75	.87	.87

political behavior, and hence in political outcomes (Fenton, 1966; Key, 1949; Lockard, 1968). Our findings suggest that regional variations are, at best, law specific. Equal pay legislation, for example, has been staunchly resisted by the southern states because it constitutes a form of civil rights legislation. Although the South lags behind other regions in allocating coverage under wage and hour laws to employees (Table 5.4), it generally catches up with the other regions. This has not been the case for equal pay laws, in part because the South has historically demonstrated a disdain

Table 5.4. Employee Coverage by Region, 1900–1970
(in percent)

Law	Year	Northeast	North Central	South	West
WP/WC	1900	.46	.15	.04	.00
	1920	.56	.41	.28	.88
	1940	.59	.64	.32	.94
	1960	.64	.75	.43	.98
	1970	.80	.80	.56	.99
MH	1900	.11	.03	.01	.03
	1920	.19	.10	.08	.13
	1940	.20	.13	.13	.19
	1960	.24	.20	.17	.14
	1970	.15	.16	.13	.19
NW	1900	.04	.01	.00	.00
	1920	.10	.02	.02	.01
	1940	.14	.01	.02	.01
	1960	.09	.03	.02	.03
	1970	.08	.03	.02	.04
MW	1940	.58	.42	.29	.46
	1960	.77	.53	.45	.61
	1970	.97	.88	.88	.85
OT	1940	.48	.38	.27	.40
	1960	.51	.49	.39	.48
	1970	.83	.68	.66	.68
EP	1960	.84	.33	.03	.70
	1970	.95	.74	.67	.81

for civil rights legislation, and in part because our data only capture changes in variations in coverage over a ten-year period.

The fact that regional variations in coverage under these laws decline over the twentieth century is no doubt partially a function of the pattern of industrialization across regions during this period. Whether measured in terms of per capita income (Easterlin, 1971; Perloff and Dodds, 1963) or rates of economic growth (Grey and Peterson, 1974), a convergence in the economic characteristics of regions occurred between 1920 and 1950. It clearly parallels the decline in coverage differentials across regions. Thus, as the United States becomes an industrial society nationally, regional economic differences decline. In other words, our findings suggest that growing regional similarities over time transcend the historical and cultural characteristics unique to each region—especially with respect to legislation establishing uniform minimum standards for hours and wages. Moreover, a further contribution to the growth of uniformity of coverage across regions is the enactment of federal legislation. As regions become more similar in their levels of industrialization, they become more similar in the distribution of their labor force. This means, of course, that the impact of federal legislation on employee coverage at the state level becomes more uniform. This results in uniform standards, which remove the competitive disadvantages of states that have extended legal protections to employees. (This theme is discussed further in Chapter 7.)

INDUSTRY GROUP

Variations in coverage by industry group were initially large; they decreased substantially over time. Table 5.5, which lists the percentage of employees covered by industry under each law, shows how the gradual extension of coverage to employees moves from the secondary to the tertiary sector. Coverage under wage and hour standards laws increased in scope through a series of steps. Employees in the secondary sector—that is, mining and manufacturing—were covered first. Coverage was next greatest for contract construction and transportation and communication, tertiary sector industries most closely linked to the expansion of production in the secondary sector. Coverage for employees in clerical and service sectors slowly caught up to the level of coverage provided to manufacturing and mining employees.

What these data reflect is a process by which coverage is extended from work settings that are industrial in the narrow sense to all work settings in an industrial society. (Indeed, by 1970, a small minority of employees engaged in agriculture and domestic service were covered.) As new groups of employees come to perceive their work situations as similar to the ones faced by industrial employees, narrowly defined, they demand the same protections as their industrial counterparts. Thus, this step-by-step imitation process results in a gradual decrease in the variations in coverage across industry groups.

The pattern by which coverage diffuses is similar for early and modern labor standards laws. This is especially interesting in light of the fact that the percentage of employees in manufacturing in the United States has remained roughly constant since 1920 (Heilbroner, 1973:164). Yet, this

Table 5.5. Employee Coverage by Industry, 1900–1970 (in percent)

Law	Year	Agriculture[a]	Mining	Contract construction	Manufacturing	T/C/PU	Trade	Personal service	Clerical	Domestic service
WP/WC	1900	.08	.58	.18	.48	.24	.18	.14	.22	.06
	1920	.21	.79	.46	.68	.54	.42	.39	.37	.22
	1940	.28	.85	.51	.78	.64	.54	.51	.51	.28
	1960	.36	.89	.59	.82	.68	.61	.57	.58	.34
	1970	.52	.90	.71	.82	.77	.72	.69	.69	.46
MH	1900	.00	.04	.14	.20	.00	.02	.01	.00	.00
	1920	.00	.28	.27	.23	.03	.11	.13	.11	.00
	1940	.00	.29	.29	.21	.10	.16	.24	.17	.00
	1960	.01	.26	.21	.20	.10	.23	.31	.20	.00
	1970	.00	.27	.19	.13	.10	.15	.24	.12	.00
NW	1900	.00	.00	.00	.10	.00	.00	.01	.00	.00
	1920	.00	.00	.00	.10	.01	.05	.04	.08	.00
	1940	.00	.00	.00	.09	.01	.06	.09	.08	.00
	1960	.01	.00	.00	.05	.01	.07	.05	.05	.01
	1970	.00	.00	.01	.04	.01	.05	.05	.06	.00
MW	1940	.01	.95	.41	.82	.81	.30	.27	.58	.11
	1960	.03	.95	.40	.86	.85	.47	.47	.73	.11
	1970	.46	.98	.98	.98	.98	.86	.88	.94	.11
OT	1940	.00	.95	.57	.85	.80	.20	.05	.40	.01
	1960	.00	.95	.46	.90	.80	.20	.06	.40	.01
	1970	.00	.96	.96	.96	.66	.47	.62	.81	.07
EP	1960	.21	.26	.40	.52	.44	.43	.43	.50	.16
	1970	.56	.83	.84	.86	.85	.72	.76	.84	.26

[a] Includes forestry and fishing

replication of pattern is rendered more understandable once we realize that, since 1920, there has been an enormous shift out of the agricultural and into the tertiary sector.

Most discussions of the process of industrialization and the growth of the economy fail to acknowledge that the rise of the service sector is a continuation of the transition from an agrarian to an industrial society (see, for example, Bell, 1973). While industrialization has an impact on the structure of society in general (Hofstadter, 1965; Wiebe, 1967), the concrete modifications in work relations occur gradually over an extended period, during which periods of greater than average change are followed by periods of less than average change. Most citizens living in a society undergoing industrialization are cognizant of the drastic changes occurring in the non-agricultural goods-producing sector. But not all employees undergo this shift simultaneously. This continuation and solidification of industrialization are reflected in the gradual extension of the social rights embodied in wage and hour legislation.

Take, for example, the case of the federal Fair Labor Standards Act. Coverage under federal legislation is based on whether an employee is engaged in interstate commerce. At first, covered occupations included mining, manufacturing, transportation, and communication, the industries associated with the first stage of industrialization. The legal definition of interstate commerce was initially very rigid. Since the enactment of the FLSA, however, the meaning of "interstate commerce" has been significantly reinterpreted, and the concept has gradually come to encompass a wide variety of occupations in which the direct connection to interstate commerce is, at best, tenuous. It is no coincidence that the changing definition of interstate commerce paralleled shifts in the labor force between 1920 and 1970. In the 1970s, legal coverage even came to include agricultural workers employed on large farms.

Wage and hour standards laws, which arise directly from the upheavals of industrialization, are thus extended initially to the employees who feel those changes most directly. The employees demand these changes in law—as ample historical evidence confirms—and are acknowledged as the legitimate recipients of such protection. Other employees—especially in occupations within the tertiary sector—come to enjoy the same legal protection some twenty years later.[2] Because of the changing distribution of the labor force, revisions in the scope of coverage are not only a reflection of but also a spur to changes in the perceptions determining which employees are legitimate recipients of government protection.

If, then, these laws mirror the changing perceptions of who needs protection in the labor market, these findings suggest that the separation of employees by the industry in which they work should largely disappear from the coverage provisions in these laws. This is, in fact, the case for equal pay laws, the most recently enacted of the standards laws. By 1960, the amount of variation in coverage attributable to industry was quite small for the five other laws as well.

Many recent books on the sociology of work—especially those written from a Marxist perspective—take as their central theme the transformation of white-collar and service jobs and the increasing similarity between jobs in the tertiary sector and traditional blue-collar jobs (Braverman, 1974; Edwards, 1979; Gordon, 1972). In an impersonal labor market organized around the imperatives of a fully developed industrial society, they argue, all work displays similar characteristics: impersonal social relations between employers and employees, increasing specialization, increasing alienation, decreasing job security, and increasing employer control over the labor process, to name but a few qualities of the world of work in contemporary society. Braverman's interpretation of the nature of work in the tertiary sector, for example, flows from this perspective. He contends that service and clerical work have come to assume the same form characteristic of blue-collar work in the secondary sector. He concludes that

> the traditional distinctions between "manual" and "white collar" labor, which are so thoughtlessly and widely used in the literature on this subject, represent echoes of a past situation which has virtually ceased to have meaning in the modern world of work. . . . In the history of capitalism, while one or another form of productive labor may play a greater role in particular eras, the tendency is toward the eradication of distinctions among its various forms. . . . As the varied forms come under the auspices of capital and become part of the domain of profitable investment, they enter for the capitalist into the realm of general or abstract labor, labor which enlarges capital (Braverman, 1974: 325–326, 365).

The gradual uniformity in coverage under these laws across industry groups adds further inferential support to such arguments: as the characteristics of jobs in different sectors of the economy become more uniform, all employees who must sell their labor in the industrial market require protection, regardless of the industry in which they work.

The decrease in the variation in legal coverage by industry and region of employee, therefore, carries with it a story about the changing meaning of industrialization over time. Industrialization grows unevenly across industries and across regions. These time series data provide a useful road map for tracing the route along which industrialization travels. As Harry Braverman has argued, as an ever greater number of employees discover themselves subject to work relationships particular to an industrial society, they legitimately obtain the same legal protection.

SUMMARY AND CONCLUSIONS

In this chapter, the determinants in coverage under wage and hour standards laws were systematically analyzed in terms of three factors—demographic group, region, and industry. All contribute somewhat to an explanation of the variations in coverage, though industry emerged consistently as the strongest determinant. Furthermore, variations in coverage by demographic group for early wage and hour standards laws increased over the twentieth century, and variations in coverage attributable to industry and region declined dramatically.

These declines in variations in coverage were attributed to the extension to all work settings of work conditions associated with the secondary sector. Moreover, regions have grown more uniform in the occupational distribution of their labor force. Finally, federal legislation, covering certain groups of employees regardless of where they lived, contributed to this growing uniformity in coverage among regions.

Industrialization transformed the nature of work. Coverage under these laws was initially restricted to employees engaged in industrial work, narrowly defined. Gradually, the laws were extended to employees in the tertiary and primary sectors, as it was recognized that all work in an industrial society occurs in a similar environment—an environment formerly associated predominantly with traditional blue-collar jobs. Industrialization affects all regions and all groups (albeit at differing historical moments), and its impact on the structure of legislation transcends other considerations that may affect coverage under any particular law. To the extent that variations in coverage persist, they reflect the social meaning of industrialization as it interacts with legal, historical, and cultural factors relevant to a particular piece of legislation.

III

STATE PATTERNS
OF CHANGE

6
THREE MODELS OF
LEGAL DEVELOPMENT

The discussion thus far has focused on the development of wage and hour standards legislation at the national level. The social rights embodied in early labor laws were distributed to a limited subset of employees. This situation arose in part because the restrictive legal norms that organized social relations in the labor market were biased in favor of the interests of employers. The Great Depression of the 1930s paved the way for federal involvement in this legal domain. As a consequence of federal legislation, coverage under modern labor legislation was far more extensive than coverage under early labor legislation. Federal legislation transformed the legal basis upon which rights were extended. What had previously been stop-gap legislation for employees who were in some respect marginal to the normal relations in the labor market became an ordinary right accorded to (almost) all who exchanged their labor for wage income.

This analysis of the national pattern of change in labor standards legislation obscures, however, other important dimensions of the growth of these laws. For example, the adoption of these laws at the state level was quite extensive: over 90 percent of the states at some time had adopted some version of each of the three early labor laws. Most states had also adopted minimum wage and equal pay laws, even though federal legislation had been enacted. An examination of national patterns disregards the nature of state action on any particular law. Chapters 6 and 7 are concerned with patterns of growth in wage and hour standards laws at the state level. This chapter examines three hypotheses on variations in growth and change in these laws subsequent to their adoption at the state level. Chapter 7 assesses the effect of state legislation on congressional voting on the Fair Labor Standards Act.

MODELS OF LEGISLATIVE CHANGE

The three models that could account for differential growth in these laws at the state level are the convergence model, the imprinting model, and the crisis model. The *convergence* model regards the growth of public policy as a product of changes in the economic, political, and social characteristics of a state. Proponents of this position contend that since states have become more uniform in socioeconomic and political characteristics, the content of social policy across states will also become increasingly similar. A corollary of this perspective, which will be tested here, is that similar types of laws within a state will become more uniform over time. In other words, within a state, the coverage and standards of the different wage and hour laws at the time of adoption may vary widely. The convergence model predicts, however, that over time, the levels of coverage and standards become increasingly similar.

The *imprinting* model suggests that the level of coverage and standards reached during the initial period of state adoption sets the limits and possibilities for further growth in these laws.[1] It predicts that state laws strongest at the time of adoption will be strengthened the most subsequent to adoption, and vice versa. In short, the imprinting model points to growth during the period of state adoption as the crucial determinant of subsequent growth.

Finally, the *crisis* model views growth of established legislation as being unrelated to either earlier growth or the general socioeconomic climate. Rather, changes in the content of legislation result from periodic crises. These crises bring to the fore new problems which become associated with the purposes of a law. The law becomes visible and takes on a new meaning. Since the impact of these crises will vary across states, the rank ordering of the provisions of state laws from strong to weak will shift greatly during or following these periods.

To determine which of these three models most accurately captures the actual change in coverage and standard under wage and hour standards legislation, a comparative framework is used. The quality of the provisions of the laws in one state are defined in terms of the range of legal provisions found in all states. These working definitions of higher quality or stronger legislation are stated in terms of what is of benefit to employees: the higher the percentage of employees covered, the better the quality of the law; the more restrictive the direct standards imposed on employers, the higher the quality of legal provisions. To be sure, the provisions of these laws are highly limited in an absolute sense. Yet, whatever their shortcomings, the laws in some states do cover a larger percentage of employees and provide stronger protection than the laws in other states (Ratner, 1977a; see Appendix).

CONVERGENCE OF LAWS OVER TIME

The convergence approach to social policy is, first and foremost, part of a general theory of the growth of industrial societies. It is associated with the writings of Clark Kerr and his colleagues, and is most clearly stated in their book *Industrialism and Industrial Man* (1964). As summarized by Robert Jackman, "The major proposition relating to the *convergence* model is that the 'logic of industrialization' leads to a decrease in the degree of material differentiation . . . stress is placed on the standardizing effects on social structure of advancing economies and modern technology which lead to a convergent pattern of development" (1975:30).

Harold Wilensky and other functional-evolutionary theorists of the welfare state link this view of a converging social structure to policy outcomes. Wilensky suggests that as countries become more urban and more highly industrialized, their social welfare programs become more similar to one another. "Scholars impressed by the convergence of urban-industrial societies toward some common post-industrial condition can see in every rich country seven or eight health or welfare programs with *similar content* and *expanded funding*—even some convergence in methods of financing and administration" (1975:1–2, italics added).

Stated as an empirical generalization, Wilensky is saying that countries that share economic and social features will have similar social security programs. This is similar to Ogburn's (1912) finding that, as states converged in certain economic characteristics, the provisions of their child labor laws also converged.

These findings across political units carry with them an implicit assumption about the growth of social policies within a political unit. The logic of the argument suggests that laws addressed to the same issue and same population subgroups within a state will grow more uniform. Thus, all the laws in some states will become stronger, while all the laws of other states will become weaker. Indeed, according to a more dynamic version of the convergence model than the one entertained by Wilensky, one would expect that, within a state, the quality of legal provisions across labor standards laws would become more consistent over time.

Furthermore, a convergence model implies the following dynamics of legislative change: the early period of legal enactment is chaotic. Laws are at their most visible when they are first being considered for enactment. Many factors within the state, such as its industrial composition, the political orientation of its administrative elites and its courts, and the conjunction of organized interest groups, result in similar laws having idiosyncratic policy outcomes (Ratner, 1977a:Chapter 6). After the period of adoption passes, these laws are affected primarily by organized groups who have something to gain or lose from further strengthening of laws and by general labor market conditions—a much more uniform set of forces. Furthermore, once all laws have been adopted, they are treated as a coherent subset. Thus, some states have wage and hour laws of uniformly higher quality than other states.

IMPRINTING: THE STABILITY OF LEGAL PROVISIONS OVER TIME

The imprinting model is taken from two related studies of the politics of the budgetary process (Davis, Dempster, and Wildavsky, 1966; Wildavsky, 1964). Both studies found that the best predictor of an annual budget was the annual budget for the preceding year. Wildavsky insists, for example, that "the largest determining factor of the size and the content of this year's budget is last year's budget. . . . Budgeting is incremental; not comprehensive . . . it is almost never actively reviewed as a whole every year in the sense of reconsidering the value of all existing programs as compared to all possible alternatives. Instead, it is based on last year's budget with special attention given to a narrow range of increases or decreases" (1964:13–15). Therefore, since budgeting decisions are made in terms of an existing base, adapted more or less to a narrow range of increases or decreases (Davis, Dempster, and Wildavsky, 1966:529–530), the increase in the allocation of funds to an item in the budget at one point should be highly related to preceding increases in funding for that budget item.

The imprinting model suggests that, for any specific law, there will be a consistent ordering of states with respect to the quality of legal provisions over time. Laws that have more extensive legal provisions during the period of state adoption will expand more extensively than would be expected if chance or random factors alone were operating and vice versa. If legislative growth follows this process, the state ranking immediately following the period of adoption should remain stable over time. This stability of state ranking would result from the differential growth that occurred after the period of adoption. All states would gradually strengthen their laws, but state laws that grew the most would be those in which early growth was greatest.

CRISIS THEORY: SYSTEM SHOCK AND LEGISLATIVE CHANGE

Budget decisions are the only set of legislative decisions that must be made annually. While investigation into the budget-making process can provide many insights into how legislators make decisions, budget decisions might prove inadequate as a model for understanding the process by which other laws are amended. While the imprinting model may capture the process by which budgets are revised, it might not be useful in understanding the more general process of legislative change.

Both Congress and state legislatures must consider an enormous number of bills each session. To handle this massive work load, legislators (or, more accurately, legislative leadership) rank legislation to be acted upon in some order of priority. This feature of informal legislative procedure is especially characteristic of state legislatures—where the resources available to legislators are highly inadequate. Malcolm Jewell (1962) points to several factors that contribute to this lack of resources: "Most state legislatures meet only a few months every other year giving committees very little time for any careful review of bills. Committees seldom have any staff assistance, legislative turnover is high, a seniority system is not as prevalent as it is in Congress, and committee members seldom acquire the experience and expertise of their Congressional counterparts" (as summarized in Dye, 1965: 179). Similarly, John C. Wahlke remarks: "We have seen that individual legislators generally get little staff assistance, that most legislatures are desperately short of committee working space, of facilities for reproducing and distributing copies of bills and amendments, and of other necessities. State legislative committees in only the rarest of instances have staffs, counsels, and work forces like those of Congressional committees" (1966: 143–144).

Thus, it is reasonable to assume that amendments to existing legislation are acted on infrequently unless there is good reason. Perhaps the most effective stimulus of legislative change is the rise of a social, political, or economic crisis. The crisis model predicts that bills are considered and amended only when a situation arises in which the types of legal changes being considered have a visible connection to a pressing social need. There are two types of crisis situations: one affects the entire society and has specific implications for certain groups—wars and economic depressions are examples. The second can be called a socially constructed crisis and is often created by the rise of new social movements with new political demands (Marx and Wood, 1975).

The belief that crises such as wars and economic depressions stimulate social reform is widely held. Wilensky, for instance, points to the importance of World War II in furthering income equality in the United States and Great Britain: "World War II was oddly egalitarian . . . the argument of 'equality of sacrifice' became irresistible . . . the United States adopted excess profit taxes, steeper income taxes, rationing wage-price controls with a massive enforcement machinery. . . . In Britain, the welfare state made great strides as Conservative Party leaders pushed Labour Party programs. In 1940, only one child in thirty was fed in school; in 1945, it was one in three" (1975:71–72). Moreover, he points out that "from 1915 to 1918, as the United States approached World War I and finally entered it, a drive for compulsory health insurance was mounted from New York to California; sixteen states actually introduced such legislation. . . . Similarly, except for Workmen's Compensation, the United States did not join the general trend toward old-age pensions and unemployment insurance until the country reached the depths of the Great Depression, when President Franklin Roosevelt was able to put the Social Security Act on the books" (Wilensky, 1975: 73–74).

But all of Wilensky's examples involve the development of new programs rather than the strengthening of existing ones. *The Growth of Public Expenditure in the United Kingdom* (Peacock and Wiseman, 1961:27) points to the impact of wars on expanding the level of expenditures for existing programs:

> People will accept, in a period of crisis, tax levels and methods of raising revenue that in quieter times they would have thought intolerable, and this acceptance remains after the disturbance itself has disappeared. As a result, the revenue and expenditure statistics of the government show a displacement after periods of social disturbance. Expenditures may fall when the disturbance is over, but they are less likely to return to the old level. The state may begin doing some of the things it might formerly have wanted to, but for which it had hitherto felt politically unable to raise the necessary revenues.

Crisis situations can, however, also be created. The 1911 Triangle Shirtwaist fire in New York City, for example, became the symbol used by unionists and feminists to spur more and better factory legislation. Following this horrible fire, which took the lives of 145 workers, mostly young girls, "a widespread demand for government action in this field led to the appointment of the Factory Investigating Commission. . . . Its investigations and recommendations were far more extensive than at first contemplated. The public and the legislature were in a receptive mood. As a result the whole New York labor code was remade—36 laws were passed in the years 1912 to 1941" (Brandeis, 1935:478). The Women's Trade Union League led the campaign for legal reform in New York State: "Twenty-four hours after the fire, the New York League began to make plans for a public meeting of protest which was held in the Metropolitan Opera House. Rose Schneiderman voiced the indignation of the workers: 'Citizens, you have been tried time and again and found wanting. It would be treachery and treason to those burned bodies if I came here to talk fellowship. Too much blood has been spilled.' This meeting started a campaign for better fire protection throughout the State" (Boone, 1942:99–100).

Social movements that organize to achieve their political demands use "events," whether or not of their own making, to gain visibility for programs for which they are fighting. In his study of budgetary politics, Wildavsky points to the use of crisis strategies by program administrators to win a greater share of the federal budget. For these crisis strategies to be successful, however, requires that program administrators tie their demands to relevant concerns of the general public. "Events do not have meaning in themselves: they are given meaning by observers. From time to time situations arise—war, drought, depression, plant disease, atomic energy—which virtually everyone recognizes as crises. The agency in a position to meet a crisis . . . can greatly increase its appropriations. . . . There is also a borderline area of discretion in which crisis may be made to appear more real. . . . By publicizing a situation, dramatizing it effectively, and perhaps asking for emergency appropriations, an agency can maneuver itself into a good position of responsibility for large programs" (Wildavsky, 1964:119).

Consequently, change in the provisions of existing legislation may have little to do with the past history of a law. Rather, observed change may be the outgrowth of more immediate events and social disturbances that bring with them the need to reassess public policy. If the crisis model holds, then, for labor standards legislation, either general crises that have an impact on the labor market or a crisis orchestrated by employee groups will result in change in the provisions of these laws. Moreover, since these factors affect states differently, change should show the greatest variation during crises.

DATA

Data on the coverage and legal standard of the three early labor standards laws compiled for 1920 to 1970 at ten-year intervals were used to examine which model best explains change in the quality of legal provisions. Attention was restricted to these laws in order to grasp the process of change subsequent to the period of state adoption. Preliminary analysis of these laws reported elsewhere (Ratner, 1977a) indicates that their growth during the period of adoption displayed no consistent patterns, which make their development after state adoption subsided of particular interest. Because most states had adopted these laws by 1920, changes in their content over five decades can be analyzed. Two simplifying assumptions were made: first, as in Chapter 3, adoption of a state law was assumed to have occurred when 1 percent of employees had been covered for at least six years. Second, since this is an examination of the growth of actual legislation, analysis of MH was limited to female adults and of NW to minors. (The raw data used in this chapter are listed in the Appendix.)

A TEST OF THE THREE MODELS

CONVERGENCE

Do the legal provisions in labor standards laws become more uniform within states between 1920 and 1970? To answer this question, the data on the percentage of employees covered and on the average legal standard for the three early labor laws were analyzed in a series of steps: first, for each of these two legislative dimensions, we calculated the zero-order correlation between pairs of laws at each ten-year period (Table 6.1). Second, we computed the average correlation of the three zero-order correlations for coverage and standard separately for each ten-year period (Table 6.2). For example, the average correlation for coverage in 1920 (r = .31) is the mean of the three correlations between pairs of laws for portion covered in 1920.

In both tables, an increasingly positive correlation over decades would suggest a trend toward convergence in the quality of legal provisions in laws of benefit to subordinate groups. This can be assessed systematically by calculating a Spearman rank-order correlation between time and the strength of the relationship for each pair of laws and for the average correlation (Table 6.3). A strong, positive correlation indicates convergence.

With a few exceptions, the results indicate that there appears to be no necessary connection in the level of coverage across laws. At best, relationships are law and time specific: there is a strong and significant relationship in state ranking on coverage for WP/WC and NW in 1920 and 1930 which disappears during the decade of the depression. By 1940, almost no relationship exists between coverage in these laws. Coverage for MH and WP/WC remains moderate but insignificant throughout the fifty-year period (with a range of r = .11 in 1960 to r = .39 in 1970). Similarly, the average correlations for percentage covered display a slight to moderate relationship over this period.

Table 6.1. Zero-Order Correlations of Legal Provisions
between Pairs of Labor Standards Laws across States, 1920–1970

Year	Law	Coverage		Legal standard	
		MH	NW	MH	NW
1920	WP/WC	.17	.51*	.38*	− .09
	MH		.26		− .22
1930	WP/WC	.26	.61*	.30	− .11
	MH		.01		− .38*
1940	WP/WC	.26	.06	.12	.04
	MH		.04		− .02
1950	WP/WC	.34*	.29	.19	− .02
	MH		.16		.05
1960	WP/WC	.11	.15	.16	.06
	MH		.16		.08
1970	WP/WC	.39	.22	− .13	.05
	MH		.26		.26

*Significant at the .10 level.

Table 6.2. Average of Zero-Order Correlations of Legal Provisions
between Pairs of Labor Standards Laws across States, 1920–1970

	Coverage	Legal standard
1920	.31	.02
1930	.29	− .06
1940	.12	.05
1950	.27	.08
1960	.14	.10
1970	.29	.06

By contrast, for legal standard and average correlation, the relationship between laws remains weak over the entire fifty years. For WP/WC and MH, the one pair of moderately correlated laws, the quality of legal provisions gets *less* uniform over time. In short, the trends in correlations on average and across pairs of laws lend no support to the convergence model. Indeed, if the correlations indicate anything, it is that state laws are at their most uniform immediately following the period of greatest state adoption.

Table 6.3. Spearman Rank-Order Correlation of Time and
Legal Provisions

Law	Coverage	Legal standard
WP/WC and MH	.43	−.83
WP/WC and NW	−.47	.83
MH and NW	.37	.94
Average correlation for three early laws	−.49	.77

Certainly, the results in Table 6.3, at least for the percentage of employees covered, should dispel any remaining hopes that the convergence model is useful for explaining within-state changes in the content of state laws.

Upon first glance, however, the correlations for legal standard support the convergence model. Yet, even this result is called into question when we look at the original correlations: if it can be said that these laws are converging at all, it is because they have remained so highly *unrelated* over the fifty years under observation. In general, then, although wage and hour laws are analytically a coherent set of laws, there is little evidence that they are treated as a class of legislation, at least in terms of changes in their provisions. Nor is there evidence that these laws are treated more as a group over time: the ordering of the quality of legal provisions in state laws does not converge; nor do we find even a more limited pattern of consistent state ranking across any pair of laws for any decade between 1920 and 1970.

IMPRINTING

Is the change in the legal provisions of labor standards legislation after state adoption a function of the growth in legislation during the period of adoption? If the imprinting model best captures the process of legislative growth and change at the state level, states in which the scope of coverage is greater relative to other states should continue to have better coverage. Similarly, state laws that have strict legal standards relative to other state laws should maintain that relative strength over time. Stability in state ranking in the quality of legal provisions could, however, arise from either of two factors. First, there could be so little change in the content of these laws that the original rank ordering of states remained intact throughout the century. Second, subsequent legislative change could be a function of earlier legislative change, and states would then demonstrate a consistent ranking in the extent to which they *changed* the content of their laws.[2]

To test for both of these factors, the data were analyzed in the following way. First, for each law, we related the percentage of employees covered at one ten-year period to the percentage of employees covered for the subsequent ten-year period. For instance, zero-order correlations between the percentage covered (PC) under WP/WC in 1920 and in 1930, 1940, 1950, 1960, and 1970 were obtained. A similar procedure was followed for the average legal standard. The results of this analysis are listed in Table 6.4 for coverage and Table 6.7 for standard. Further, for each correlation, we calculated an expected correlation, that is, a correlation one would expect to obtain simply by relating the same legal dimension at two points in time. This reveals what the correlation would be if there were no relationship

Table 6.4. Zero-Order Correlation of Coverage
under Early Labor Legislation, 1920–1970

Law	Year	Coverage				
		1930	*1940*	*1950*	*1960*	*1970*
Coverage	1920	.99*(26)	.90*(26)	.84*(26)	.74*(26)	.54 (26)
under	1930		.91*(26)	.85*(26)	.76*(26)	.55*(26)
WP/WC	1940			.93*(26)	.83*(26)	.61*(26)
	1950				.91*(26)	.65*(26)
	1960					.63*(27)
Coverage	1920	.87*(25)	.81*(25)	.80*(25)	.74*(24)	.84*(14)
under	1930		.90*(26)	.89*(26)	.84*(25)	.79*(15)
MH	1940			.97*(26)	.89*(25)	.80*(15)
	1950				.91*(25)	.76*(15)
	1960					.63*(15)
Coverage	1920	.89*(17)	.51*(15)	.36 (19)	.30 (19)	.52*(19)
under	1930		.76*(16)	.57*(19)	.52*(19)	.71*(19)
NW	1940			.72*(17)	.71*(17)	.76*(17)
	1950				.95*(26)	.92*(26)
	1960					.90*(26)

NOTE: Numbers in parentheses indicate number of cases.
*Significant at the .10 level.

Table 6.5. Expected Values: Zero-Order Correlation of Coverage
under Early Labor Legislation, 1920–1970

Law	Year	Coverage				
		1930	*1940*	*1950*	*1960*	*1970*
Coverage under WP/WC	1920	.98(15)	.89(18)	.86(21)	.80(21)	.72(22)
	1930		.90(14)	.86(20)	.80(21)	.71(22)
	1940			.91(19)	.84(20)	.71(21)
	1950				.88(17)	.72(21)
	1960					.72(16)
Coverage under MH	1920	.84(23)	.81(25)	.79(26)	.74(26)	.59(26)
	1930		.91(25)	.90(26)	.83(26)	.55(26)
	1940			.97(25)	.86(25)	.55(25)
	1950				.89(20)	.58(25)
	1960					.54(25)
Coverage under NW	1920	.89(18)	.65(20)	.60(26)	.59(25)	.64(25)
	1930		.74(18)	.68(27)	.68(26)	.74(26)
	1940			.84(26)	.83(26)	.85(25)
	1950				.91(22)	.89(23)
	1960					.90(22)

NOTE: Numbers in parentheses indicate number of cases.

between the level of the legal dimension at the first time point and the change in that legal dimension between two time points.[3] In other words, we calculated what correlation to expect if all changes in the legal provisions were entirely the product of random factors. The expected values of the correlations of legal dimensions are listed in Table 6.5 for coverage and Table 6.8 for standard.

Next, for each correlation, we calculated the difference between each obtained and expected correlation. This difference measured the extent to which the change in the value of the legal dimensions between two points in time (or deltas) was *related to* the level of the legal dimension at the earlier point. Or, put somewhat differently, this difference indicated the extent to which subsequent growth in legislation was a function of the previous level of legislation. These differences are listed in Table 6.6 for coverage and Table 6.9 for standard. A positive value means that the difference in growth between the laws with higher quality legal provisions and those with lower quality legal provisions was greater than expected by chance.

Table 6.6. Differences between Obtained and Expected Correlations:
Coverage under Early Labor Legislation, 1920–1970

Law	Year	Coverage				
		1930	*1940*	*1950*	*1960*	*1970*
Coverage	1920	.01	.01	−.02	−.06	−.18
under	1930		.01	.01	−.04	−.16
WP/WC	1940			.02	−.01	−.10
	1950				.03	−.07
	1960					−.09
Coverage	1920	.03	.00	.01	.00	.25
under	1930		−.01	−.01	.01	.24
MH	1940			.00	.03	.25
	1950				.02	.18
	1960					.09
Coverage	1920	.00	−.14	−.24	−.29	−.12
under	1930		.02	−.11	−.16	−.03
NW	1940			−.12	−.12	−.09
	1950				.04	.03
	1960					.00

Conversely, a negative value means that the difference in growth between laws with higher quality legal provisions and those with lower quality legal provisions was less than expected by chance.

Fourth, these sets of differences were summarized by averaging, for each law, all the ten-year differences for each legal dimension. For example, we averaged the difference measures for 1920 and 1930, 1930 and 1940, 1940 and 1950, and so on. We repeated this procedure for the twenty-, thirty-, forty-, and fifty-year differences as well. The results of this analysis are found in Table 6.10. In addition, we generated an average difference score across the three laws (also listed in Table 6.10). This involved calculating the mean ten- to fifty-year differences in percentage covered and legal standard for WP/WC, MH, and NW.

The summary differences over decades found in Table 6.10 indicate that the imprinting model also does not account for legislative change: there is no relationship between legal change at different periods, whether among labor laws in general or for any specific law. Almost all of the differences between the obtained correlations and the expected correlations are trivial,

Table 6.7. Zero-Order Correlation of Average Standard
under Early Labor Legislation, 1920–1970

Law	Year	Average standard				
		1930	*1940*	*1950*	*1960*	*1970*
Average standard under WP/WC	1920	.79*(26)	.69*(26)	.58*(26)	.55*(26)	.28 (26)
	1930		.89*(26)	.74*(26)	.70*(26)	.35*(26)
	1940			.83*(26)	.80*(26)	.46*(26)
	1950				.96*(26)	.57*(26)
	1960					.57*(27)
Average standard under MH	1920	.93*(25)	.26 (25)	.24 (25)	.30 (24)	.12 (15)
	1930		.32 (26)	.31 (26)	.35 (25)	.16 (16)
	1940			.94*(26)	.94*(25)	.84*(16)
	1950				.98*(25)	.84*(16)
	1960					.88*(16)
Average standard under NW	1920	.86*(25)	.85*(24)	.88*(25)	.68*(25)	.66*(25)
	1930		.92*(26)	.77*(27)	.55*(27)	.64*(27)
	1940			.81*(26)	.63*(26)	.58*(26)
	1950				.78*(27)	.74*(27)
	1960					.90*(27)

NOTE: Numbers in parentheses indicate number of cases.
*Significant at the .10 level.

and the direction of the differences is inconsistent: for percentage covered under WP/WC and NW, for example, growth at a later period is negatively related to growth at an earlier period. By contrast, growth at an earlier period "predicts" growth at a later period for percentage covered under MH and for legal standard under NW. Indeed, for the legal standard under WP/WC and MH, the relationship between growth in provisions shifts over time: ten-year changes and twenty-year changes are positively related to the earlier quality of the legal standard, whereas thirty- to fifty-year changes are inversely related to the previous level of the legal standard.

What we do find out from the correlations between the actual level of the legal provisions at two points in time for coverage (Table 6.4) and standard (Table 6.7) is that there is little change in state ranking between 1920 and 1970 because there is little growth and change in the content of state laws subsequent to the period of state adoption. It is the stability of state ranking with respect to the quality of legal provisions after the early

Table 6.8. Expected Values: Zero-Order Correlation of
Average Legal Standard under Early Labor Legislation, 1920–1970

Law	Year	Average standard				
		1930	1940	1950	1960	1970
Average standard under WP/WC	1920	.67(8)	.61(12)	.57(14)	.60(16)	.53(21)
	1930		.76(10)	.65(13)	.66(15)	.55(20)
	1940			.64 (9)	.67(14)	.55(19)
	1950				.86(10)	.65(16)
	1960					.67(15)
Average standard under MH	1920	.47(9)	.50(16)	.50(17)	.41(18)	.26(21)
	1930		.61(13)	.62 (6)	.48(16)	.31(21)
	1940			.88(11)	.49(14)	.27(21)
	1950				.42(10)	.26(21)
	1960					.27(18)
Average standard under NW	1920	.37(14)	.30(18)	.40(20)	.39(21)	.38(21)
	1930		.48(16)	.76(18)	.64(19)	.67(19)
	1940			.51(19)	.48(19)	.45(17)
	1950				.72(13)	.76(26)
	1960					.83(13)

NOTE: Numbers in parentheses indicate number of cases.

period of development of these laws that accounts for the high correlations between the quality of the legal provisions at two points in time. Once we compare these correlations to expected correlations, however, we find that the amount of change in the quality of the legal provisions between 1920 and 1970 is both small and unrelated to previous growth. While imprinting theory may be a good explanation of *lack* of legislative change, it does not contribute much to an understanding of the development of the content of legislation subsequent to the period of adoption.

CRISIS

Finally, are the observed variations in the modification of coverage and standards across states between 1920 and 1970 a function of crises that affected the labor market? From Tables 6.4 and 6.7 we can observe that in certain decades the ordering of states with respect to the quality of legal provisions shifted. These shifts in state ranking are indicated by a lower

Table 6.9. Differences between Obtained and Expected Values:
Average Legal Standard under Early Labor Legislation, 1920–1970

Law	Year	Average standard				
		1930	*1940*	*1950*	*1960*	*1970*
Average standard under WP/WC	1920	.12	.08	.01	−.05	−.25
	1930		.13	.09	.04	−.20
	1940			.19	.13	−.19
	1950				.10	−.08
	1960					−.10
Average standard under MH	1920	.46	−.24	−.26	−.11	−.14
	1930		−.29	−.31	−.13	−.15
	1940			.04	.45	.57
	1950				.56	.58
	1960					.61
Average standard under NW	1920	.49	.55	.48	.29	.28
	1930		.44	.01	−.09	−.03
	1940			.30	.15	.13
	1950				.06	.01
	1960					.07

Table 6.10. Differences between Observed and Expected
Zero-Order Correlations of Legal Provisions

Average differences	Coverage				Average legal standard			
	WP/WC	MH	NW	Average of three laws	WP/WC	MH	NW	Average of three laws
Over 10 years	.00	.03	−.01	.00	.09	.28	.27	.21
Over 20 years	−.02	.05	−.09	−.02	.06	.12	.18	.12
Over 30 years	−.05	.09	−.16	−.04	−.05	−.06	.17	.02
Over 40 years	−.11	.12	−.16	−.05	−.13	−.13	.13	−.04
Over 50 years	−.18	.25	−.12	−.02	−.25	−.14	.28	−.04

than average zero-order correlation for ten-year changes in the value of legal provisions. Lower correlations are found for

1. WP/WC—coverage between 1960 and 1970: $r = .63$;
2. WP/WC—legal standard between 1960 and 1970: $r = .57$;

3. MH—coverage between 1960 and 1970: $r = .63$;
4. MH—legal standard between 1930 and 1940: $r = .76$; and
5. MH—legal standard between 1940 and 1950: $r = .72$.

A more direct indication of the decades when the largest amount of change in these laws occurred can be obtained by calculating the mean and the variance of the ten-year changes in the provisions of the law. The larger the mean and the variance, the greater the differential change.

Table 6.11, which displays the means and the variances of the ten-year changes in the legal provisions of wage and hour standards laws, suggests that with two exceptions, the decades listed above are the ones during which the greatest amount of change in state ranking took place. The exceptions are:

1. MH—legal standard between 1930 and 1940: the low correlation does *not* appear to have been a function of a large amount of change in this provision relative to other decades; and

2. MH—legal standard between 1960 and 1970: state ranking changed substantially.

Substantial legislative activity for WP/WC and for MH seems to have occurred between 1960 and 1970. By taking the ratio of the average variance for the decades 1920–1960 to the variance for 1960–1970, we can gauge more directly how much change occurred in those ten years relative to the previous forty:

1. WP/WC—coverage: $227.74/1316.85 = 0.17$;
2. WP/WC—legal standard: $10753.69/24790.12 = 0.43$;
3. MH—coverage: $104.99/1230.64 = 0.09$;
4. MH—legal standard: $6628.04/26423.83 = 0.25$.

This shift does not occur for night-work laws, where similar ratios were 1.23 for coverage and 5.59 for standard. In addition, the mean change between 1960 and 1970 for WP/WC–coverage, WP/WC–legal standard, MH–coverage, and MH–legal standard was approximately two and one-half times the mean change for any other decade. But, whereas the provisions of WP/WC were strengthened during this decade, the provisions of MH were dramatically limited. To what crises can we attribute these findings?

All of the observed shifts in the content of laws between 1960 and 1970 find their source in crisis situations created by the rise of social movements. The renewed interest in WP/WC is associated with the prominence of the civil rights movement and the concern with MH with the contemporary women's rights movement. Both movements saw these laws as relevant to

Table 6.11. Changes in State Wage and Hour
Standards Laws, 1920–1970

Law	Provision	Decade	Mean	Variance	Explanation
WP/WC	Coverage	1920–1930	2.13	37.12	
		1930–1940	10.79	267.29	
		1940–1950	9.11	235.43	
		1950–1960	7.29	371.10	
		1960–1970	25.00	1,316.85	Pressure of civil rights movement
	Standard	1920–1930	62.50	11,252.00	
		1930–1940	70.80	7,626.62	
		1940–1950	61.67	17,206.25	
		1950–1960	43.10	6,929.88	
		1960–1970	127.87	24,790.12	Pressure of civil rights movement
MH	Coverage	1920–1930	3.17	189.51	
		1930–1940	8.92	81.74	
		1940–1950	6.96	24.46	
		1950–1960	−1.05	124.26	
		1960–1970	−28.16	1,230.64	Pressure of women's movement
	Standard	1920–1930	56.67	10,678.25	
		1930–1940	63.54	5,812.93	
		1940–1950	1.00	636.20	
		1950–1960	−27.10	9,384.77	
		1960–1970	−166.78	26,423.83	Pressure of women's movement
NW	Coverage	1920–1930	−.22	40.65	
		1930–1940	3.94	146.76	
		1940–1950	9.50	150.50	
		1950–1960	1.09	73.61	
		1960–1970	−.18	83.97	
	Standard	1920–1930	17.00	1,299.85	
		1930–1940	−10.31	939.70	
		1940–1950	2.90	984.54	
		1950–1960	1.85	328.47	
		1960–1970	−2.62	158.92	

their political goals: the civil rights movement (in coalition with the labor movement) fought to win new WP/WC laws and increase their implementation in ghetto areas. It was found that black and other minority employees often needed the intervention of state departments of labor to receive wages for the work they had performed. In 1961, Pennsylvania rewrote its WP/WC law, for example. This constituted the first substantial revision of that law since 1891. Coverage was made universal, and the list of procedures to be followed by employers in paying employees included six of the seven possible procedures. Laws with universal coverage also were adopted in Virginia in 1962 and in Delaware in 1965. As recently as 1973, Illinois passed an entirely new and "complete" WP/WC law, in which all workers were covered and seven procedures specified.

The women's movement, on the other hand, saw maximum hours laws for women as standing in the way of equal treatment of women in the labor market. Title VII of the 1964 Civil Rights Act, which contains a prohibition against discrimination in compensation, brought the opportunity to translate insights on women's treatment into concrete changes in their role in the economy. Instances surfaced repeatedly showing that laws such as MH restricted job opportunities and potential mobility. Cases were taken to court. Ironically, after some hesitation, the same court system that earlier had sustained and even fostered the openly separate and unequal treatment of women now invalidated laws that were not sex neutral (Ratner, 1980). By the early 1970s, MH had been struck down by the courts in nine states, repealed by state legislatures in twenty-one states, and ruled against by attorneys general in twenty-three states (Babcock et al., 1975:262–263). In fact, states with MH laws with extensive coverage provisions, such as New York and New Jersey, were among the first either to limit coverage under these laws severely or to repeal them entirely.

In each case, crises created by organized interest groups concerned with the way certain employees were being treated in the labor market facilitated change in the content of legislation. To the extent that states responded to the interest groups' pressure and modified their laws, they changed in their ranking relative to other states on the quality of legal provisions.

The crisis model, therefore, accounts for whatever change is observed better than either the imprinting or the convergence models. Yet, the stability in state ranking on the quality of provisions in these laws over the twentieth century is, perhaps, an equally impressive finding. State laws that ranked high in 1920 relative to other state laws continue to rank high in 1970, in large measure because modifications in these laws have been weak or nonexistent.

SUMMARY AND CONCLUSIONS

In this chapter, legal growth after the period of state adoption was examined in the light of three theories of legislative change: the convergence theory, the imprinting theory, and the crisis theory. Neither the convergence theory nor the imprinting theory explained the observed change. State laws did not become uniform over time as the convergence model would predict. Later change in the content of legislation was unrelated to the earlier growth in these laws as the imprinting model would hold. Differential growth in these laws can best be accounted for by the successful implementation of crisis strategies on the part of organized groups acting in the political arena.

These groups mobilized political support for their demands by making increasingly visible the problems employees faced on the labor market, be it the discrimination a woman suffered by being "protected" from better paying jobs, or the exploitation of blacks who performed work and remained uncompensated by fly-by-night firms. The success of organized groups in making these troublesome labor market conditions generally visible was, in large part, a function of the general climate in the country. A social climate favorable to the civil rights of blacks and women in general will be more receptive to demands that their civil and social rights in the labor market be respected.

In short, the same law carries a new meaning in a different historical epoch. What was once adopted to protect immigrant workers became attached to the protection of the rights of blacks. Similarly, a set of laws enacted to protect women from harsh and exploitative treatment came to be regarded as a barrier to their advancement. Laws enacted at the turn of the century have been modified to make them relevant to the socioeconomic conditions of the 1970s.

7

CONGRESSIONAL VOTING ON THE
FAIR LABOR STANDARDS ACT

The development of modern labor laws was characterized, in Chapter 4, as a process in which there were long stretches of modest growth in coverage resulting from state legislative activity followed by a large increase in coverage resulting from congressional action. Because the federal government enacted the Fair Labor Standards Act in 1938, the number of employees covered under a minimum wage law or an overtime law trebled. The federal courts and the Wage and Hour Division of the United States Department of Labor were given the power to determine what constituted "interstate commerce" and concluded that approximately one-third to one-half of all United States workers were engaged in such employment. Chapter 4 concluded as well that coverage under state minimum wage laws subsequent to a revision in the FLSA seemed to remain unaffected by the federal reforms.

But there is reason to believe that revisions in the definition of interstate commerce were based on prior amendments to more innovative state laws, amendments enacted between 1938 and 1960 and between 1961 and 1966. In 1960, the New York legislature, for example, revamped its 1937 minimum wage law. It established a statutory minimum wage rate of $1.00 per hour, a significantly higher rate than the one provided in the federal law at that time. In addition, the scope of coverage was expanded to include all employees except those in agriculture, domestic service, nonprofit organizations, and government. The 1961 and 1966 amendments to the coverage provisions of the FLSA followed the lead of this New York State and other minimum wage laws by covering certain employees in construction, wholesale and retail trade, and personal service who had previously been excluded from coverage under the federal law. New York was not the only state to enact a more comprehensive minimum wage law before 1961. Other states included North Carolina (1959), Maine (1959), Rhode Island (1956), Vermont (1957), Idaho (1955), and New Mexico (1955). The probable interplay between the scope of coverage in state and federal legislation suggests that congressmen were well aware of the advances in coverage at the state level, and that congressional voting patterns were influenced, to some extent, by these state advances. In this chapter, the precise relationship between the scope of state minimum wage laws and the voting patterns of state congressional delegations is examined.

Economic theory would suggest that employers in states where the scope of coverage under minimum wage laws was extensive operate at a competitive disadvantage to employers in states with either no minimum wage law or a very limited one. Since labor costs are likely to be lower in states with no minimum wage law, employers in low-wage states could pass these savings on to consumers through lower prices. This would suggest that employers staunchly resisted the implementation of minimum wage laws at the state level. The historical evidence supports the theory. For example, when the Massachusetts legislature was considering the adoption of the first United States minimum wage law in 1912, "representatives of textile and other manufacturers opposed the bill, maintaining that they could not raise wages and still meet competition from outside the state" (Brandeis, 1935:509). In the early 1920s, the Ohio state legislature considered a bill to establish a minimum wage. In 1922, the Ohio Manufacturers' Association continued its long campaign to defeat such a measure. "An interesting bulletin to its members on April 21, 1922 was headed by the question: 'Are you contributing to these Organizations?' There followed a list of the organizations conducting a campaign for a minimum wage law. . . . Further on came the statement: 'The organizations which are doing this work are largely supported but not directed by you' and the suggestion: 'You might stipulate . . . that no part of it shall be used to promote the passage of legislation . . . for the social service labor program adopted by these organizations'" (Brandeis, 1935:521). The Ohio bill was delayed until after the Supreme Court declared a similar law unconstitutional. A committee did investigate the condition of wages in Ohio, however. "After a thoroughly biased and unscientific investigation, obviously dominated by the Ohio Manufacturers' Association, five of the six members of the [investigating] committee signed a report opposing any minimum wage legislation. The reasons given for their stand . . . that such legislation would have a detrimental effect on Ohio industries" (Brandeis, 1935:520–522). Finally, in 1934, several New England states agreed to maintain the same minimum wage standards in their minimum wage laws. Such "an interstate compact on minimum wage standards was endorsed by official representatives of seven eastern states. This compact . . . aimed to secure uniformity in state laws by prescribing general standards substantially the same as those already enacted in 1933. . . . It was ratified first by Massachusetts in 1934, New Hampshire in 1935, and Rhode Island in 1936." By agreeing on uniform standards, each state protected its industries from operating at a competitive disadvantage to industries in adjacent states (Commons and Andrews, 1936:57–58). In threatening to shift their firms out of the state to one more sympathetic to pure profit-making motives, employers were well aware that such a move would mean a loss of jobs and revenues for the state considering the adoption of a minimum wage law.

Congressional representatives from such a state thus proved eager to support a federal law on at least two related grounds. First, federal legislation would place those firms remaining in states with minimum wage laws in a more favorable competitive position vis-à-vis similar firms in other states. Second, national labor standards would deter shifts by employers in highly industrialized states engaged in low-wage, labor-intensive industries (Silberman and Durden, 1976:320). One would expect, therefore, that support for the enactment of federal minimum wage laws would come from both employers and employees in industrial states and in states with minimum wage laws. Reformulated as hypotheses: (1) the stronger the legal provisions of a state minimum wage law, the greater the likelihood that congressmen from that state will support the FLSA and amendments to it; and (2) the more industrialized a state, the greater the likelihood that congressmen from that state will vote for the FLSA and amendments to it.

DATA

To test these hypotheses, three sets of data were used: roll calls of the Senate and the House of Representatives on the FLSA; measures of the scope of coverage and the average legal minimum wage rate by state; and measures of the extent of industrialization.

ROLL CALL

We examined roll calls taken for the FLSA at three points: 1938, 1961, and 1966.[1] These constitute the years of enactment and of major amendments to the law. A major amendment was defined as one that both extended the scope of coverage and raised the minimum wage rate. Although several other amendments to the FLSA were made between 1938 and 1961—as, for example, in 1949 and 1955—these were limited to raising the minimum wage for workers who were covered under the 1938 law.

Moreover, roll calls were measured by the percentage of a state delegation voting in favor of the FLSA. A congressional delegation consisted of all senators and representatives from a particular state. This departs from other studies of the correlates of congressional voting on FLSA amendments. Silberman and Durden (1976) and Bloch (1975) look at the voting patterns of individual congressmen. Since interest here is in the relationship between state legislation and the voting behavior of congressmen and senators from that state, however, the combined vote of the state delegation seemed a better indicator of the impact of state law on congressional votes.

Furthermore, because the congressional delegation was used as the unit for measuring voting behavior, the likelihood of bias toward states with small congressional delegations was great, because the smaller a state's delegation, the more likely its voting pattern was to fall at one extreme or the other. To remove that effect, states in which the total number of senators and members of the House of Representatives was less than five were excluded.[2] Finally, to ensure that senators and congressmen were voting on equivalent bills, roll calls were used only for the version of the bill approved by the Joint Senate and House Conference Committee.

The data on roll calls therefore consisted of a twenty-state sample measuring the percentage of congressmen voting favorably for the FLSA in 1938 and for the amendments to that law in 1961 and 1966.

STATE MINIMUM WAGE LAWS

Data on the employee coverage and the legal standard by state were compiled for the three years before congressional action was taken. These data enabled us to gauge the precise relationship between the scope of preexisting minimum wage laws and subsequent voting behavior. For coverage, for 1937, we simply calculated the percentage of employees covered under a state law. For 1960 and 1965, we calculated the percentage of employees in a state covered by the provisions of state or federal wage laws or both. Data on both state and federal laws were included in order to capture the differential impact of federal legislation on states arising from differences in the industrial composition across states. For legal standard, for 1938, we measured the average minimum wage standard for employees covered by state laws in 1938. For 1960 and 1965, we used the combined average minimum wage rate established through state or federal legislation or both.

Including coverage and standard from the federal law for 1960 and 1965 meant that in some states employees were only covered by federal laws. Yet, once the FLSA had been enacted, the combined indices offered a more complete picture of the factors that congressmen had to consider when making a decision to amend or not to amend the federal law. Given the fact that coverage was coded under federal legislation as if twenty-eight states had adopted this law, it also would have proven quite difficult to disaggregate coverage resulting from state and federal legislation at the state level.

INDUSTRIALIZATION

The level of industrialization of a state was measured in two ways: as the ratio of manufacturing employees to the total state population; and as the value added in manufacturing per capita.[3] For the first measure, we used as our denominator the total population rather than total employees, so that the measures of industrialization for the three time points would be consistent. In addition, it was necessary to interpolate data on the year before and the year after the FLSA was adopted or amended for both indices. For example, we calculated the percentage of employees in manufacturing in 1938 by adding the total number of employees in manufacturing in a state for 1937 and 1939, and dividing it by the sum of the population for that state for 1937 and 1939. Similarly, value added in manufacturing per capita for 1938 was computed by adding the value added in manufacturing for 1937 and 1939 and dividing it by the total population in a state for 1937 and 1939. The basic data sets used in this analysis are listed in the Appendix.

DATA ANALYSIS AND RESULTS

The zero-order correlations among congressional voting, minimum wage law coverage, minimum wage law standard, and industrialization are listed in Table 7.1 for 1938, Table 7.2 for 1961, and Table 7.3 for 1966. The

Table 7.1. Zero-Order Correlations of Congressional Vote,
Minimum Wage Coverage and Standard, and Industrialization, 1938

	Value added in manufacturing per capita	Minimum wage coverage, 1937	Minimum wage standard, 1937	Congressional vote, 1938
Percent manufacturing	.93*	.29	− .42	− .05
Value added in manufacturing per capita		.42	− .34	.18
Minimum wage coverage, 1937			− .19	.48*
Minimum wage standard, 1937				.21

*Significant at the .05 level.

Table 7.2. Zero-Order Correlations of Congressional Vote,
Minimum Wage Coverage and Standard, and Industrialization, 1961

	Value added in manufacturing per capita	Minimum wage coverage, 1960	Minimum wage standard, 1960	Congressional vote, 1961
Percent manufacturing	.93*	.74*	− .43	.41
Value added in manufacturing per capita		.60*	− .51*	.41
Minimum wage coverage, 1960			− .45	.54*
Minimum wage standard, 1960				− .64*

*Significant at the .05 level.

Table 7.3. Zero-Order Correlations of Congressional Vote, Minimum Wage
Coverage and Standard, and Industrialization, 1966

	Value added in manufacturing per capita	Minimum wage coverage, 1965	Minimum wage standard, 1965	Congressional vote, 1966
Percent manufacturing	.90*	.71*	− .30	.51*
Value added in manufacturing per capita		.57*	− .42	.62*
Minimum wage coverage, 1965			− .34	.66*
Minimum wage standard, 1965				− .47*

*Significant at the .05 level.

results confirm the hypothesis on the relationship between state law and congressional delegation voting pattern for all three years and confirm the hypothesis about the relationship between industrialization and congressional voting for 1961 and 1965.

CONGRESSIONAL VOTING AND STATE LAW

The extent of employee coverage under existing minimum wage legislation was consistently the variable most strongly correlated with congressional vote: $r = .48$ for 1938, .54 for 1961, and .66 for 1966. By contrast, the relationship between congressional vote and the legal standard was somewhat complicated: while there was a moderate, positive relationship between legal standard and congressional vote in 1938 ($r = .21$), the correlations between legal standard and congressional vote were strong and negative for 1961 and 1965 with $r = -.64$ for 1961 and $-.47$ for 1965. These seemingly inconsistent results fall into place when we realize, however, that the 1937 legal standard index was substantively different from the index in 1960 and 1965. Many states had *no* minimum wage law in 1937. The moderate positive relationship between legal standard and congressional vote in 1938 indicates, therefore, that representatives and senators from states that had a minimum wage law were somewhat more likely to vote for the adoption of the FLSA than congressmen from states with no law. Once the federal law was enacted, however, all states had some minimum wage standard applying to at least a portion of their workers (even if it was only the federal standard). And, since state laws usually covered a broader population of workers than the FLSA, but covered them at a lower wage rate, states with state and federal laws generally had a lower average legal standard. (Note that for 1960 the correlation coefficients for coverage and legal standard were negative: $r = -.45$; for 1965 $r = -.34$.)

Thus, employees covered under state laws pressed for a federal minimum wage standard to raise their wages. Furthermore, even a low minimum wage rate can be costly to employers who have competitors not subject to any minimum wage standards. Consequently, employers subject to state minimum wage standards might have been willing to accept a higher minimum wage rate as long as it extended uniformly to all competitors. Whether we look at coverage or standard, the correlations indicate that for all three roll calls, congressmen from states in which a large percentage of employees were covered under state and federal minimum wage laws were more likely to vote for the FLSA amendments.

CONGRESSIONAL VOTE AND INDUSTRIALIZATION

The relationship between industrialization and congressional vote increased over time. In 1938, industrialization and voting were only slightly related, with $r = .05$ for percent employees and .18 for value added by manufacturing. By 1961, however, that relationship had grown much stronger with $r = .41$ for percent employees and .42 for value added by manufacturing. By 1966, $r = .51$ for percent employees and .62 for value added by manufacturing.

This increasing correlation over time could have been the product of various factors. First, during the Great Depression, minimum wage laws became a means for buttressing the pay of employees operating in a slack labor market, and many congressmen from less industrialized states voted for them. In 1938, for example, delegations from several southern and southwestern states, such as Alabama, Kentucky, and Oklahoma, voted for these laws. Indeed, it was Senator Black from Alabama who introduced and fought unsuccessfully for a national law establishing a thirty-hour workweek with the purpose of spreading existing work to more employees. He was also a strong advocate of the FLSA (Brandeis, 1972:201–204, 219). Yet, by 1966 southern congressmen were less likely to vote for the amendments to the FLSA than were representatives from other regions. Perhaps this shift resulted from the 1961 and 1966 amendments, which brought low-wage labor-intensive occupations such as retail trade and personal service under the law. Although the southern states industrialized at a greater rate than the rest of the country between 1938 and 1966, they remained among the less industrialized states.

Moreover, one way to convince employers to move to the South and continue this trend of high industrial growth was to stress low labor costs. Consequently, southern congressional delegations were acting in their constituents' self-interest by voting against the 1961 and 1966 amendments to increase the scope of coverage under these laws.

By contrast, as discussed in Chapter 4, in 1961 and 1966 Presidents Kennedy and Johnson repaid their debt to the labor vote by, among other things, actively supporting these amendments to the FLSA. The 1965 congressional delegations from nonsouthern states constituted an overwhelmingly Democratic majority, one ushered in by the Johnson landslide victory. It was easy, then, for those Democratic representatives from more industrialized states to vote in accordance with the economic interests of both the employers and employees in their states.

Finally, the results indicate that each industrialization variable was strongly related to coverage, especially in 1961 ($r = .74$ for percent employees and .60 for value added in manufacturing) and 1966 ($r = .71$ for percent employees and .57 for value added in manufacturing). These strong relationships are plausible in light of the economic assumptions discussed above, which rest on similar strands of thought: industries in more industrialized states and in states with stronger minimum wage laws operated at a competitive disadvantage to those in states without one or both of these characteristics. These simple relationships among industrialization, provisions in minimum wage legislation, and congressional vote are summarized diagrammatically in Figure 7.1 for 1938, Figure 7.2 for 1961, and Figure 7.3 for 1966.

Figure 7.1. Zero-Order Correlations between Congressional Vote, Legislation, and Industrialization: Significant Relationships, 1938.

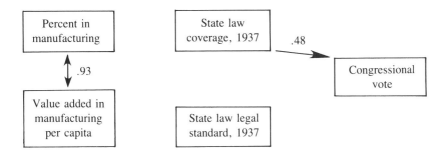

Figure 7.2. Zero-Order Correlations between Congressional Vote, Legislation, and Industrialization: Significant Relationships, 1961.

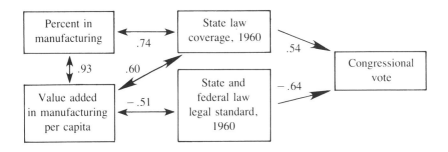

PARTIAL CORRELATION: CONGRESSIONAL VOTE,
STATE LAW, AND INDUSTRIALIZATION

It is clear from Figures 7.1–7.3 that, for each year, legislation was more strongly related to congressional voting patterns on the FLSA than was industrialization. These results suggest that the zero-order correlations between industrialization and congressional vote mask the fact that employees in more industrialized states were able to exert pressure on *state* legislatures to enact minimum wage laws. If this were the case, we would expect the extent of industrialization to be only indirectly related to congressional vote, or related only insofar as it had already affected state action on minimum wage laws. Does the relationship between industrialization and congressional

Figure 7.3. Zero-Order Correlations between Congressional Vote, Legislation, and Industrialization: Significant Relationships, 1966.

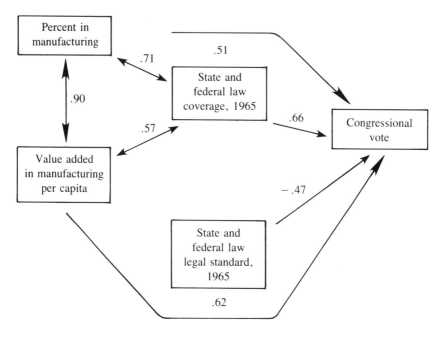

vote disappear, therefore, when we control for employee coverage and standard in existing minimum wage laws?

The partial correlations between the measures of industrialization and congressional vote, controlling for employee coverage or standard under minimum wage laws in 1938, 1961, and 1966, are listed in Table 7.4, along with the original zero-order correlations between industrialization and congressional vote. With one exception, the relationship between industrialization and congressional vote fell sharply when state legislation was controlled. The relationship between industrialization and congressional vote dropped more sharply controlling for coverage than controlling for standard. Thus, while industrialization independent of state law remained slightly related to congressional vote, its impact on congressional vote dropped significantly in 1961 and 1966. Therefore, the findings support the contention that industrialization affects congressional voting through its impact on the development of legislation. This sets the stage for a more complete model of the determinants of congressional voting patterns.

Table 7.4. Zero-Order and Partial Correlations of Industrialization and Congressional Vote, 1938, 1961, 1966

| Industrialization | Provision of law controlled for | Congressional vote | | | | | |
| | | 1938 | | 1961 | | 1966 | |
		Zero order	Partial	Zero order	Partial	Zero order	Partial
Percent employees in manufacturing	Coverage		−.22		.01		.08
	Legal	−.05		.41		.51	
	standard		−.05		.18		.44
Value added in manufacturing per capita	Coverage		−.03		.14		.40
	Legal	.18		.42		.62	
	standard		.27		.14		.52

A MODEL OF CONGRESSIONAL VOTING PATTERNS ON THE FLSA

The analysis thus far has confirmed the hypothesis that the scope of existing state minimum wage laws and congressional voting are highly correlated. The level of industrialization in a state was also found to affect congressional vote indirectly through its effect on the adoption of state laws. These results can be reorganized into the simple model shown in Figure 7.4.

In this and in previous chapters, I have stressed that the power position of interest groups is a major determinant of the quality of these laws. In fact, I argue that it is the behavioral mechanism underlying the relationship between these structural characteristics. Because more industrialized states are likely to have a larger portion of the labor force organized in unions than less industrialized states, employees in these states can be expected to have more power relative to employers than do employees in nonunionized states. Unionization, therefore, should be an important medi-

Figure 7.4. Simple Model.

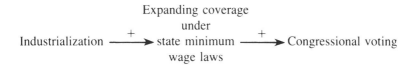

ating variable linking industrialization and the expansion of coverage under *state* minimum wage laws. Indeed, the two recent studies of congressional voting on the FLSA mentioned previously (Bloch, 1975; Silberman and Durden, 1976) found that unionization was the single most important factor predicting congressional voting. Bloch analyzed Senate voting on the 1966 and 1973 amendments to the FLSA and concluded that "senators favoring passage of these bills are likely to come from states with high union membership and, to a lesser extent, high wage levels" (1975:17). Silberman and Durden developed a more complicated model to predict the vote on the 1973 amendment to the FLSA in the House of Representatives and also reported that unionization had the largest influence on the voting behavior of members of the House of Representatives.[4] Neither study introduced state legislation as a variable in its model of the determinants of congressional voting. Here, however, unionization is introduced as an important explanatory variable both of congressional voting patterns on the FLSA and its amendments and of the level of coverage under state legislation.

Adding unionization to the simple model produces the following path model: state legislation and unionization have a direct, positive effect on congressional voting. Industrialization has a direct, positive effect on unionization and on the progressiveness of state legislation. It also has an indirect and positive effect on the congressional vote through its impact on unionization and the state law. Its direct effect on congressional vote is unclear. Finally, unionization has a direct, positive effect on the strength of state legislation. This path model is represented in Figure 7.5.

Figure 7.5. Path Model.

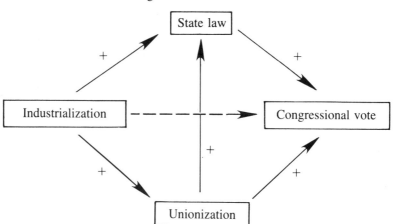

DATA AND DATA ANALYSIS

The path model was analyzed for 1961 and 1966 congressional votes on amendments to the FLSA using the same data as in the preceding analysis, with two exceptions. First, for state legislation, the analysis was restricted to employee coverage because its relationship to the other variables was more straightforward than it was for legal standard in the earlier analysis. Second, for industrialization, only the percentage of the total population employed in manufacturing was used in 1961 and 1966 because the two measures of industrialization were so highly correlated ($r > .90$) that their multicollinearity would have distorted the results. Data estimating the percentage of the labor force in a state that was unionized were also collected. Because of data limitations, 1953 estimates of union membership calculated by Troy (1957) were used for the analysis of the 1961 congressional vote. Data for 1965 were gathered from Friedheim (1968).

These data were analyzed by using a series of simultaneous equations. The results of the path analysis are displayed in Figure 7.6 for 1961 and Figure 7.7 for 1966.

DISCUSSION OF MODEL: GENERAL FINDINGS

In general, while the beta coefficients are not identical, the strength and the signs of the relationships are basically the same in 1961 and in 1966. First, the direct effect of industrialization is negative. Second, state legislation and unionization had a strong, direct, positive effect on the patterns of congressional voting on the FLSA. Third, the direct effect of unionization on the scope of coverage under state laws was positive.

Figure 7.6. Path Analysis of Industrialization, Unionization, State Legislation, and Congressional Vote: Minimum Wage Legislation, 1961.

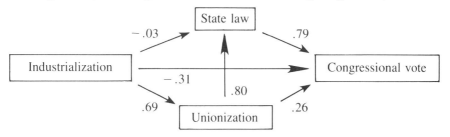

Figure 7.7. Path Analysis of Industrialization, Unionization,
State Legislation, and Congressional Vote, 1966.

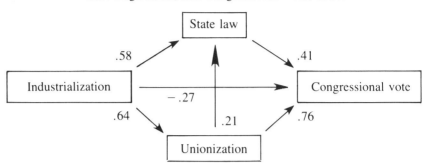

An important difference between 1961 and 1966 is in the indirect effect
of industrialization, which influences congressional voting through its effect
on state laws. Specifically, the relationship was small and negative in 1961
and strong and positive in 1966. This finding points to what is perhaps
one of the more interesting patterns in the path diagram: the effects of
industrialization on congressional voting. Industrialization had a direct but
negative effect, and an indirect positive effect on congressional voting. In
other words, the level of industrialization of a state is related to voting
favorably on the FLSA by that state's congressional delegation because it
facilitates unionization and more extensive laws within the state. Once its
effect on those variables is taken into account, the level of industrialization
hinders congressional support for the FLSA. If the combination of high
industrialization, sparse unionization, and poor state legislation is considered
to be evidence that employers have substantially greater power than employees, the meaning of these seemingly paradoxical results falls into place.

Employees in more industrialized states are more likely to be unionized.
Through these unions, they have more ability to influence state and federal
legislation. Congressmen from highly industrialized states with low unionization, however, do not face the pressure of union opposition in the next
election if they vote against labor-supported legislation. They are free to
vote in the interests of employers. If these employers could deter union
organization in industrial settings, they certainly could successfully oppose
further amendments to this federal wage legislation.

At the other extreme, congressmen from less industrialized states can
operate with some independence from the influence of employer interests.
In these states, employers are only one of many interest groups, and a
congressman could vote in favor of raising the minimum wage and expanding

the scope of coverage for several reasons. He or she could have voted affirmatively as part of a bargain with another congressman. He or she could have voted for the FLSA amendments to repay labor interests for their support in the last election. Or, he or she could have voted to demonstrate a general concern with the needs of lower paid employees.

Whatever the reason, congressmen from less industrialized states can support the FLSA amendments and lose little if they alienate industrial interests. In general, however, industrialization appears to have stimulated a variety of mechanisms that furthered the interests of employees. It did so because, under certain conditions, the interests of employees and employers converged. Unionization and state laws put the more industrialized states at a competitive disadvantage to the less industrialized ones, especially in a national economy. It was in the interests of both employers and employees in these states to support federal legislation to adjust these economic imbalances. In estimating their cost-benefit calculus, therefore, congressmen from states with state wage laws and high unionization found their political interests heavily weighted in the direction of support for federal minimum wage standards.

DISCUSSION OF MODEL: DIFFERENCES IN RESULTS

While in major respects, the findings were similar for 1961 and 1966, the strength of the relationships among variables shifted in several interesting ways between those years. In 1961, for example, the dominant path accounting for congressional voting patterns went from industrialization to unionization to state legislation to favorable congressional voting patterns. That is, the more industrialized a state was, the greater the number of unionized employees in that state. The more unionized a state was, the broader the scope of coverage under its minimum wage laws. And, the stronger the coverage under minimum wage laws in a state, the higher the percentage of congressmen from that state to vote for the amendments to the FLSA. In 1966, by contrast, industrialization affected congressional voting through its impact both on unionization and on the level of coverage in existing state laws. In addition, unionization bore strongly and directly on congressional voting patterns. The strong link between unionization and state law found in 1961 had weakened considerably by 1966. Instead, unionization directly affected congressional voting on the FLSA.

The major difference between the two path models hinges on the change in the locus of unions' political activism. In Chapter 4, it was noted that the antiunion sentiment following World War II found expression in, among other things, a low interest in labor's political priorities. Inertia over the FLSA was reflected in frequent wavering over the definition of interstate commerce. Given the political environment of the late 1950s and early 1960s, labor concentrated on state legislation in states in which it carried political weight. Once it had made progress in enough states, the balance of forces supporting uniform federal standards tipped in its direction. By 1961, with Kennedy in office and a sufficient number of progressive state laws, labor was able to reform the FLSA substantially. The findings for the 1961 data indicate that labor activism affected federal legislation through its impact on the scope of coverage under state laws.

The 1961 amendments to the FLSA were the first to provide a broadened definition of interstate commerce. The courts sustained this definition and provided the breakthrough needed by organized labor to modify and further expand the meaning of interstate commerce. Interstate commerce was defined so as to make coverage under the FLSA consistent with coverage under more innovative state laws. Labor responded to the changes in the political environment of the 1960s in an economically rational way. By redirecting its efforts for legislation to Congress, it could gain benefits for its members in the fifty states. By 1966, what had been a strong but indirect effect of unionization on congressional voting became, instead, a strong factor acting directly on Congress.

SUMMARY AND CONCLUSIONS

This chapter has examined the relationship between the scope of coverage under minimum wage laws at the state level and congressional voting on the Fair Labor Standards Act and amendments to it. While previous studies had investigated these patterns of voting, none had introduced the scope of existing legislation into their models. Since, however, employers in more industrialized states with state minimum wage laws operated at a competitive disadvantage to similar employers in other states, it would be in the interests of both employers and employees in these states to support federal legislation that would uniformly affect the same categories of employees in every state.

A strong positive relationship was found between the scope of coverage under minimum wage legislation in a state and congressional voting on the FLSA. The level of industrialization in a state was also found to be related to a state delegation's congressional vote for the FLSA. But the partial correlation of industrialization and congressional vote, controlling for state law, showed a much weaker relationship between industrialization and congressional vote. The relationship between industrialization and state law, therefore, is indirect and is mediated by the scope of existing state laws.

On the basis of these findings and the results of earlier studies of voting on the FLSA, the following causal model was proposed: the level of industrialization is directly and positively related to the extent of unionization in a state and to coverage under existing minimum wage legislation. But it is only indirectly related to congressional vote through its effect on these two factors. The strength of this basic model of the determinants of congressional voting is reinforced by the fact that the findings for 1961 and 1966 were essentially the same: as expected, unionization and state law had direct and positive effects on congressional voting.[5] These factors were, in turn, positively affected by industrialization. In addition, industrialization was found to have a direct negative effect on congressional voting.

There were differences between the two models, however, especially in the dominant paths determining congressional voting. In 1961, the indirect effect of unionization on congressional voting (through existing state legislation) was stronger than its direct effect. By 1966, the direct effect of unionization on congressional voting outweighed its indirect effect. While existing legislation directly affected congressional voting in 1966, it did so to a much lesser extent than in 1961.

This change was attributed to a shift in strategy by organized labor, which was facilitated by a changing political environment. In 1961, the more industrialized states were also the more highly unionized states and the states with more progressive minimum wage laws. The congressmen from these states voted for the 1961 amendments to the FLSA, and a larger portion of workers were covered under federal law than had been the case previously. Once the lid had been lifted from the restricted definition of interstate commerce, organized labor could press for further extension of coverage at the national level. The labor movement socialized the conflict by bringing it to national attention, to return to Schattschneider's phrase. Through a single lobbying effort, it could change the provisions of a law to the benefit of employees in fifty states. And, labor was aided, no doubt crucially, by employers' groups from states with progressive laws, who wanted more uniform standards across states.

This analysis also has more general implications. It suggests the fruitfulness of looking at the behavior of congressional delegations in terms of the competitive position of a state relative to other states concerning the issue at hand. In the case of minimum wage laws, firms in states where coverage was extensive were operating at a competitive disadvantage to firms in states without laws or subject only to the FLSA. Furthermore, the results point to the important interplay between policy decisions at different levels of government. Not only did Congress look to states for innovative approaches to domestic policy, but members of Congress clearly based their decisions on the possible impact of such measures on constituents in their states.

Finally, it is highly probable that the constellation of forces actively supporting or opposing legislation varied both with the level of government and with the distribution of interest groups within a state. Employers worked hard to deter the enactment of state minimum wage laws. Once defeated, however, they turned to the federal government to enact uniform standards to ensure that competitors in other states would be subject to the same labor costs. To a certain extent the conflict over the FLSA and amendments to it transcended the conflict between employers and employees observed at the state level. Added to this class-based conflict is a conflict between states with firms already "handicapped" by government intervention and states with firms operating in unrestricted labor markets.

IV

CHANGE IN
LABOR STANDARDS
LEGISLATION

8
UNIONIZATION AND SOCIAL REFORM
To Them That Have Shall Be Given

The broad sweep of historical development of the modern economy from one based on principles of laissez-faire to one in which such tenets co-exist in uneasy tension with social rights is comprised of many separate but related strands of change. One of these—the entrance of the state into the regulation of economic transactions—has been the primary focus of the book thus far. Just as those social rights embodied in labor standards legislation have become gradually institutionalized into the American legal system over the twentieth century, so the organized labor movement has become increasingly incorporated as a participant in American politics. A second path of change, therefore, takes the form of the growth of unions.

In several preceding chapters, a great deal of emphasis has been placed on the role of organized labor both in facilitating the enactment of wage and hour standards legislation and in maintaining the achieved legislative gains over time. In the last chapter, for example, a strong positive relationship was found between the extent of unionization in a state and support for the FLSA by a state's congressional delegation. In this chapter, an implicit theme of this study is examined directly by asking what the relationship between unionization and social reform in twentieth-century America is. Although it is not possible to gauge directly the extent of organized group support for every wage and hour law and amendments to it, it is possible to ascertain whether union members were covered under these laws and what the dynamic relationship between these two forms of worker self-protection was.

Specifically, this chapter addresses three sets of questions about the relationship between the *growth* in social reform legislation and the *growth* in unionization. First, is the most extensive coverage under labor standards laws provided to workers in industries that are most heavily unionized? Or, do these standards serve as a substitute means of protection for employees who lack union organizations with which to bargain collectively? Second, is the growth in unionization related to the growth in the scope of social reform legislation? More generally, how much does a change in one of these variables relate to prior, contemporary, or subsequent change in the other measure? Third, to what extent is the change in unionization and social reform a consequence of some third independent factor?

TESTING THE RELATIONSHIP BETWEEN UNIONIZATION AND SOCIAL REFORM

Early twentieth-century proponents of labor standards legislation argued that the rights embodied in these laws should be extended to unorganized employees. Protective labor laws were envisioned as a substitute for the power of labor unions to garner benefits for workers through collective bargaining. For example, a delegate from the Women's Trade Union League to an early twentieth-century AFL convention argued to her union brothers that the convention should pass a resolution supporting maximum hours laws for women because they would serve as "another weapon in the hands of the trade union women to protect not only themselves and their children but the great mass of unorganized women to whom has not yet come the social visions which will redeem the world" (Beyer, 1929:10–11). Probably the most vocal advocates of the law-as-substitute position were John R. Commons and John B. Andrews, who remarked that: "in any modern industrial community, large numbers of unorganized workers are found, still bargaining individually, employed at low wages and apparently unable to make any effective efforts themselves to improve their condition. If they are to be helped toward an equality in bargaining power with the employer, the state must take the initiative" (1936:43).

These supporters not only argued, however, that these rights *should* be extended to the unorganized, they also believed that these laws *were* being adopted for unorganized workers. In the case of the 1867 Ten Hour Law in Massachusetts, for example, "the emphasis on the textile industry was natural since it included most of the incorporated companies in which hours were especially long. Moreover, the preponderance of women and children in that field had made organization particularly difficult. The legislation was really desired to bring the textile mills up to the ten-hour standard which had been secured in other trades largely through trade union action" (Brandeis, 1935:462). The motivation underlying the adoption of an hours law for all minors under 18 and women under 21 in New York State in 1869 was similar: "The act was secured largely by the efforts of the Consumers' League of the city of New York, an organization which grew out of a large public meeting held 'to consider the condition of working women in New York retail stores.' Attempts to organize these women had previously been abandoned as hopeless" (Brandeis, 1935:469). Members of the Consumers' League worked successfully for the enactment of legislative standards for unorganized employees. (See also Baer, 1978; Foner, 1979; Wertheimer, 1977).

But the idea that benefits will be given by political decision makers to unorganized constituencies flies in the face of what is probably the most taken-for-granted assumption about political change: power begets reform; organization begets power. In other words, power resources can be mobilized for political reform, and organization is one of the most significant resources available to subordinate groups (Korpi, 1978). Commons and Andrews, when they turn from being advocates of what should be to being analysts of what is, understand this straightforward political dictum: "It seems no exaggeration to say," they remark, "that the majority of low-skilled industrial workers in the United States receive wages too small for decent self-support. This fact explains the demand for legislation as necessary to social welfare. . . . The almost entire absence of strong labor organizations and collective bargaining among this group of wage earners is an important factor in producing the low wage scale" (1936:47). In other words, where workers are organized, they create the potential power to obtain the benefits they seek.

This formulation sounds strangely reminiscent of a similar analysis first put forth by Karl Marx and Friedrich Engels in *The Communist Manifesto* on the relationship between the organization of workers and their subsequent political success. It also underlies Marx's analysis of the ten-hour laws in England in volume one of *Capital*. (The similarity is strange because Commons and Andrews and Marx are, in other respects, ideologically so divergent.) Marx and Engels posit that all change in the labor market in capitalist society is an outgrowth of class-based conflict. At the same time, the very existence of a labor market organized around private property norms creates the conditions under which class-based conflict may emerge. This class-based conflict—that is, the dynamic of change—can take the form of sets of political demands being identified with the interests of opposing groups. Class-based conflict, therefore, is at the root of the sweeping transformation of the modern political economy.

Marx and Engels view the political response of the working class to the organization of industry as moving through three stages: during the first stage, "individual laborers . . . direct their attacks not against bourgeois

conditions of production, but against the instruments of production themselves." At a second stage, integrally tied to the first, the laborers still
form an incoherent mass, but "if anywhere they unite to form more compact
bodies, this is not yet the consequence of their own active union, but of
the union of the bourgeoisie, which class, in order to attain its own political
ends, is compelled to set the whole proletariat in motion." At this point,
"every victory so obtained is a victory for the bourgeoisie. . . . But,"
continues Marx, moving on to the third stage, "with the development of
industry the proletariat not only increases in number; it becomes concentrated in greater masses, its strength grows, and it feels that strength more.
. . . Thereupon the workers begin to form combinations (trades' unions)
against the bourgeoisie. This organization . . . is continually being upset
again. . . . But it ever rises up again, stronger, firmer, mightier. *It compels
legislative recognition* of particular interests of the workers. . . . Thus,
the ten-hour bill in England was carried" (Marx and Engels, 1955:18–19,
italics added). In a letter to the 1854 Chartist congress, Marx returns to
this issue: "By creating the inexhaustible productive powers of modern
industry . . . the labouring classes have conquered nature, they have now
to conquer man. To succeed in this attempt they do not want strength, but
the *organization* of their strength, organization of the labouring classes
on a national scale" (Avineri, 1968:147). For Marx, the fact that an objective
need exists is not a sufficient condition for the passage and extension of social legislation. This is where he parts ways with the functional-evolutionary
theorists discussed in Chapter 1. Rather, to Marx, a necessary condition is
an organized constituency that can translate demands for legal rights into
effective political action.[1] If Marx and Engels are correct, one would expect
to find that social rights are distributed to unionized employees. Formulated
in terms of a testable hypothesis: the greater the unionization within an
industry, the more extensive will be the distribution of these social rights
to employees in that industry.

The proposition that employees must organize to obtain legal rights
implies first that the political machinery in a pluralist democracy in which
some interest groups are significantly more powerful than others responds
to discontent and that the elected representative who initiates social legislation in a vacuum is rare indeed. Second, it assumes that organized groups
of employers resisted and opposed the political demands made by employees.
Historical accounts of key legislative decisions, some of which were docu-
mented in Chapters 3 and 4, suggest that both of the assumptions reasonably
reflect the structure of actual events surrounding the enactment of labor
standards legislation.

DATA AND DATA ANALYSIS

To test the unionization hypothesis, 1970 data on the national estimate of coverage by industry under each of the six wage and hour laws were used. In addition, the average percentage covered across the six laws within each industry category (hereafter referred to as "average law") was calculated. (The raw data are presented in the Appendix.) The strength of unionization was measured by both the absolute number of union members in an industry and the percentage of employees unionized (U.S. Department of Labor, Bureau of Labor Statistics, 1974). With the first indicator, one can examine whether there is some minimum critical mass of union membership— independent of the total number of employees in that industry who could be unionized—that is correlated with coverage under labor standards legislation. Unfortunately, data for these two measures had only been calculated for seven of the nine industry groups.[2] The total number of employees in an industry also was gathered and is discussed more fully below.

The first step in testing this hypothesis is to examine whether the six types of law have similar patterns of coverage by industry. In Chapter 5, industry was found to be the most important determinant of coverage. Such similarity in coverage by industry is a necessary (but not sufficient) condition for unionization by industry to be linked systematically to coverage by industry. If the patterns were dissimilar, unionization could be related to a subset of the laws at best; it could not be a universal correlate of the patterns of the full set of laws.

The findings in Table 8.1 indicate that coverage by industry group is highly correlated between laws. Government activity is quite industry spe-

Table 8.1. Zero-Order Correlations of Employee Coverage, by Industry, 1970

	MH	NW	MW	OT	EP	Average law
WP/WC	.78*	.22	.89*	.87*	.86*	.93*
MH		.29	.75*	.77*	.69*	.81*
NW			.44	.31	.41	.39
MW				.88*	.99*	.98*
OT					.86*	.96*
EP						.96*

*Significant at the .05 level.

cific: if an industry group has a higher level of coverage under one law, it has a higher level of coverage under all laws. While the relationship is not quite as strong with night-work laws, a moderate correlation is found. The lower correlation coefficients associated with night-work legislation seem most likely to be a consequence of the generally low levels of coverage under this type of legislation.

Given these results, to simplify the analysis of unionization and social reform, each of the three indicators of worker strength and organization will be correlated separately with average law. As expected, average law correlates very strongly with all of the labor standards laws except night-work laws, facilitating its use as a simple overall index of the degree of government activity. Average law is a better overall measure than any particular labor law because it reflects the entire domain of labor standards legislation. The influence of any idiosyncratic factors connected with specific law is thereby reduced.

With this groundwork laid, the unionization and social reform hypothesis can be tested. As can be seen from the results displayed in Table 8.2, there is a very strong relationship between the distribution of social rights within an industry category and the extent of organization among employees within that industry ($r = .72$). There is, as well, a moderate positive relationship between the number of union members in an industry and the extent of social reform ($r = .45$).

Recall that in his letter to the Chartist congress, Marx explicitly distinguished between the potential strength of workers (as evidenced by their numbers) and the organization of that strength into unions. One might conjecture that latent groups (such as unorganized employees) receive benefits from the political process independent of manifest groups (organized workers or unions). This would lead to the hypothesis that the larger an industry group is, the more powerful the employees in that industry group will be, and the more extensive the distribution of social rights to employees in that industry group. The simple correlation between legal coverage and the size of an industry group ($r = .09$) suggests that no relation exists between these two variables. A more careful inspection of the relationships among the variables listed in Table 8.2, however, reveals that there is a sizable negative relationship between the percentage of employees unionized in an industry group and the number of employees in that group ($r = -.40$). The extent of unionization may be suppressing the relationship between average law and industry size. When the partial correlation between coverage under average law and number of employees by industry group controlling for the percentage unionized is computed, a strong relationship between coverage and number of employees does in fact emerge ($r = .61$).

Table 8.2. Zero-Order Correlations between Coverage and
Unionization, by Industry, 1970

	Percent unionized	Number of union members	Total number of employees
Average law	.72*	.45	.09
Percent unionized		.33	−.40
Number of union members			.59*

*Significant at the .05 level.

Given that controlling for the extent of unionization reveals a strong
relationship between coverage under average law and number of employees,
might not an even stronger relationship than was observed for the simple
correlation exist between unionization and legal coverage controlling for
employee size of industry? The partial correlation of these two variables
controlling for number of employees (r = .83) is indeed stronger than
the simple correlation (r = .72). Moreover, if the two industry group
characteristics are combined as a battery, the multiple correlation of coverage under average law and the battery measure is very strong (r = .83).
These findings thus suggest that both extent of unionization and the number
of employees in an industry group are highly related to the allocation of
social rights. Of the two factors, however, unionization has the stronger
effect.

Regressing average law on unionization and size of industry gives a
precise estimate of the degree of change in the dependent variable—average
law—that is associated with a unit change in each of the independent variables. Since the purpose of this regression analysis is to map out analytically
the relationship of the two independent variables to the dependent variable,
the standardized regression equation is introduced:

$$Z_I = b_1 U_I + b_2 S_I$$

where Z = percentage covered by labor standards legislation;
$\quad U$ = percentage of employees unionized;
$\quad S$ = number of employees; and
$\quad I$ = industry group

Regressing coverage under average law on extent of unionization and number
of employees, we find

$$Z_I = (0.91)U_I + (0.46)S_I$$

The equation reveals that when an industry category increases one standard unit of change in the percentage of unionized employees, there is an increase of .91 standard units in the percentage of employees covered under labor standards legislation when employee size of that industry group is controlled. On the other hand, one standard unit change in the size of an industry group yields only .46 of a standard unit of change in coverage under this legislation controlling for the extent of unionization. Thus, the regression analysis further illustrates the primary importance of unionization relative to employee size of industry as a correlative of extensive legal coverage. Unionization and legal rights go hand in hand.

LEGAL REFORM: SUBSTITUTE OR SUPPLEMENT?

These statistical findings indicate that unionized industries also are covered by reform legislation. Historical accounts suggest, however, that unionized employees within these industries may not be the direct beneficiaries of the social rights embodied in labor standards laws.

Consider the following examples of instances in which representatives of the labor movement explicitly supported the enactment of specific pieces of wage and hour legislation. In Massachusetts in the mid-1880s, textile manufacturers extended the length of the working day from 6:00 P.M. to 10:00 P.M. In response to this unilateral action, organized textile workers brought pressure to bear on the state legislature, and the first night-work law was passed. The bill, however, contained a sufficient number of loopholes to render it ineffectual. Organized labor's efforts to win an enforceable night-work law is a clear case of the preceding Marxian model in practice:

> In order to put an end to evening overtime work the men workers in the textile mills made a long and determined fight for a nightwork law for women which should prohibit their employment after 6 p.m. and thus force the closing of the mills at that hour. In 1901 the bill was within one vote of passing; in 1904 it went through both houses but was vetoed by the governor. Aroused by the textile unions, all the labor groups launched a campaign to prevent the re-election of the governor guilty of this veto. His defeat in the following year was attributed to this labor opposition. . . . The next two years, however, the bill was defeated in the Senate. Labor then launched a campaign against the senators responsible for the defeat and secured their retirement. Finally in 1907 the bill passed with only one dissenting vote, and was promptly signed by the governor (Brandeis, 1935:473).

Another historical instance refers to further efforts of organized labor in Massachusetts: again the textile workers convinced other unions affiliated with the AFL to support maximum hours legislation. Such legislation, the textile unionists felt, would facilitate the enforcement of their union contracts (Beyer, 1929). A third example reveals the direct connection between organized workers' sponsoring and winning labor standards legislation—in this case a California maximum hours law.

> In 1905 and 1906 the State Federation of Labor introduced a women's eight-hour bill as a possible means of shortening hours generally. No real fight was made to secure its passage, and it died in committee. Meanwhile organization among working women was spreading and the eight-hour day was being secured by union action. In 1910 a small group of union women and unionists' wives suggested that the State Federation take action to secure an eight-hour law for women workers. The suggestion was welcomed as a chance to show labor's political strength and to bolster up the eight-hour standard secured through union activity . . . the credit for California's eight-hour law belongs almost entirely to organized labor. Aside from one "prominent Suffragist" identified with the waitresses' union, practically no other influence was brought to bear on the legislature (Brandeis, 1935:476).

A final, more recent example, concerns support given for the extension of coverage to unorganized workers under minimum wage legislation by the national political arm of the AFL-CIO: "A major effect of this legislation would be a reduction in the nonunion lower-wage areas' attractiveness to businessmen considering the location of new factories. The issue was, therefore, very important to several individual unions in the garment trades" (Greenstone, 1969:334). Each of these historical illustrations reveals the interest taken by those who were unionized in extending government-set labor standards to nonunionized employees in the same industries. The extension of these rights to comparable groups of workers was to the advantage of unionized workers.

Unionized employees based their support for these reforms on a different rationale in the early period of industrialization from the one they used later. The two early Massachusetts cases suggest that workers fought for legislation on the premise that standards that would apply legally to only a segment of the workers in an industry would actually be implemented industrywide. By the time of the more recent example, however, the gains made by labor unions through their collective bargaining agreements often far surpassed the standards set by legislatures. The support of organized workers for these legal rights was guided by a new purpose: to see to it that government standards were stringent enough to deter the shift of industries from highly unionized states to other, nonunionized areas within the United States. In other words, both national labor standards and strong laws in states where unions were weak decreased the competition between unionized and nonunionized workers within the same industry. As labor economists have noted, "through minimum wage legislation . . . the government acts to raise both union and nonunion wages and hence tends to cause similar rates of change in wages" (Burtt, 1963:368). Moreover, gradual improvement in government-enacted labor standards may even narrow the differential in rewards to workers who occupy different labor grades within the same industry.

In addition, these findings reveal a relationship between the size of an industry and coverage under these laws when the effect of unionization is controlled. This secondary effect of employee size of industry may be a function of employer attempts to avoid unionization. It is well known that many firms—especially the larger ones and those using modern management techniques—have extended benefits to employees without the labor struggles of the mid-nineteenth century that initiated the very idea of an employee benefit. Employers may view legal rights that are distributed uniformly within an industry as a preferable alternative to the unionization of the workers in their firm. For example, one of the conclusions reached in a 1928 Women's Bureau study on the impact of maximum hours laws was that managers of retail stores frequently endorsed such legislation because it eliminated competition over hours among stores in a community (Winslow, 1928). The rationale underlying employer preference is clear-cut: if employees are given legal rights, the discontent that might otherwise channel itself into union organizing activity can be checked. Moreover, the cost of such government regulation does not put one firm at a competitive disadvantage.

The preference among United States employers for welfare state measures to damp the extent of unionization has also been noted by labor economists. "The welfare approach," says H. B. Davis in a classic article on the growth of labor unionism, "which had been adopted by individual employers already before the First World War, principally in Germany but also in other countries, was much advertised in the United States from 1923 to 1929. The purpose was partly to keep labor contented and cut down labor turnover . . . and partly to head off unionism. . . . the union movement was checked for the time being" (1941:611–613).

In sum, even if union members are not covered by the provisions of a wage and hour standards law, there is a great overlap between those industries that are highly unionized and the industrial categories in which the distribution of legal rights to employee groups is most extensive. Furthermore, the size of an industry is also related to the widespread distribution of social rights when the fact that employees in larger industry categories are less likely to be unionized is taken into account. Finally, when unionization and employee size of an industry are combined, they are very powerfully related to the widespread distribution of legal rights ($R^2 = .70$).

A FURTHER TEST

Having shown that organization is related to reform, the next question is whether the growth in the organization of employees begets growth in reform. Ordinarily, the results of a cross-section analysis permit only the most tentative conclusions concerning causal relationships that underlie the correlation between the growth in the percentage of the employee population that is unionized (hereafter unionization) and the growth in the percentage covered under labor standards legislation (hereafter, the extension of social rights). At least five causal models would be consistent with the preceding cross-section findings. The first two models posit that a change in one of the two variables preceded and induced a change in the other variable. If we let A = unionization and B = legal reform, the previous results would support either of the following causal models:

$$1.\ A \longrightarrow B$$
$$2.\ B \longrightarrow A$$

Equally likely, however, is a set of models that specify the concurrent growth of A and B. The simplest model of concurrent growth specifies that A and B are reciprocal, such that

$$3.\ A_1 \rightleftarrows A_2$$
$$B_1 \longrightarrow B_2$$

A fourth causal model assumes that the relationship found for cross-section data is, in fact, spurious, and that the growth of unionization and social reform is caused by some third factor or factors, C:

$$4.\ C \begin{array}{c} \nearrow A \\ \searrow B \end{array}$$

A fifth model posits that a change in factor C preceded and accounts for the concomitant changes in A and B. However, the coterminous changes of A and B interact with and reinforce one another:

The social indicators approach adopted here makes it possible to move one step closer to an understanding of the causal relationship between these variables. Since causality implies ordering in time, the time series data on coverage and on the extent of union membership (constructed by Leo Troy, 1965:2) offer the opportunity to determine whether change in one of the two variables preceded change in the other (that is, models 1 and 2) or whether changes in the two variables covary (models 3–5).

DATA AND DATA ANALYSIS

To test for the temporal ordering between growth in unionization and extension of social rights, time series data for unionization and social reform were compiled for 1900 to 1960 at five-year intervals.[3] Unionization was measured as the percentage of nonagricultural employees who were unionized, and social rights were measured as an index of cumulative growth of labor standards legislation or average law, which was computed by averaging the national percentage covered across all six labor standards laws. (Obviously, annual data would have been preferable; however, data obtained at five-year intervals proved sufficient to determine the general relationship between these data.)

Figure 8.1 shows the growth in unionization and in the percentage covered by average law between 1900 and 1960. (It also includes a third variable— the percentage of nonagricultural employees—which is treated later in the chapter.) Both unionization and social reform have grown substantially over the twentieth century. At the same time, however, these avenues for worker self-protection proved to be open to only a significant minority of all employees by 1960. Indeed, labor standards legislation extended to a larger portion of employees than did union organization—certainly a somewhat surprising fact in light of how little scholarly attention has been paid to these laws compared to that lavished on the dynamics and correlates of union growth. While the growth of both labor standards legislation and unions is clearly constrained, the patterns of growth are quite different. The fluctuations in the extent of unionization for five-year intervals between

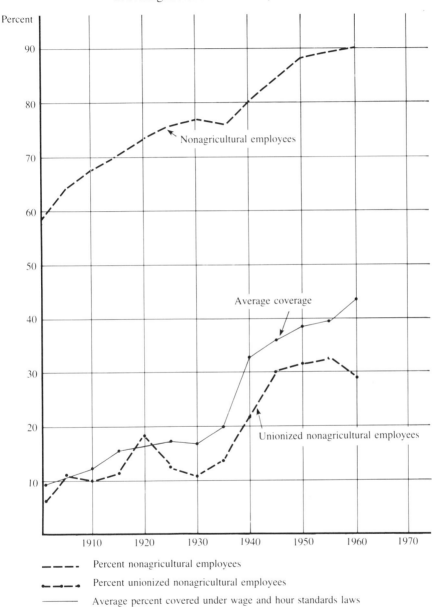

Figure 8.1. Employees Covered under Legislation, in Unions and in Nonagricultural Industries, 1900–1960.

- - - - Percent nonagricultural employees

- - - - Percent unionized nonagricultural employees

———— Average percent covered under wage and hour standards laws

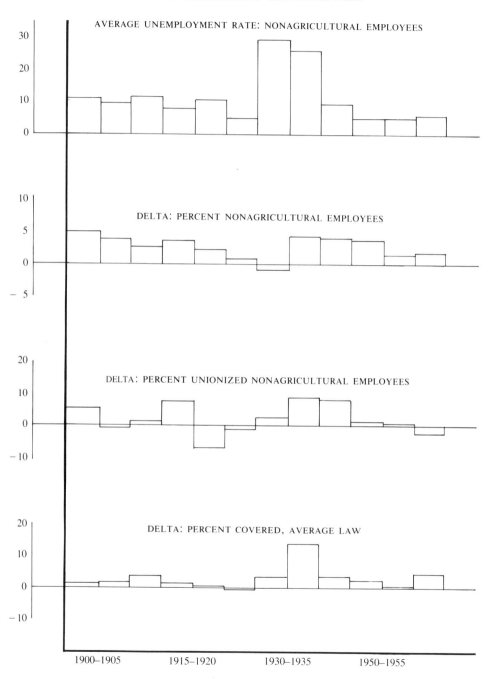

Figure 8.2. Five-Year Changes or Deltas of Variables Indicating Unionization, Social Reform, Unemployment, and Industrialization Used in Correlations of Time Series Data.

1900 and 1930 are far more extreme than those observed for coverage under average law.

To measure the growth over a five-year period (and consequently arrive at a more precise understanding of how change in one of these variables relates to change in the other), we calculated the first difference of each variable over the five-year period. As the two lower graphs in Figure 8.2 indicate, the five-year changes or deltas in unionization are more extreme than the five-year changes in coverage under labor legislation. This difference in the pattern of growth between these two variables is further reflected in the standard deviation of the two variables: $s = 4.41$ for delta unionization and 3.37 for delta average law. Indeed, if the percentage growth in average law for the period 1935–1940 (clearly an atypical period of growth) is removed, the standard deviation for delta average law drops to 1.33.

The differences in the pattern of growth in percentage of employees unionized and percentage of employees covered by labor standards legislation can be seen even more clearly by a simple inspection of the deltas for these two time series. There is less homogeneity and greater variability in the five-year changes in average law. Union growth is intermittent, with four periods of high growth, three periods of moderate growth, and three periods of decrease in the percentage unionized. Growth of average law is, on the other hand, more gradual and more uniform: there is almost no contraction in coverage and only one period of high growth. Yet changes in unionization and social reform seem to occur contemporaneously. In addition, both sets of variables seem to have the same high points of change. While this pattern of seemingly simultaneous change is most clearly discerned between 1930 and 1950 it seems to hold to a lesser extent for the entire sixty-year span.

To ascertain precisely how change in unionization related to change in the distribution of social rights, the deltas were correlated as follows: first, the deltas were correlated for the same five-year period (in other words, without lag or lead). Next, change in one variable during a given five-year interval was correlated with change in the other variable during the preceding five-year period (that is, a five-year lead was introduced for each variable). Clearly, correlating two variables by leading one or the other made it possible to gauge how the change in one of these measures related to prior, contemporary, or subsequent change in the other measure.

RESULTS AND DISCUSSION

Table 8.3 lists the zero-order correlations between changes in extent of unionization and changes in the distribution of legal rights introducing no

Table 8.3. Zero-Order Correlations of Five-Year
Changes in Unionization and Extent of Coverage
under Legislation, 1900–1960

Lead or lag	Correlation of Average law and percent unionized
Unionization leads average law by five years	.09
No lead or lag	.52*
Average law leads unionization by five years	.52*

*Significant at the .10 level using two-tail test.

lead, a five-year lead in unionization, and a five-year lead in average law. First, there is almost no relationship between unionization and social reform when we lead unionization by five years ($r = .09$). Thus, model 1 can be rejected: growth in organization does not beget growth in the distribution of legal rights.

Rather, coverage under labor legislation seems to grow at the same time as unionization. Indeed, what the results reveal is that although there is a five-year period during which coverage under work-related legislation is made more extensive, the concomitant growth of unionization begins during that five-year period and continues over the following five years. The correlations for average law and unionization when no lead or lag is introduced ($r = .52$) and when average law leads unionization by five years ($r = .52$) suggest that the growth in average law might well begin several years before the percentage of union members expands.

The idea that the growth of unionization occurs over a longer period is entirely plausible and may well reflect the difficulty of organizing individualistic employees into organizations premised on collective action for economic betterment. Consider these two avenues of change: passing a piece of legislation ultimately involves a decision by a group of selected political elites. Certainly, getting the political decision makers to act (be it through pressure from electoral returns or from lobbying) occurs more quickly than organizing hundreds and thousands of individual workers.

But, as was suggested earlier, it may also be true that employers resist uniform standards legislation less than they resist the organization of their employees into a trade union. For minimum standards governing the terms and conditions of work might prove less costly to them than the unionization of their workers. At the very least, labor standards would apply uniformly to an employer's competitors as well as to himself, or herself; unionization of a single firm, on the other hand, might well put an employer at a great economic disadvantage to his or her competitors.

The patterns of growth of unionization and social reform laws thus narrow down the choices to one of the three models of concurrent growth—with the change in legal coverage beginning somewhat sooner and moving from start to finish somewhat more rapidly than the change in the unionization of the labor force. Although it is difficult to decide on the basis of the empirical analysis, between model 4, in which the relation between unionization and legal change is spurious, and model 5, in which it is not, both of these changes may to some extent be the consequence of a third independent process of change. The next section discusses what this other change might be.

THE POLITICAL CONSEQUENCES OF SOCIAL DISLOCATION: UNEMPLOYMENT AND INDUSTRIALIZATION

Because there has been little systematic empirical analysis of the preconditions of change in the distribution of legal rights, any clues that might help us discover such prior changes will have to be sought in the literature addressed to explaining union growth.[4] But, as a recent study (Bain and Elsheikh, 1976) has concluded, relatively little is known about the determinants of union growth. The research on union growth that does exist can be divided into two schools of thought. The first, associated most closely with the writings of Leo Wolman, ties union growth to an upturn in the business cycle. Summarizing Wolman's position, "the upswing of the business cycle improves the bargaining position of unions. Employers faced with expanding markets but low inventories, are eager to obtain high levels of output, more workers, and uninterrupted production, and are therefore more likely to accede to union demands and threats of strikes. At the same time workers are likely to be motivated to join together to present their demands because consumer prices are rising while wages remain unchanged; moreover, *the workers may have grievances that have accumulated during the previous period of depressed conditions*" (Burtt, 1963:101, italics added; see also Wolman, 1924:33; 1936).

The other perspective, advanced most effectively by Irving Bernstein, links the growth of unions to protracted social crises: "An acceleration in the secular rate of trade union expansion stems from crisis, whether a domestic social cataclysm or a war. Of the five periods studied, two related to profound internal unrest (1884–1886 and 1933–1938), two arose out of great international conflicts (1917–1920 and 1942–1944), and one was based on a combination of both factors" (1954:313). Bernstein (1960:78) also contends that the cyclical phases of the business cycle occur too quickly to accommodate the more sluggish process of unionization.

The difference between Wolman and Bernstein hinges on the strength of the relationship between unionization and unemployment. Moreover, Wolman's emphasis on the changing power position of employees relative to employers at different phases of the business cycle suggests that during any business downturn, when unemployment is high and the labor market is slack, employees will not be in a good position to press for improvements in their contract. As business conditions begin to improve and the rate of unemployment drops (with a lag), union membership is likely to grow. Bernstein makes a similar connection but contends that the level of unemployment must be high and of long duration to stimulate union growth.

To be sure, there is some evidence that the growth in unionism is related to changes in the rate of unemployment. In 1941, H. B. Davis explored the relationship between unemployment and the growth of unionism by what he called "a partial test." He "examined twenty cases of revival from depression in four countries, and in sixteen of them, or 80 percent, union membership increased markedly, while in only two of them did it decline" (1941:200). But he did not investigate the extent of union growth in periods of prosperity to determine what, if any, relationship exists between favorable economic conditions and union growth.

A counterhypothesis is suggested in the extensive literature—both theoretical and empirical—on the relationship between social reform and industrialization. In Chapter 5, for example, industry groups were found to be the most significant determinant of coverage under these laws. And, in Chapter 7, the level of industrialization was found to affect the scope of coverage under state minimum wage laws. Does the growth of industrial enterprises also account for the general growth in coverage at the *national* level? Historical treatments (Brandeis, 1935; Commons and Andrews, 1936; Polanyi, 1957) link the initial adoption of labor standards legislation to the rise of industrial production. General analyses of welfare state policies have found that the greater the extent of industrialization, the higher the level of expenditures devoted to welfare state programs (Hofferbert, 1974). There is, however, little understanding of the dynamic relation between industrialization and social reform legislation—that is, between the growth of the industrial (nonagricultural) labor force and the growth of coverage under labor standards legislation. An alternative explanation for the growth of these channels of worker self-protection could be the following: once a society has undergone the initial process of industrialization, additional industrialization paves the way both for amendments to social legislation and for the organization of employees into unions.

Two plausible explanations for change in average law are put forward: first, laws may be extended and unions may expand for the same reason that they first come into existence—that is, because of the dislocation associated with *shifting* of employees from a traditional to a modern labor market. Alternatively, these two channels for worker self-protection may be strengthened because of unemployment suffered by employees already familiar with the conditions of work in the industrial labor market. Both of these hypotheses rest on the assumption that shifts in the social (and economic) position of members of a society are an important precondition of other types of changes. Where they part ways is in locating the source of the social dislocation that results in changes in both unionization and the extension of social rights.

DATA AND DATA ANALYSIS

To test these competing hypotheses on the kinds of structural factors that precede changes in the legal and organizational forms available to subordinate groups, two additional indicators were introduced into the analysis: the five-year average unemployment rate and the five-year change (or delta) in the percentage of nonagricultural employees in the labor force.

The time series plotted in Figure 8.1 suggest that, while average coverage, unionization, and percentage of nonagricultural employees have all steadily increased between 1900 and 1960, during any particular five-year period the direction of change for unionization and average law seems to be opposite to that for the percentage of nonagricultural employees. The clearest differences in the direction of change occurred between 1925 and 1940. This impression is confirmed by the plots of the deltas of these variables in Figure 8.2. At least for the first forty years of the twentieth century, changes in the percentage of nonagricultural employees during a five-year period seem to be in the opposite direction from changes in unionization during the subsequent five-year period. This seems to be generally true for the deltas of industrialization and average law as well. Inspection of the unemployment rate and the deltas for unionization and average law suggests that unemployment for the five years preceding unionization and legal reform might well be directly related to the changes in the extent of unionization and the distribution of social rights. Let us ground these impressions in a more systematic analysis of the data.

The labor force variables were correlated with the variables on unionism and legal change with no lead or lag introduced (Table 8.4) and with each of the four variables leading each of the other variables by five years (Table 8.5). The results indicate that all the processes of change being observed occur fairly rapidly: a high rate of growth in one five-year period for any of these indicators did not strongly relate to growth in that same indicator in the subsequent five-year period.[5]

It is also clear that there is a strong, positive relationship between unem-

Table 8.4. Correlation Matrix of Five-Year Changes or Averages
in Indicators, 1900–1960

	Average law	Percent unionized	Unemployment rate
Percent unionized	.52*		
Unemployment rate	.64*	.36	
Percent labor force, nonagricultural	.27	.46**	−.28

*Significant at the .05 level.
**Significant at the .10 level.

Table 8.5. Correlation Matrix of Five-Year Changes or Averages
in Indicators, with a Five-Year Lead, 1900–1960

	Average law	Percent unionized	Unemployment rate	Percent labor force, nonagricultural
Average law	.14	.52*	−.14	.40
Percent unionized	.09	.08	−.12	.51
Unemployment rate	.68*	.57*	.30	.36
Percent labor force, nonagricultural	−.58*	−.40	−.61*	−.02

*Significant at the .10 level, using two-tail test.

ployment with a five-year lead and both unionization ($r = .57$) and social rights ($r = .68$). These results suggest, therefore, that a prolonged period of high unemployment is followed by the growth of unionism and legislative reform. In addition, the two forms of worker self-protection are *not* related to an increase in the extent of industrialization. Rather, there is a moderate, negative relationship between both unionization and social reform and the percentage of workers employed in nonagricultural pursuits—providing even greater evidence in support of the hypothesis that the unemployment rate is a key factor stimulating these political changes.

Returning to the models of concurrent change, the findings support either model 4 or 5. In both models, a third factor, C (an increase in the unemployment rate), leads to a change in both A and B. The next section suggests one way in which a prolonged period of high unemployment could create the conditions under which these modes of worker self-protection are strengthened.

UNIONIZATION AS A PRECONDITION TO REFORM

During a period of high unemployment, gains in the standards of employment that were achieved during more prosperous times are halted or eroded. Elections are one mechanism open to those who are demoted, laid off, or fired. Moreover, during periods of economic depression, employees can count on more generalized public support for the political reforms they are seeking. Because every citizen is likely to know personally and therefore identify with an employee who has lost her or his job, the norms guiding work relations and the transactions in the labor market are seen to be of questionable legitimacy. Constituents (both those who have lost their jobs and the general public) indicate to political elites that they are no longer satisfied with politics as usual. Through this regularized channel of political expression, elites who demonstrate that they support the kinds of policies that will benefit subordinate groups are rewarded and allowed to replace less sympathetic elites. This is especially true during times of economic downturn when the decisions that elites in office make about laws directly affecting employees are more visible. The threat of replacement because of an unacceptable voting record becomes a more pressing reality.

The period immediately following the bottoming out of the business cycle is especially advantageous to the bargaining position of employees vis-à-vis employers. At this time, employers cannot resist worker demands as effectively as they can when economic conditions are at their worst, because they have lost the excuse that they are suffering as much as or more than employees. This situation improves the power position of organized workers who have the capacity to mobilize themselves at least to restore the gains they made during previous periods of prosperity. One consequence of this mobilization is to organize more employees into unions.

The preceding discussion renders more understandable as well the earlier finding that legal reform occurs somewhat sooner than unionization. An election provides an immediate opportunity for an employee, his or her dependents, and the general public to signal their discontent with economic conditions. It operates independently of the power relationship of employers and employees in any particular work setting. Consequently, dissatisfaction over the state of the economy can be registered when conditions are at their worst. But unionization appears to be more directly connected to the power resources available to the organizational actors in the labor market at any point in time. As a result, the conditions that facilitate unionization emerge at a later point in the cycle than do the conditions that facilitate voting for political elites favorable to legal reform.

An additional factor suggesting that the relationship between unionization and social reform is *not* spurious hinges on the actions of political elites. They can shape the legal environment so as to facilitate or deter union organization. Positive action on labor standards legislation creates a more receptive climate for other avenues of worker self-help. In turn, additional unionization of employees enhances the power position of representatives of labor who come into contact with political elites: threats of punishment to those who part ways with labor's political program are taken more seriously. Moreover, this explanation draws additional strength from the findings of the earlier, cross-section analysis of unionization and the extension of social rights: those who benefit from these two types of political outcomes are the same or a similarly situated group of employees who have the power resources to make these political outcomes happen.

The discussion thus far hinges on the assumption that the level of unionization is crucial in facilitating both the growth of unionization and the growth of social reform. It is much easier for organized workers to translate their economic and political dissatisfaction into demands for economic and political reform. Their representatives can lobby for additional reforms and institute an organizing drive to expand union membership and create new unions. The political demands of union leaders carry with them the threat to legislators that the channels of communication among members of unions can be used against them fairly rapidly. Obviously, it is easier to mobilize the membership of an existing organization behind a political measure than to organize the general electorate. Similarly, an existing union can rely on the dues of its members to mount an organizing drive should conditions encourage such activity. Consequently, while rejecting the hypothesis that growth in unionization leads to growth in social reform, I continue to conclude that organization is an important precondition of reform.

SUMMARY AND CONCLUSIONS

In the *Communist Manifesto*, Marx and Engels argued that organization of subordinate groups is the essential precondition to political reform. This premise is further supported by historical evidence on the adoption of wage and hour standards laws in the United States. While unionization and legal reform have been seen to be parallel processes of change in an industrial society with a capitalist political economy, this chapter examines the precise relationship between workers organizing into unions and workers reaping the benefits of statutory labor standards.

First, the validity of the hypothesis that the extensive distribution of social rights was a function of unionization was tested on 1970 data disaggregated by industry. Not only did a strong positive relationship between the extent of unionization in these industry categories and the extent of coverage of employees under labor standards laws emerge, but the results were also found to hold across all six laws.

Having shown that organization is related to reform, the next question was whether growth in employee organization was a prior condition to legislative reform. Time series were analyzed to gauge how much the change in one of these variables related to prior, contemporary, or subsequent change in the other measure. Coverage under labor legislation seemed to grow concomitantly with unionization. While there was a five-year period during which coverage under work-related legislation was made more extensive, the concomitant growth of unionization began during that five-year period and continued over the following five years. The development of labor standards legislation took less time than the growth of unions.

The suggestion that both these changes might result from change in a third, independent factor was explored, and it was found that improvement in these forms of worker self-protection grew out of prolonged periods of high unemployment. Once the growth of industrial (that is, secondary) workers had reached an equilibrium, unionization and extension of coverage were *not* found to be related to the further growth in the nonagricultural labor force.

There are several mechanisms through which a prolonged period of high unemployment is translated into the strengthening of institutions for worker self-protection. Elections provide an immediate opportunity for employees and their dependents to signal their discontent with economic conditions. Unionization, which is more closely tied to the power resources available to groups of actors in the labor market, takes place when there is an upswing in the economy because the improvement of economic conditions strengthens the power position of existing unions to organize more employees. Consequently, unionization occurs somewhat more slowly and somewhat after the reform of social legislation, which begins to happen when the level of unemployment has bottomed out.

The results of the analysis point to a broad process of social change connecting industrialization, unemployment, unionization, and legal reform. The process begins when there is a period of growth in the industrial labor force. During this initial period, few gains are made either in the scope of coverage under existing legislation or in the unionization of workers. As the dynamics of production in a capitalist society play themselves out in what is often referred to as the business cycle, unemployment increases. Shortly after the level of unemployment has reached its highest level, workers begin to respond to protect themselves. First, laws such as labor standards legislation are amended. Several years later, the successes of labor organizers begin to be registered through growth in the extent of unionization. By this time the rate of unemployment has begun to drop. Industrial growth continues along with the last stages of unionization. The increasing distribution of legal rights to employee groups is simultaneously the result and a reflection of the larger dynamics of the long waves of the business cycle, because of its impact on the power positions of employers and employees. For this reason, the growth of labor legislation is also cyclical, with the growth of coverage following a cyclical form around an upward trend.

9

A MODEST MAGNA CHARTA

The results of this study of the development of a set of social rights in the United States over the twentieth century have led to many insights about the dynamics of social reform in an advanced industrial society with a capitalist political economy. This chapter pulls together the major features of the patterns and correlates of legislative development and suggests some additional avenues for research. Using the findings as a springboard, some tentative conclusions are offered about the general nature of social reform. Before turning to a discussion of these substantive issues, however, the fruitfulness of using a social indicators approach to study legislative change is assessed.

METHODOLOGICAL CONCLUSIONS

The study was designed to use a social indicators approach to convert the provisions on coverage and standards contained in a law into the percentage of employees covered and the average legal standard. Quantitative estimates of these two provisions of each of six wage and hour standards laws were generated at twenty-four points in time between 1900 and 1973. While a few studies have used quantitative indices of law as a variable, I am not aware of any study in which information from legal statutes is combined with historical census data on the extent and distribution of private, non-professional and nonmanagerial employees to construct measures of the scope and distribution of legal rights. I believed this technique to have many methodological virtues; yet, I had no guarantee that this major effort at data construction would prove fruitful in uncovering meaningful patterns of legal change. Consequently, I approached the findings with a good deal of caution. In a sense, the time series data constituted a methodological experiment which, if worthwhile, would prove to be one of the major contributions of this research.

   The findings suggest that it is extremely fruitful to organize legal data into time series. The imprecision of the procedure for constructing this set of data was far from trivial, but the measurements used were sufficient to uncover a wide range of meaningful patterns. In Chapter 3, for example, the logistic, decaying exponential, and linear curves fit to the time series data on adoption and employee coverage for the three early wage and hour standards laws fit the data quite well and painted a reasonable picture of the process of change underlying the observed patterns. Similarly, in Chapter 8 on the relationship between social reform, unionization, industrialization, and unemployment, a plausible model of long-term legislative change was uncovered.

The fact that these time series data did bring out systematic patterns of change argues well for their use in research. While qualitative studies are important—especially as a first, exploratory step and for explaining quantitative results—they fall far short of capturing systematically the major aspects of change occurring across the universe of units. It is questionable whether one can generalize from detailed qualitative analysis of a few cases; at best, such a study has to justify the selection of cases on the basis of information about all the cases. A case study can never be a substitute for the social indicators approach in capturing, in summary measures, the range, breadth, and complexity of such dimensions of legal change as the scope of coverage and the legal standard.

PATTERNS OF CHANGE

The patterns of change must be considered in relation to two distinguishing characteristics of wage and hour standards as a category of legislation. First, since they constitute direct government intervention into setting the terms and conditions of the labor contract, they meet head-on the freedom-of-contract doctrine, the property norm dominating transactions in the labor market. By this is meant that "the wage-earner's 'property' becomes his right to seek an employer and to acquire property in the form of wages; his property in the sense of liberty is his right to refuse work or to quit work if the conditions are not satisfactory. The employer's 'property' is, in part, his right to seek laborers and to acquire their services; his property, in the sense of 'liberty,' is his right to run his business in his own way, that is, in part, to withhold employment or to discharge the laborer if the bargain is unsatisfactory" (Commons and Andrews, 1936:508). Second, the enactment and extension of these laws required an uphill battle by employees who operate in a subordinate power position in this market against sustained and often fierce opposition of employers.

GROWTH OF EMPLOYEE COVERAGE

While the national pattern of state adoption was strikingly uniform across these laws, there are significant differences among wage and hour laws in the scope of employee coverage at the national level. These variations become understandable when viewed in the context of two additional attributes of these laws. A first important factor is whether the legal stipulation restricts the discretion or autonomy of the employer in the organization of the workplace. The more a law restricts the discretion of an employer, the greater the employer resistance, and the more restrictive its coverage. In contrast to a more simplistic conception of employer opposition as based on the economic cost of a legal regulation, the conclusion here is that the employer's attachment to the ideology of capitalism—that is, to her or his right to full discretion in conducting transactions in the marketplace—is also a powerful component in any reaction to government interference.

A second attribute encompasses both the period during which these laws emerged as significant political demands and the presence of federal legislation. The six wage and hour laws conceptually divide into early labor laws, which arose as political demands in the mid- to late nineteenth century and were adopted by most states between 1900 and 1920, and modern labor laws, which received widespread acceptance by the federal and state legislatures during and subsequent to the Great Depression. Employee coverage under modern labor laws grew more quickly and reached substantially higher levels than was the case under early labor laws. It appears that modern labor laws built upon their predecessors: the gains in a legislative domain made during one historical period became the starting point for new laws in that same legislative area. Furthermore, the introduction of the federal government into a legal area that was formerly the exclusive domain of state legislatures led to a significant increase in the scope of coverage under these laws, because federal legislation led to court reversal of several important precedents barring certain groups from coverage under state legislation.

When wage and hour legislation is grouped according to these two features, as in Table 9.1, the variations in coverage fall into place. Minimum wage and equal pay laws are less restrictive of employer discretion than the other wage and hour standards laws. They were also enacted after 1930 by both the federal and state legislatures. The scope of coverage under these laws is more extensive than is coverage under the other labor standards laws. Perhaps even more telling are the severe constraints on coverage found for maximum hours and night-work laws. These laws placed a significant burden on employers to revise their operating procedures to conform to a legally

Table 9.1. Wage and Hour Standards Laws
by Effect on Employer Discretion and Period of Adoption

Effect on employer discretion	Period of adoption	
	Early (no federal)	Late (federal)
More restrictive	Night work (4%) Maximum hours (15%)	Overtime (71%)
Less restrictive	Wage payment/wage collection (76%)	Minimum wage (90%) Equal pay (78%)

NOTE: Number in parentheses indicates percentage of all employees covered under a law in 1970.

delimited workweek. Moreover, no such legislation was ever enacted by Congress. The result is clear: by 1970, a mere 4 percent of the employee population was covered under night-work legislation, and 15 percent was protected by a weekly hours ceiling. Thus, even within a category of legislation with similar analytic features, distinct variations occur in the distribution of legal rights.

LEGAL BASIS OF COVERAGE

The legal basis on which coverage was extended also was profoundly transformed over the twentieth century. Labor standards legislation was initially regarded as legitimate protection for employees who either were not subject to the right to contract by virtue of some characteristic or were employed in highly unusual settings that rendered their contract rights effectively null and void. After some time, such legal rights became a precondition essential to the adequate functioning of the marketplace. In other words, they became the basis for restoring to the employee his or her equal legal status. This equality was the legal precondition for the operation of smooth transactions in a labor market based on principles consistent with freedom of contract. Starting as stop-gap legislation under extraordinary conditions, wage and hour standards laws became an ordinary right accorded to those who must bargain their labor.

The same category of reform can emerge as a result of different social impulses at different stages in its development. When political demands first arise, the reference points of constituents are past conditions as they believe them to have existed. The type of legislation sought is structured so that roles and relationships in industrial settings conform to preconceived images of roles and relationships prevailing in traditional society. Even more enlightened reformers who accepted the fact that the new social relationships constituted permanent features of the economy used these conservative and restorative sentiments to gain some legal protection for industrial employees.

This general framework explains why early labor laws were differentially extended to women and children. The employment of women and children in the labor market runs counter to the more traditional view of the role of women and children. While it is certainly legitimate for such persons to be economically productive in cottage industry, their entrance into the world of the factory and the department store created new problems concerning their legal status. After all, only men were perceived as capable of bargaining on their own behalf in the labor market. Rather than being given a legal status in the labor market equal to that of men, women and children were provided with an alternative set of rights in which the government, in effect, bargained for them. In other words, government replaced the family—read husband or father—as the source of protection for family members who were believed to be incapable of taking care of themselves in the public domain. Rather than being given the resources to be autonomous and independent individuals, they were offered a new source of protection (Smelser, 1959: 266–269, 293–295). The introduction of these reforms, therefore, rested on highly conservative impulses.

The fact that government would intervene in the economy for *some* workers was an entering wedge, however, suggesting the possibility that government might intervene in the labor market on behalf of most (or even all) workers. It offered a precedent that could be built upon and transcended when conditions warranted. When women and children entered the industrial labor market, it became necessary to introduce new legislation to regulate social relationships that fell outside of the existing legal framework. When the Great Depression brought home to people the extent to which their position in the labor market rested on tenuous legal fictions, political leaders could turn to past innovative legislation as one possible solution to the problem. Law was no longer used to create new social relationships through contractual means, but rather was introduced to compensate workers for the political inequalities that underlay all social relationships in the labor market. The concept of protection was completely severed from notions of the distribution of roles and responsibilities in the traditional family. Instead, all employees (regardless of their age and sex, but varying somewhat by their occupation) needed government protection to remain independent operators in the labor market.

Early labor laws that emerged in the new industrial society rested upon the legal assumptions of the old laissez-faire state. The basis for coverage under the modern labor standards laws, on the other hand, reflected more closely the legal realities operating in modern industrial society. With modern labor laws, the new industrial state had been created out of the old industrial society.

CORRELATES OF CHANGE

One important finding that emerged throughout this book is that wage and hour standards laws develop and change as a result of crises, especially economic downturns that lower the bargaining position and the status of workers. A second, related finding is that the crucial ingredient that translates a crisis situation into the enactment and survival of legislation of this type is the sustained interest of organized groups in creating, maintaining, and strengthening the social rights of subordinate groups. Third, it appears that a subset of employers must support a reform for it to be enacted, especially by Congress. These themes are only analytically separable because an economic crisis can only lead to legislative action if groups of people develop a set of political demands to which government elites can then respond. Indeed, since 1960 new social movements, which regarded existing legislation as relevant to their larger political aims, have created the crisis situations that result in a reconsideration of existing legislation. These groups use crisis strategies to create a general political climate favorable to their political goals. In less favorable economic circumstances, such a sympathetic climate already exists.

CRISIS AND LEGISLATIVE CHANGE

Significant amendments to the provisions of any particular law occur when the goals of the law bear some connection to an immediate economic or social problem. Legislative change appears to be an outgrowth of immediate events. Whereas changes in maximum hours laws, for example, are sensitive and responsive to changes in the role of women in the labor market, changes in wage and hour legislation in general are clearly related to the changes in the level of employment and unemployment. Specifically, the scope of coverage under wage and hour standards laws is extended following a severe downturn in the economy.

This relationship is nowhere more clearly observed than in the enactment of the Fair Labor Standards Act. Not only did the scope of coverage expand under existing state legislation, but the federal government enacted legislation in a legal area that had previously been the exclusive domain of state legislatures. In addition, since the economic crisis touched the lives of all employees, the basis of coverage under these laws was transformed.

Similarly, the rise of equal pay laws corresponds to the shortage of manpower in the war production industries of World War II. The use of women in historically male production jobs reached unprecedented levels at that time. Equal pay legislation was necessary to ensure that the higher wage scale associated with jobs for white male adults would not be undermined by the fact that female employees had been a cheap source of labor. The development and change in these laws, therefore, were intricately tied to the nature of a social, economic, or political crisis as it affected social relations in general, and the economic relations in the labor market in particular.

POLITICS AND LEGISLATIVE CHANGE

Crisis is only a necessary condition for the enactment and modification of these laws. A further ingredient is the support of organized groups who can convince political elites that their demands are supported by the general electorate. Organized labor, for example, was quite unsuccessful in obtaining legislation restricting the length of the working day in the late nineteenth century. When such laws became a demand of visible and articulate segments of the middle class—such as the National Consumers League and other Progressive era organizations—their adoption took off. Coverage under these laws grew very little after 1920. Organized labor had turned its attention to other pressing issues, and many of the Progressive era women's organizations disbanded. Gains that had been made up to that time were sustained primarily because the Women's Trade Union League and the Women's Bureau of the United States Department of Labor continued to have an interest in these laws.

The legal provisions in the Fair Labor Standards Act were maintained and strengthened subsequent to adoption because the organized labor movement regarded them as high on its list of political demands. It was no coincidence that the major amendments to the FLSA immediately followed elections in which organized labor played a significant role in voter turn-out on behalf of the winning presidential candidate. When groups favoring legislation for those in a subordinate power position legitimized their de-mands through voting returns, Congress was more likely to adopt or amend a piece of legislation they supported.

The results of the time series analysis also reinforce these particular historical examples. First, a high level of unionization is found in states with progressive minimum wage laws. The extent of unionization also affects positively congressional voting on the federal minimum wage law. Finally, the greater the unionization in an industry, the more extensive is the scope of coverage under wage and hour standards laws to employees in that in-dustry.

In the preceding chapter a broad process of social change that linked economic crisis to the rise of several forms of worker self-protection was sketched out. Shortly after unemployment reached its highest level, the processes of political change began. First, laws such as labor standards laws were amended. Several years thereafter, increases in the percentage of organized workers became apparent. The unemployment rate dropped to a lower level. Industrial growth started up while unions continued to grow.

FUTURE RESEARCH NEEDS

Because of the exploratory nature of this study, it was only possible to begin to answer some of the more general and overriding questions con-cerning the dynamics of social reform. Several directions for future research, however, flow from this first effort.

LEGAL IMPACT STUDIES

In Chapter 2 it was argued that a complete investigation into these laws would focus not only on their formal provisions, but also on the extent to which the laws were implemented and on their impact on the relations between employers and employees in the labor market. To measure the strength of enforcement of a wage and hour standards law across states in terms of the number of inspectors assigned to oversee compliance, data are also needed on the number of covered employees so that the measure can be standardized. When the number of inspectors is increased, are these empty gains because the employee population being protected has also in-creased? Do gains in coverage result from legal change or from change in the composition of the labor force? Similar information on employee coverage is needed to standardize the amount of expenditure allocated to enforcement.

To design an adequate impact study, it is also necessary to know the range of legislation across states and the comprehensiveness of legislation within a state. A sample of states and a set of industries within states could then be systematically selected so that the results would be generalizable. Harold Wilensky (1975, 1976) used this two-stage research design in his cross-national study of the correlates of social security expenditures. He developed a model that differentiated among the social security programs in the twenty-two countries with the highest level of social security spending as a percentage of GNP. He then analyzed the structural and political correlates of the level of expenditures on a subset of welfare state leaders and laggards.

These data can also be used to assess which groups in the labor market benefited from the existence of these laws. For example, feminists and others have argued successfully for the repeal of maximum hours laws on the grounds that they restricted the employment opportunities of women. These groups held that employers used such laws (with the tacit, or even open, consent of male employees and male-dominated unions) to keep women from competing for higher paying jobs (Baer, 1978; Kanowitz, 1969; Ratner, 1980; Ross, 1970). Similarly, such revisionist historians as Gabriel Kolko (1963) and James Weinstein (1968) contend that many employers welcomed government regulation of the labor market because it further rationalized the labor market by reducing interfirm competition, among other things. The data generated for this study can be combined with data on court cases to assess the actual uses to which these laws were put. Did women or government officials initiate court cases against employers because they failed to comply with the laws? Or did women go to court to protest against losing a job because of a restriction in a law? Did both of these types of cases occur, but at different historical periods? And so on. A study that relates legislative change to litigation could uncover important insights into the changing functions of laws over time.

TYPOLOGY OF SOCIAL LEGISLATION

This study of the development of wage and hour standards laws can also serve as a model for empirical studies of other categories of social legislation. In Chapter 1, work-related legislation was divided according to the type of employment process the law regulated: normal, on-the-job conditions, or contingencies that remove an employee from the labor market. Each of these types of social policies involves different costs to the employer. Each of these laws bears a different relationship to the dominant legal and ideological norms informing transactions in the labor market. Equal opportunity laws, for example, are buttressed by the fact that they resonate with the prevailing ideology of an individualistic, achievement-oriented society. To hire the best qualified applicant regardless of ascriptive characteristic is economically efficient, at least in theory. But, equal opportunity laws do restrict the discretion of an employer concerning which employees she or he can choose to hire. On the other hand, occupational safety and health laws potentially are very costly to employers. Such laws also restrict employer discretion. We would expect these and other types of social legislation to display different patterns of legislative development. The scope of coverage and the stringency of standards under these laws should vary because of their differing impact in the labor market.

A series of studies can be designed that look at other types of social legislation using a social indicators approach. The state labor force population weights by age-by-sex-by-industry categories generated here can be used by others, which simplifies the coding of additional laws. This study constitutes the first step of a larger endeavor that would map the development of different types of social reform and construct a typology of reform, leading toward an empirically grounded theory of social reform in capitalist society.

REFLECTIONS ON SOCIAL REFORM

This study has highlighted the connection between a particular type of social reform and the power position of organized interest groups in conflict over these reforms. To be sure, several theoretical schemas, including Marxist and non-Marxist conflict approaches, are broadly consistent with these findings, and Marxist and non-Marxist scholars alike have demonstrated a long-standing interest in the nature of social reform. To draw out some implications of this work for the process of social reform in general, however, the Marxist approach introduced in Chapter 1 will be used here as an orienting framework.

Although Marx's theory of the revolutionary transformation of society is widely known, his writings on social reform in capitalist society are rarely discussed, despite the fact that many Marxist political sociologists have an interest in this issue (for an exception to the lack of discussion, see Harrington, 1976). In volume one of *Capital,* in the chapter on the enactment of the ten-hour law in England, for example, Marx contends that the working class could and did achieve self-interested reform in capitalist society, and by so doing, could and did change the distribution of power in that society: "For 'protection' against the 'serpent of their agonies,' the labourers must put their heads together, and, as a class, compel the passing of a law, an all-powerful social barrier that shall prevent the very workers from selling, by voluntary contract with capital, themselves and their families into slavery and death. In place of the pompous catalogue of the 'inalienable rights of man' comes the modest Magna Charta of a legally limited working day, which shall make clear 'when the time which the worker sells is ended, and when his own begins.' Quantum mutatus ab illo! [and what a great difference that will make!]" (Marx, 1906:330).

In the *Communist Manifesto,* quoted at length in Chapter 8, Marx envisioned a stage building up to the revolutionary transformation of society in which the working class organizes and achieves reform of the property relations within capitalist society. "The proletariat," wrote Marx, "will use its political supremacy to wrest, by *degrees,* all capital from the bourgeoisie. . . . Of course, in the beginning, this cannot be effected except by means of *despotic* inroads on the *rights of property,* and on the conditions of bourgeois production: by means of measures, therefore, which appear economically insufficient and untenable, but which, *in the course of movement outstrip themselves,* [and] necessitate further inroads upon the old social order" (Marx and Engels, 1955:31, italics added). Marx clearly regarded laws restricting the length of the working day as a constraint on the capitalist's use of labor power. Since labor power is, for Marx, the source of capitalists' profits, such reforms are seriously detrimental to the long-run objective interests of capitalists. This objective situation is the driving force behind the staunch opposition of employers to these laws, at least initially. "The creation of the normal working day is . . . the product of a protracted civil war, more or less dissembled, between the capitalist class and the working class" (Marx, 1906:327).

In opposition to this Marxist perspective on social reform, American revisionist historians have developed a counterperspective that may be labeled a theory of corporate liberalism. "The expansion of the role of the state was designed by corporate leaders and their allies to rationalize the economy and society." Kolko, for example, has argued that "big business needed state regulation to stabilize the business environment because the persistence of small firms and high levels of competition endangered the newly formed corporate giants" (Block, 1977a:352–353). While these historians have acknowledged that class conflict can generate reforms, they regard it as secondary to the support of enlightened liberal businessmen for these reforms. For example, in *The Corporate Ideal in the Liberal State* James Weinstein argues that: "the original impetus for many reforms came from those at or near the bottom of the American social structure, from those who benefitted least from the rapid increase in the productivity of the industrial plant of the United States. . . . But in the current century, particularly on the federal level, few reforms were enacted without the tacit approval, if not the guidance, of large corporate interests. . . . [Their] ends were the stabilization, rationalization, and continued expansion of the existing political economy" (1968:ix).

The suggestion that the Marxist class-based conflict model is invalid because some large corporate interests favored reform is unwarranted. The weight of historical evidence, including the findings in this study, indicates that these reforms were enacted in steps, and that, although some employers supported the laws, they did so because they had lost the battle at an earlier stage. Small segments of more powerful workers were able to obtain social rights through collective bargaining agreements or legislation. They used a variety of power resources such as unionization, strikes, and for women and children, ideological justifications. Once a subset of employees was covered, it was to the competitive advantage of their employers to fight for uniform standards. It is quite likely that employers in larger, more bureaucratic enterprises could absorb the cost of reforms more easily than employers in smaller enterprises. Indeed, firm size restrictions were a prevalent feature of the coverage provisions of wage and hour standards laws. So it is quite plausible that these employers (who had lost in a conflict with their employees) worked to achieve uniform standards in concert with uncovered workers.

I have found little evidence that employers who had not already extended these rights in their labor contracts supported labor standards laws. On the contrary, most businessmen did not support the adoption of these laws. And, after the laws were enacted, business interests opposed their extension to new groups of uncovered employees. Throughout the twentieth century, business spokesmen have appeared before legislatures to argue against these legal reforms.

Some of our findings also indirectly indicate that employers resisted this government intervention in the labor market. One interpretation of the differences in coverage across laws is that employers opposed reforms that would make any significant inroads in their property rights in the labor market. In addition, the analysis of the correlates of congressional voting on the Fair Labor Standards Act (Chapter 7) suggested that businessmen would support federal legislation when they were already subject to similar legislation at the state level. The state laws had put them at a competitive disadvantage to competitors from other states. A federal law removed this differential impediment.

The fact that wage and hour standards laws (and other related reforms) have not undermined the capitalist mode of production, and have probably further rationalized it, should not be confused with the completely separate issue of the political factors that brought the laws into being. I agree with Block's argument that social reforms are "forced on capitalism from below." The extent to which businessmen express interest in social reform is, in large measure, motivated by a desire "to shape and control the process of change" (1977a:357).

In part, the conclusions of revisionist historians are shaped by an over-arching assumption that all social reform is conservative. Kolko, for example, regards the Progressive era as "a conservative triumph in the sense that there was an effort to preserve the basic social and economic relations essential to a capitalist society" (1963:2). He goes on to indicate that he uses "the attempt to preserve existing power and social relationships as the criterion for conservatism because none other has practical meaning." If one's criterion for assessing reform is whether it transforms basic social and power relations, however, then one is defining away all reform as conservative. For, again by definition, only a revolution will bring with it the possibility of a fundamental transformation of power relations in a society. And, depending upon the nature of the revolution, it too may, by definition, be conservative.

While there is a distinction between revolution and reform, not all reform is conservative. Of course, the enactment of wage and hour standards laws did not eliminate or reverse the dominance of employers over employees. In that sense, the labor market was rearranged, not reformed. But the terms upon which that dominance could be exercised and the nature of its impact on subordinate employees were unquestionably altered.

In establishing a dichotomous and extreme criterion, the revisionist his-torians lose sight of the more continuous, gradual, and moderate process of change that takes place in the so-called welfare state. In a political economy with formal democratic rights, reform is the outgrowth of a crisis in the legitimacy of that political economy. The Great Depression was one such crisis of legitimacy. When a democratic government does act, be it to give employees the right to organize and bargain collectively or to impose direct restrictions on employers, it acts not anew but builds from the political outcomes achieved during the last period of crisis. In other words, the outcomes achieved during one period become the starting point for change in another era.

But even more important is the fact that each of these outcomes changes the meaning of the ideology that legitimizes the structure of authority in the labor market. This new definition of authority relations moves in the direction of enlarging the power of employees to shape the terms and conditions of the work process. This process of change results, therefore, in a complicated revision of key legal concepts over time. In the case of wage and hour standards laws, these legal rights simultaneously transform the concrete application of freedom of contract and reestablish it as the primary norm guiding economic relations. Therefore, what occurs over the twentieth century is "the repeated correction or improvement of government policies to bring them more in line with traditional political values *as they are understood* to apply to current circumstances" (Dolbeare, 1974:65, italics added; see also Johnson, 1972:364).

As the noted historian E. P. Thompson has concluded:

> We reach, then, not a simple conclusion (law = class power) but a complex and contradictory one. On the one hand it is true that law did mediate existent class relations to the advantage of the rulers. . . . On the other hand, the law mediated these class relations through legal forms, which imposed again and again, inhibitions upon the actions of the rulers. . . . The rhetoric and rules of a society are something a great deal more than a sham. In the same moment they may modify in profound ways, the behavior of the powerful and mystify the powerless. They may disguise the true realities of power, but at the same time, they may curb that power and check its intrusions (1975: 264–265).

Reform, then, is Janus-faced: from one perspective it tends to co-opt groups that fight for its passage and lead them to accept legal norms that keep them in a subordinate position. Yet, ironically, it may serve as a resource for its own transformation from the symbolic realm into a potentially effective regulation. To change the meaning of key legal concepts by changing their practical applications is, as Marx wrote, to change those property relations and to change the larger social order organized on the basis of them.

APPENDIX, NOTES,
BIBLIOGRAPHY
AND INDEX

APPENDIX

Table A.1. State Adoption and Employee Coverage under Early Labor Laws, 1900–1973 (in percent)

Year	Wage payment/ Wage collection		Maximum hours		Night work	
	State adoption	Employee coverage	State adoption	Employee coverage	State adoption	Employee coverage
1900	29	19	26	4	14	1
1905	41	24	28	5	26	2
1910	53	27	58	7	54	3
1913	66	38	66	10	68	4
1915	76	38	76	12	79	5
1918	88	40	76	12	79	5
1920	92	45	76	12	79	4
1925	92	47	84	12	83	4
1930	92	48	84	12	83	4
1935	92	52	88	17	88	4
1937	92	55	88	15	88	5
1938	92	55	88	15	88	5
1940	92	56	88	15	88	5
1943	92	58	88	13	88	4
1945	92	59	88	14	88	4
1947	92	59	88	16	88	4
1950	92	62	92	18	92	5
1955	92	65	92	18	92	5
1960	96	67	92	19	92	4
1961	96	71	92	21	92	5
1965	96	75	92	22	92	5
1966	96	75	92	22	92	5
1970	96	76	92	16	92	4
1973	96	78	92	15	92	4

NOTE: Once a state had enacted a law, it remained in this tabulation, even when the law was rescinded.

Table A.2. Employee Coverage by Industry, 1900–1970 (in thousands)

Law	Year	Agriculture[a]	Mining	Contract construction	Manufacturing	T/C/PU	Trade	Personal service	Clerical	Domestic service
WP/WC	1900	831	291	261	2,134	356	357	541	193	80
	1920	2,371	793	1,464	5,977	1,543	1,660	676	1,047	288
	1940	2,517	732	998	7,703	1,779	4,127	1,976	1,596	560
	1960	1,619	502	2,040	13,018	2,649	7,186	3,095	3,329	570
	1970	1,551	468	2,881	15,295	3,393	11,063	4,709	5,631	481
MH	1900	0	20	203	889	0	40	39	0	0
	1920	0	281	859	2,021	86	435	225	311	0
	1940	0	250	568	2,074	278	1,223	930	532	0
	1960	45	147	726	3,175	390	2,703	1,683	1,148	0
	1970	0	140	771	2,425	441	2,305	1,638	979	0
NW	1900	0	0	0	445	0	0	39	0	0
	1920	0	0	0	879	29	198	69	226	0
	1940	0	0	0	889	28	459	349	250	0
	1960	45	0	0	794	39	823	271	287	17
	1970	0	0	41	746	44	768	341	490	0
MW	1940	90	818	802	8,098	2,251	2,293	1,046	1,815	220
	1960	135	536	1,383	13,653	3,312	5,523	2,552	4,189	184
	1970	1,372	510	3,977	18,279	4,325	13,214	6,005	7,671	115
OT	1940	0	818	1,115	8,394	2,223	1,528	194	1,252	20
	1960	0	536	1,591	14,288	3,117	2,350	326	2,296	17
	1970	0	499	3,896	17,906	2,913	7,223	4,231	6,610	73
EP	1960	944	147	1,383	8,256	1,714	5,053	2,334	2,870	268
	1970	1,670	432	3,409	16,041	3,751	11,063	5,186	6,855	272

[a] Agriculture, forestry, and fishing.

Table A.3. Employee Coverage by Region, 1900–1970
(in thousands)

Law	Year	Northeast	North Central	South	West
WP/WC	1900	3,343	1,299	357	0
	1920	5,714	4,817	3,359	2,640
	1940	6,596	8,256	4,124	3,892
	1960	8,719	12,377	6,484	7,526
	1970	12,333	15,025	10,137	9,627
MH	1900	799	260	89	59
	1920	1,939	1,175	960	390
	1940	2,236	1,678	1,674	787
	1960	3,270	3,300	2,563	1,075
	1970	2,312	3,005	2,353	1,848
NW	1900	291	87	0	0
	1920	1,020	235	240	30
	1940	1,565	129	258	41
	1960	1,226	495	302	230
	1970	1,233	563	362	389
MW	1940	6,484	5,423	3,734	1,904
	1960	10,490	8,746	6,786	4,685
	1970	14,954	16,527	15,929	8,265
OT	1940	5,366	4,906	3,477	1,656
	1960	6,948	8,086	5,881	3,686
	1970	12,795	12,771	11,947	6,612
EP	1960	11,443	5,446	452	5,376
	1970	14,645	13,676	12,128	7,876

Table A.4. Employee Coverage by Demographic Group, 1900–1970
(in thousands)

Law	Year	Male adult	Female adult	Male minor	Female minor
WP/WC	1900	3,565	820	473	219
	1920	12,311	2,165	1,416	713
	1940	16,847	4,080	1,240	733
	1960	23,546	8,421	1,950	1,191
	1970	28,645	13,018	3,307	2,158
MH	1900	188	570	177	229
	1920	1,338	2,010	337	763
	1940	1,478	3,702	396	679
	1960	1,385	6,751	810	1,002
	1970	1,488	5,454	1,262	1,237
NW	1900	0	214	89	104
	1920	0	670	371	415
	1940	0	1,209	448	380
	1960	0	936	870	567
	1970	0	352	1,349	777
MW	1940	11,527	4,306	1,108	747
	1960	18,352	9,223	1,800	1,305
	1970	33,109	16,010	3,829	2,561
OT	1940	11,822	2,267	791	407
	1960	17,659	4,946	1,170	624
	1970	27,157	12,139	2,872	1,928
EP	1960	14,543	6,149	990	775
	1970	29,017	13,195	3,785	2,503

Table A.5. Number of Employees in United States,
by Industry, Region, and Demographic Group, 1900–1970
(in thousands)

				Industry					
Year	Agriculture[a]	Mining	Contract construction	Manu-facturing	TC/PU	Trade	Personal service	Clerical	Domestic service
1900	10,388	502	1,451	4,445	1,483	1,983	3,864	877	1,331
1920	11,290	1,004	3,183	8,789	2,858	3,953	1,734	2,829	1,307
1940	8,989	861	1,957	9,875	2,779	7,642	3,875	3,129	2,000
1960	4,496	564	3,458	15,876	3,896	11,751	5,429	5,739	1,675
1970	2,983	520	4,058	18,652	4,413	15,365	6,824	8,161	1,046

[a]Agriculture, forestry, and fishing.

	Region				Demographic group			
Year	Northeast	North Central	South	West	Male adult	Female adult	Male minor	Female minor
1900	7,268	8,663	8,924	1,469	18,763	3,564	2,956	1,041
1920	10,204	11,748	11,995	3,000	26,762	5,155	3,372	1,658
1940	11,179	12,911	12,877	4,140	29,556	7,555	2,638	1,358
1960	13,623	16,502	15,079	7,680	34,626	13,367	3,000	1,891
1970	15,416	18,781	18,101	9,724	37,201	17,593	4,351	2,877

Table A.6. Employee Coverage
under Wage Payment/Wage Collection Laws, 1920–1970
(in percent)

State	1920	1930	1940	1950	1960	1970
Alabama	0	0	0	0	0	0
Arizona	86	82	99	98	98	100
Arkansas	100	100	100	100	100	100
California	100	100	100	100	100	100
Delaware	0	0	0	0	2	100
Georgia	42	53	61	75	88	94
Idaho	100	100	100	100	100	100
Illinois	32	33	83	82	81	81
Iowa	4	4	3	3	2	2
Kentucky	44	44	44	45	45	46
Maine	52	53	50	66	69	70
Michigan	59	79	83	91	93	99
Montana	57	58	64	71	79	83
Nebraska	3	3	3	4	3	3
New Jersey	95	96	100	100	100	100
New Mexico	20	19	58	74	86	91
New York	46	51	51	52	53	51
North Carolina	1	1	1	1	1	1
North Dakota	3	3	2	2	3	99
Ohio	58	57	58	93	93	94
Oklahoma	16	16	17	20	100	100
Oregon	100	100	95	96	97	97
Pennsylvania	47	43	41	43	40	100
Rhode Island	39	38	39	100	99	99
Texas	16	17	36	40	45	48
Vermont	16	16	43	46	48	100
Virginia	24	25	27	28	30	97
Wisconsin	61	62	100	100	100	99

Table A.7. Average Legal Standard under Wage Payment/Wage Collection Laws for Covered Employees, 1920–1970

State	1920	1930	1940	1950	1960	1970
Alabama	0.0	0.0	0.0	0.0	0.0	0.0
Arizona	3.0	3.0	2.6	2.6	2.5	3.3
Arkansas	2.0	3.0	3.0	3.0	3.0	3.0
California	6.0	6.0	6.0	6.0	6.0	6.0
Delaware	0.0	0.0	0.0	0.0	2.0	4.0
Georgia	2.9	2.9	2.9	2.9	2.9	2.9
Idaho	1.0	1.0	1.0	1.0	1.0	6.0
Illinois	3.1	3.0	4.7	4.8	4.8	4.9
Iowa	3.0	3.0	3.0	3.0	3.0	3.0
Kentucky	3.3	3.4	3.4	3.4	3.5	3.8
Maine	3.0	3.0	4.0	4.0	4.0	4.0
Michigan	3.0	4.0	5.0	5.0	5.0	5.0
Montana	4.0	4.0	4.0	5.0	5.0	5.0
Nebraska	2.0	2.0	2.0	2.0	2.0	2.0
New Jersey	3.0	3.0	3.9	3.9	4.0	7.0
New Mexico	4.0	4.0	6.4	6.3	6.3	6.3
New York	2.6	2.6	2.6	2.6	2.6	2.6
North Carolina	3.0	3.0	3.0	3.0	3.0	3.0
North Dakota	3.0	3.0	3.0	3.0	3.0	4.1
Ohio	2.0	2.0	2.0	2.0	2.0	2.0
Oklahoma	2.0	2.0	2.0	2.0	4.0	4.0
Oregon	2.0	5.0	5.7	5.7	5.7	5.7
Pennsylvania	3.0	3.0	3.0	3.0	3.0	5.8
Rhode Island	2.0	2.0	2.0	6.0	6.0	6.0
Texas	3.0	3.0	3.0	3.0	3.0	3.0
Vermont	3.0	3.0	3.0	3.0	3.0	6.2
Virginia	2.0	2.0	2.0	2.0	0.0	3.0
Wisconsin	3.8	3.8	3.7	4.1	4.4	4.6

Table A.8. Employed Female Adults
Covered under Maximum Hours Laws, 1920–1970
(in percent)

State	1920	1930	1940	1950	1960	1970
Alabama	0	0	0	0	0	0
Arizona	25	71	80	88	87	0
Arkansas	10	14	23	16	0	0
California	43	41	55	62	21	60
Delaware	57	66	65	70	78	0
Georgia	4	5	6	8	8	10
Idaho	50	57	52	65	70	68
Illinois	45	40	70	78	79	0
Iowa	0	0	0	0	0	0
Kentucky	37	34	41	51	51	55
Maine	53	53	50	61	58	60
Michigan	64	63	68	77	77	83
Montana	50	50	57	61	67	70
Nebraska	36	33	37	40	55	0
New Jersey	49	41	53	57	56	57
New Mexico	0	40	53	67	71	11
New York	43	36	46	52	51	13
North Carolina	23	26	39	46	47	13
North Dakota	14	15	42	48	46	0
Ohio	45	41	71	79	80	85
Oklahoma	15	16	16	35	39	0
Oregon	34	34	46	48	49	0
Pennsylvania	88	75	81	89	91	0
Rhode Island	88	83	88	94	96	97
Texas	43	52	57	57	57	51
Vermont	23	18	21	26	20	0
Virginia	18	25	27	39	39	12
Wisconsin	43	44	52	56	56	0

Table A.9. Average Legal Standard under Maximum Hours Laws
for All Covered Female Adult Employees, 1920–1970

State	1920	1930	1940	1950	1960	1970
Alabama	0.0	0.0	0.0	0.0	0.0	0.0
Arizona	56.0	48.0	48.0	48.0	48.0	0.0
Arkansas	56.3	56.5	54.0	54.0	0.0	0.0
California	48.0	48.0	48.0	48.0	48.0	55.6
Delaware	54.3	54.4	55.0	54.2	54.2	0.0
Georgia	60.0	60.0	60.0	60.0	60.0	60.0
Idaho	63.0	63.0	63.0	63.0	63.0	63.0
Illinois	70.0	70.0	48.1	48.1	48.5	0.0
Iowa	0.0	0.0	0.0	0.0	0.0	0.0
Kentucky	60.0	60.0	60.0	60.0	60.0	60.0
Maine	54.0	55.4	55.2	55.1	52.0	51.9
Michigan	54.0	54.0	54.0	54.0	54.0	54.0
Montana	56.0	56.0	53.3	53.7	53.0	53.6
Nebraska	54.0	54.0	54.0	54.0	54.0	0.0
New Jersey	60.0	54.0	54.0	54.0	54.0	54.0
New Mexico	0.0	52.0	50.0	50.0	50.0	48.0
New York	54.0	51.2	49.8	49.8	49.7	54.0
North Carolina	60.0	60.0	48.2	48.3	48.3	48.2
North Dakota	48.0	48.0	48.0	48.0	48.0	0.0
Ohio	50.0	50.0	47.1	50.0	48.0	48.0
Oklahoma	59.6	58.6	57.6	56.1	56.4	0.0
Oregon	60.0	60.0	60.0	60.0	60.0	0.0
Pennsylvania	54.0	54.0	44.0	48.0	48.0	0.0
Rhode Island	54.0	54.0	54.0	48.0	48.0	50.7
Texas	54.1	54.1	54.1	54.4	54.5	54.0
Vermont	56.0	56.0	50.0	51.9	51.9	51.9
Virginia	70.0	70.0	48.9	48.6	48.9	48.0
Wisconsin	53.0	50.1	50.1	50.3	50.3	0.0

Table A.10. Employed Male and Female Minors
Covered under Night-Work Laws, 1920–1970
(in percent)

State	1920	1930	1940	1950	1960	1970
Alabama	5	4	6	14	20	23
Arizona	0	0	0	5	18	24
Arkansas	37	40	35	39	37	39
California	16	15	16	36	36	38
Delaware	0	0	0	25	0	0
Georgia	12	17	16	7	8	10
Idaho	0	0	0	11	12	14
Illinois	5	5	0	4	4	4
Iowa	1	0	0	4	5	13
Kentucky	7	6	3	22	31	7
Maine	15	6	6	4	3	3
Michigan	5	5	4	37	37	30
Montana	0	0	0	0	0	0
Nebraska	6	5	0	6	29	8
New Jersey	15	36	65	73	74	73
New Mexico	0	0	0	12	4	10
New York	29	26	43	43	42	46
North Carolina	6	6	43	46	46	32
North Dakota	7	0	0	4	6	4
Ohio	36	35	27	50	50	56
Oklahoma	0	1	0	16	19	20
Oregon	0	0	9	5	8	8
Pennsylvania	43	35	37	20	21	37
Rhode Island	13	11	16	52	47	47
Texas	0	1	2	3	4	5
Vermont	0	0	0	9	7	6
Virginia	1	2	2	25	27	31
Wisconsin	10	9	6	11	12	15

Table A.11. Average Legal Standard under Night-Work Laws
for Covered Male and Female Minor Employees, 1920–1970

State	1920	1930	1940	1950	1960	1970
Alabama	10.7	10.7	10.5	10.6	10.5	10.5
Arizona	10.0	10.8	11.2	11.0	11.4	11.4
Arkansas	9.2	9.2	9.2	8.9	9.0	8.7
California	7.1	7.1	7.1	7.1	7.1	7.1
Delaware	9.0	9.2	8.9	8.1	12.7	12.6
Georgia	9.5	9.5	9.6	8.4	8.4	8.4
Idaho	9.0	9.0	9.0	9.0	9.0	9.0
Illinois	12.0	12.0	0.0	12.0	12.0	12.0
Iowa	9.8	9.4	10.4	11.8	11.8	10.5
Kentucky	10.8	10.8	10.8	8.9	8.9	9.0
Maine	12.5	12.5	12.5	12.5	10.0	10.0
Michigan	9.8	9.5	9.1	8.6	8.6	6.8
Montana	0.0	0.0	0.0	0.0	0.0	6.0
Nebraska	8.5	8.4	6.3	8.8	7.0	7.7
New Jersey	9.1	8.5	8.0	8.4	8.4	8.4
New Mexico	0.0	12.0	12.0	12.0	12.0	12.0
New York	8.7	8.3	7.9	8.6	8.5	7.7
North Carolina	9.0	11.0	8.3	8.0	8.1	11.3
North Dakota	12.0	12.0	12.0	12.0	12.0	12.0
Ohio	9.0	9.0	8.9	9.5	9.4	8.9
Oklahoma	13.0	13.0	13.0	13.0	13.0	13.0
Oregon	9.9	10.1	9.9	9.6	9.6	8.2
Pennsylvania	9.0	9.0	9.3	7.1	10.3	9.3
Rhode Island	7.9	8.1	8.1	7.1	7.5	7.0
Texas	0.0	7.0	7.0	7.0	7.0	7.0
Vermont	11.0	11.0	11.0	11.0	11.0	11.0
Virginia	9.5	12.8	12.9	8.8	7.0	7.3
Wisconsin	10.8	10.7	11.2	11.8	11.8	11.8

Table A.12. Basic Data Set for Analysis of Congressional Voting
on the Fair Labor Standards Act, 1938

State	Value added in manufacturing per capita	Percent manufacturing	State law coverage (%)	State law standard	Congressional vote (%)
Maine	179.7	9	0	.00	40
New York	246.4	7	26	.01	73
New Jersey	351.2	11	26	.01	79
Pennsylvania	258.9	9	22	.01	81
Ohio	324.1	9	16	.01	85
Illinois	287.4	8	0	.00	81
Michigan	384.7	12	0	.00	59
Wisconsin	225.5	7	25	.01	100
Iowa	96.4	3	0	.00	63
Nebraska	50.2	1	1	.58	83
Virginia	135.5	5	0	.00	55
North Carolina	148.5	8	0	.00	45
Georgia	148.5	5	0	.00	20
Kentucky	65.9	2	2	.30	80
Alabama	86.8	4	0	.00	80
Arkansas	23.9	2	0	.00	14
Oklahoma	46.0	1	15	.01	100
Texas	70.9	2	0	.00	74
Oregon	159.8	6	19	.01	40
California	167.3	4	24	.01	95

Table A.13. Basic Data Set for Analysis of Congressional Voting
on the Fair Labor Standards Act, 1961

State	Value added in manufacturing per capita	Percent manufacturing	State law coverage (%)	State law standard	Congressional vote (%)
Maine	735.6	10	82	1.13	40
New York	1,080.2	11	91	1.13	62
New Jersey	1,461.6	13	65	.85	88
Pennsylvania	1,146.2	12	66	.85	71
Ohio	1,434.3	13	63	.87	36
Illinois	1,303.8	12	64	.81	56
Michigan	1,427.9	12	48	1.13	50
Wisconsin	1,236.6	12	64	.75	58
Iowa	701.9	6	31	1.13	20
Nebraska	457.8	4	28	1.10	17
Virginia	642.1	7	39	1.13	8
North Carolina	864.2	11	71	1.00	55
Georgia	660.0	8	38	1.13	36
Kentucky	678.3	6	56	.77	100
Alabama	606.3	7	38	1.13	64
Arkansas	458.7	6	32	1.16	29
Oklahoma	339.8	4	35	1.13	43
Texas	613.9	5	35	1.13	30
Oregon	793.2	8	60	.73	60
California	915.1	8	62	.75	63

Table A.14. Basic Data Set for Analysis of Congressional Voting
on the Fair Labor Standards Act, 1966

State	Value added in manufacturing per capita	Percent manufacturing	State law coverage (%)	State law standard	Congressional vote (%)
Maine	1,001.5	11	87	1.27	NA[a]
New York	1,317.7	11	92	1.30	100
New Jersey	1,737.2	13	77	1.08	100
Pennsylvania	1,563.7	13	98	1.21	85
Ohio	1,871.2	13	76	1.10	77
Illinois	1,743.2	13	77	1.04	79
Michigan	2,005.3	13	83	1.24	89
Wisconsin	1,580.5	12	76	.99	70
Iowa	1,065.9	7	46	1.29	57
Nebraska	701.9	5	43	1.29	40
Virginia	856.0	7	56	1.29	8
North Carolina	1,217.9	12	83	1.23	23
Georgia	983.7	9	55	1.29	30
Kentucky	1,064.6	7	68	1.05	44
Alabama	949.2	8	56	1.30	11
Arkansas	709.1	7	51	1.31	40
Oklahoma	492.9	4	76	1.22	71
Texas	908.8	6	52	1.29	44
Oregon	986.8	8	72	.98	NA[a]
California	1,123.6	8	74	1.00	84

[a]Total number of congressional representatives in House and Senate is less than five.

Table A.15. Employees Covered by Wage and Hour Standards Legislation and Measures of Unionization, 1970

	WP/WC (%)	MH (%)	NW (%)	MW (%)	OT (%)	EP (%)	Average law	Percent unionized	Number union members (in thousands)	Number employees (in thousands)
Agriculture[a]	52	0	0	46	0	56	25.7	1	24	3,462
Mining	90	27	0	98	96	83	65.7	59	369	622
Contract construction	71	19	1	98	96	84	61.5	77	2,576	3,345
Manufacturing	82	13	4	98	96	86	63.2	47	9,173	19,369
T/C/PU	77	10	1	98	66	85	56.2	73	3,286	4,504
Trade	72	15	5	86	47	72	49.5	86	1,604	18,612
Personal service	69	24	5	88	62	76	54.0	11	1,287	11,630
Clerical	69	12	6	94	81	84	57.7	NA[b]	NA[b]	NA[b]
Domestic service	46	0	0	11	7	26	15.0	NA[b]	NA[b]	NA[b]

[a]Agriculture, forestry, and fishing.
[b]Not available.

NOTES

1. Some writers, notably the revisionist historians, see the transition from an agrarian to a market-based economy as the consequence of the imperatives of capitalism (as, for example, Kolko, 1963, 1965; Weinstein, 1968). Others, notably John R. Commons (1968) and Lloyd Ulman (1955), stress the importance of the market as the driving force behind these changes. "The division of labor, stimulated primarily by the continuous extension of the market in this country, sharpened the distinction between employer and employed and generated the modern economic classes. With functional specialization there developed distinctive group interests and, particularly on the part of the employed, organization of individuals to further those common interests" (Ulman, 1955:27). Yet, even the agrarian society, with small-scale industry, operated on the basis of "free" markets, which are central to a capitalist political economy. Whether a writer chooses to attribute these late nineteenth-century changes to the market or to capitalism carries clear ideological implications; while the positions differ over the motivating force behind these changes, they both point to similar structural attributes associated with these changes. It is these structural changes and their effects on social relations in the workplace that are of primary importance here.

2. Blumer has argued that the process of industrialization does not *inevitably* lead to the outcomes indicated by Grey and Peterson and others. Rather, he says that "the nature of the early class of industrial workers may be said to depend on four more general factors: the composition of the working class; the milieu encountered in industrial establishments; the conditions of life to which workers are subject outside of industrial establishments; and the schemes or definitions which the workers use to interpret their experience . . . early industrialization is indifferent and neutral to each of these four basic conditions" (Blumer, 1972:13). While Blumer's general conclusion that industrialization is neutral to the four conditions is a bit overstated, it is nonetheless true that the response of United States workers to the transformations to which they were subjected was the product of industrialization as it occurred in the United States in the late nineteenth century. However, Grey and Peterson's general conclusions are amply supported by historical evidence of worker responses to industrialization in the mid- to late nineteenth century in the United States.

3. Government also played an important role in facilitating or deterring union organization. One of the first social rights workers attempted to obtain was the right to organize collectively to bargain for the terms and conditions of their labor contract. They met with little success over these political demands at the state level, especially before 1935. Instead, they were faced with injunctions which sharply curtailed the

extent of strike activity employees could engage in to get an employer either to recognize their union or to accept their contract demands.

Only with the enactment of the National Labor Relations Act (NLRA) during the New Deal were government-backed measures enabling workers to organize into unions and bargain collectively extended to many workers. The enactment of the NLRA preceded an unprecedented period of union organizing. Irving Bernstein (1971) and others (for example, Rayback, 1966) have linked this labor activism to the favorable conditions created by the new law.

4. The transformation of the American economy from agrarian to small-scale industrial to corporate (or monopoly) industrial capitalism has received considerable attention from social scientists (see, for example, Bell, 1973; Braverman, 1974; Edwards, 1979). The character of the society has been defined in terms of the dominant (or emerging) character of enterprises. This study examines instead the character, form, and nature of institutions of worker protection. What relationship exists between these two fundamental changes in the political economy is unclear, but unfortunately beyond the scope of this study.

5. Economists have also studied certain of these laws, especially right-to-work laws (Gilbert, 1966; Moore, Newman, and Thomas, 1974; Palomba and Palomba, 1971) and minimum wage laws (see Goldfarb, 1974, for a summary and critique of several studies). Kochan (1973) and Kochan and Wheeler (1975) have examined the correlates of the scope of state public employee collective bargaining laws.

6. To be sure, as is discussed in this chapter and in Chapter 3, these early laws were symbolic reforms (Edelman, 1967). They contained major loopholes or exceptions to coverage and virtually no mechanisms for enforcement.

7. Scholars of the structural school do not often agree on which sets of economic, political, and social changes stimulate political reform. Dye (1979), for example, summarizes a debate between political scientists—none of them Marxist—on whether economic or political factors are greater determinants of public policy.

8. While political scientists have devoted an enormous amount of attention to the legislative process, and to the impact of economic and political interests, political party structure, and legislative activity, this is not the approach taken here (see, for example, the classic study by Bailey, 1950, and a partial list compiled in Berk, Brackman, and Lesser, 1977:17–18). Chapter 8 does examine the correlates of congressional voting on the Fair Labor Standards Act from an interest-group perspective. In general, however, this study proceeds by examining systematically, over a seventy-year period, the relationship between specific policy outcomes, the economic structure, the ideological context, and the constellation of interest groups for and against the reforms. Each approach offers different insights into the process by which original demands are shaped into legislation.

CHAPTER 2

1. A seventh law calls for one day of rest per week. It was enacted in several states, although most states included it as a part of their maximum hours legislation.

2. Because of this method of sampling, it was necessary to introduce sampling weights when generating regional and national indices. The sampling weight for the six states with the largest population was 1.00. The sampling weights for the other states varied by region. They are: Northeast, 1.75; South, 1.875; North Central, 2.00; West, 2.00.

3. By 1900, most states had reference volumes that included the most recent version of all effective laws up to the year of publication of the code. These laws were organized by substantive area. For all but a few of the states, the six laws examined in this study were compiled in a separate chapter entitled either "Labor" or "Employer-Employee." In addition to compiling the most recent provisions of a law, many of these codes contained citations to the state statute books which indicated the year legislative action was taken on a law and the chapter in which the action was recorded. Consequently, the data on legal provisions collected from the annual statute books could be checked against the references to the legal provisions as listed in the code, and any oversights could be easily rectified.

4. In general, amendments to existing wage and hour laws or adoption of new laws were not compiled by subject matter in the annual or biennial state statute books. Consequently, it was necessary to locate the laws by examining the index thoroughly. Wage and hour laws were listed in the index under one or more of the following entries: antidiscrimination, child labor, children, civil rights, eight-hour law, employees, employer/employee, employment, equal employment, fifty-four-hour law, furnace men, hours of labor, labor, labor and labor unions, laborers, laundries, mines, minimum wage act, minimum wages for women, minors, newsboys, public contracts, railroads, sawmills, wage and hour law, wage law, women, women's labor, and workmen. Employees, employer/employee, employment, labor, minors, and wage law were the most frequently used headings.

5. In very few cases were provisions in a law pertaining to coverage or to the legal standard enacted *and* repealed (or declared unconstitutional) within a five-year period. Among the examples were several state laws, such as a 1919 Texas minimum wage law for all females and 14 year-old males which was suspended in 1920 and repealed in 1921. They also include two federal laws: the 1916 child labor law, which was declared unconstitutional in 1918, and the 1933 National Industrial Recovery Act (NIRA), declared unconstitutional in 1935. The NIRA was the one excluded law of major national significance. It provided for the establishment of committees organized by industry to fix codes of fair competition which set uniform maximum hours and a uniform wage rate for that industry. In selecting the nine intermediate years, however, years during which permanent federal legislation was adopted or revised and the war years took precedence over the year the NIRA was enacted.

6. Other types of coverage restrictions are discussed in Ratner, 1977a:Appendix C. These included limitation of coverage to private sector construction workers employed under public works contracts; provision for suspension of the law if an employer and employee agreed upon a contract with different (and less stringent) standards; provisions restricting coverage to employees of corporations; special provisions for learners, apprentices, and handicapped people; exclusion of students from coverage under minimum wage laws; provisions shaping coverage under age dis-

crimination legislation to subgroups of employees by age; provision of coverage to children and minors engaged in street trades; and restriction of coverage to non-migratory agricultural laborers.

7. Since the estimates of the distribution of employees gathered from census data were often imprecise, employee coverage was treated in terms of the percentile ranges used in coding the final coverage scores. The percentile ranges were: less than 1 percent; 1 to 9 percent; 10 to 29 percent; 30 to 49 percent; 50 to 69 percent; 70 to 89 percent; and 90 to 99 percent. For example, if a 1960 law covered all 14- and 15-year-old males and the 1950 census reported that 10 percent of all 14- to 20-year-old males were 14 or 15, we estimated that between 10 and 29 percent of all male minors were 14 or 15.

8. For the decades 1890 and 1900, data were taken from U.S. Department of Commerce, 1911, p. 204; for 1910 from U.S. Department of Commerce, 1911, p. 204 and 1948, p. 7; for 1920 from U.S. Department of Commerce, 1932, pp. 761–765; for 1930 from U.S. Department of Commerce, 1936, p. 761; for 1940 from U.S. Department of Commerce, 1941, p. 879; for 1950 from U.S. Department of Commerce, 1951, p. 767; and for 1960 from U.S. Department of Commerce, 1964, p. 778.

9. Sources of the estimates were: U.S. Department of Labor, Wage and Hour and Public Contracts Division, 1970, Tables 1, 3; U.S. Department of Labor, Wage and Hour and Public Contracts Division, 1964, pp. 4–7; 1967, pp. 7–9; 1974, Tables 20, 21, pp. 81–84; 1948, pp. 79–84; U.S. Department of Labor, 1950, pp. 272–274.

10. The average legal standard was not coded in constant dollars. Rather, constant dollar amounts were introduced as part of the computer program that combined data matrices into the final estimates of average legal standard.

11. The 1961 amendments to the Fair Labor Standards Act established two minimum wage rates—one for previously covered employees and a second for newly covered employees. Consequently, estimates of the average minimum wage rate by industry varied as a function of the mix of old to new covered employees in the category.

12. The fact that state-by-state time series data on the distribution of the labor force by demographic group and industry group have never been developed is further evidence of the difficulty of the task. In part, this oversight is a function of the uses to which such data would be put: labor economists, the academics most interested in such statistics, employ time series data on labor force participation to test theories on the dynamics of the labor market. Consequently, it is essential that they obtain as precise data as possible. In this study, however, state-by-state estimates of labor force participation by demographic and industry groups are used as rough population weights to be matched with the provisions of labor legislation to arrive at estimates of the extent of coverage and the average protection.

13. We used estimates on the percentage of clerical workers in each SIC from the 1950 census to generate the total number of clerical workers for each state for 1940. These estimates were generated separately for males and females. For 1940

and 1950 the source was U.S. Department of Commerce, 1952, Table 134; for 1960, U.S. Department of Commerce, 1961, Table 209; for 1970, U.S. Department of Commerce, 1972, Table 232.

CHAPTER 3

1. There were several minor pieces of federal legislation enacted before the Fair Labor Standards Act in 1938, including a maximum hours law covering construction employees engaged in federal public works projects, and an overtime law covering railroad employees. Furthermore, there were no federal standards with which state legislators had to comply, as there are, for example, for such programs as Aid to Families with Dependent Children and unemployment compensation. While not direct legislation, such programs can have considerable impact on state public policy.

2. In part, the difference between the actual workweek and maximum hours laws occurred as a result of changes during World War I. Between 1910 and 1930, the legal hours ceiling declined gradually at approximately three-quarters of an hour per decade. By contrast, by 1929 slightly more than 71 percent of manufacturing employees worked an average of fifty-four hours or less. Commons and Andrews attribute these real changes to the fact that the "labor shortage during the war and competitive conditions in the following decade stimulated employers to introduce more machinery, better equipment and improved methods, which, together with the heightened efficiency of the workers, led to a tremendous increase in the productivity of industry" (1936:84–86). The fact that the legal standards did not keep pace with actual hours indicated that the average legal standard for MH moved from one that affected the average employee to one that was relevant only to workers faced with exceptionally long workweeks.

3. It is unclear whether the employers would have withheld protection demanded by employees had there been a labor shortage. The late nineteenth century was a time of massive immigration, which, in combination with the enormous technological and organizational changes taking place in production, further undercut the power of employees relative to employers.

4. Ralf Dahrendorf (1959, 1964) has argued that dominant social classes can be analytically linked with the preservation of the status quo. In turn, subordinate groups (such as labor) seek to change the status quo (see also Bachrach and Baratz, 1970). An important arena in which these conflicting tendencies are played out is the legal system. Since dominance relations are undergirded by the legal system, labor will have a difficult time achieving legal changes in its interest. The conflict is heightened when the reform at hand is directed at making inroads into the property rights that differentially benefit dominant groups. As Dahrendorf writes: "Our model of conflict group formation involves the proposition that of the two aggregates of authority positions to be distinguished in every association, one—that of domination—is characterized by an interest in the maintenance of a social structure that for them conveys authority, whereas the other—that of subjection—involves an interest in changing a

social condition that deprives its incumbents of authority. The two interests are in conflict" (1964:106–107). "Empirically, group conflict is probably most easily accessible to analysis if it be understood as a conflict about the legitimacy of relations of authority" (Dahrendorf, 1959:176).

5. It is especially important to separate out the multiple motives of different segments of organized labor for supporting these laws because of the frequent charge that male unionists endorsed protective labor laws for women as a way to limit the entrance of women into traditionally male jobs (see, for example, Hill, 1979; Yellowitz, 1977). There is very little evidence, however, that fear of female encroachment into jobs held by men accounted for trade union support of the first female maximum hours law adopted in any state. Unions used other devices to keep women out of craft jobs, most notably apprenticeship rules and equal pay clauses (Baer, 1978). Better evidence of their discriminatory use surfaces in the first two decades of the twentieth century when male unionists used these laws to remove women from certain positions. Yet, even these instances have been cited out of all proportion to the relative number of women affected. In New York State, in particular, women in the printing trades, women messengers, and women elevator operators lost their jobs because employers did not want to be subject to government hours regulations. In a more clear-cut case of male employee collusion with employers, women streetcar conductors who had replaced men in these jobs during World War I were displaced when the men came home (Baker, 1925; Beyer, 1929). In the case of the women printers in New York State, the controversy was resolved in 1924 in favor of the women when, after an eight-year battle, they were exempted from coverage under night-work legislation (Baer, 1978:87). It has not been established that unions supported these laws entirely, or even primarily, as a device to maintain a monopolistic labor market.

6. Certain males in occupations such as underground mining were covered under maximum hours legislation. The legal justification for providing these social rights to male employees rested on the concept of "dangerous occupations." Of course, in legal proceedings, the burden of proof in defining "dangerous" rested with the employee. For example, in *Holden* v. *Hardy* (169 U.S. 366, 1898), sufficient evidence was presented to convince an unsympathetic judiciary of the dangers of mining. "While the general experience of mankind may justify us in believing that men may engage in ordinary employments more than eight hours per day without injury to their health, it does not follow that labor for the same length of time is innocuous when carried on beneath the surface of the earth" (Brandeis, 1935:668). By contrast, in *Lochner* v. *New York* (198 U.S. 45, 75, 1905), the Court concluded that "to the common understanding the trade of a baker has never been regarded as an unhealthy one." The Court thus overturned a New York State maximum hours law for male bakery employees.

7. Several other writers have noted the importance of discretion or autonomy to employers. R. D. Corwin and Lois Gray (1971:41–42) have explained businessmen's preference for the Republican party not in terms of profit—because, after all, four of the five recessions between 1950 and 1970 have occurred under Republicans—

but rather in terms of their freedom from restraint, investigation, and harassment during Republican administrations. Alvin Gouldner has also pointed to the increase in discretion as one moves up the industrial hierarchy. The industrial employee is faced with a very unpredictable environment, in large part because the rules he or she must follow are not of his or her own making. Hence, the union contract removes discretion from superordinates and "may be seen as an effort on the part of workers to establish a basis of prediction relevant to their own goals." On the other hand, employers justify their discretion as a work incentive for employees because they believe that "anxiety and insecurity are effective motivators" (Gouldner, 1948:397–398). Thus, the conflict between employers and employees is based on the extent of discretion the employer may maintain over the terms and conditions of work vis-à-vis the employee. More recently, Marglin (1974) has argued that, while it may be more profitable to increase employee discretion over certain production decisions, employers avoid doing so in order to maintain control within the firm.

8. At the same time, it is important to note that the enactment of the overtime provisions of the FLSA had rendered state maximum hours laws for women superfluous, at least for those employed in manufacturing. This is indirectly indicated by the change in attitude of Frances Perkins who had been a determined fighter for protective labor laws. As is discussed at greater length in Chapter 4, she viewed the approach taken to hours standards in the Black-Connery Bill as archaic. Yet this was the approach taken in maximum hours laws. Experience had also proven that maximum hours laws as well as other protective laws were very difficult to enforce. Furthermore, the number of hours constituting the hours threshold in the federal overtime law was significantly lower than the weekly hours ceiling provided in most state maximum hours laws. In the late 1930s, the average workweek in manufacturing was close to forty hours. Forty hours per week became the hours threshold beyond which employees received pay for additional work rendered. Therefore, the hours standard in the FLSA was closer to the actual workweek of employees than were the forty-eight- to fifty-four-hour ceilings found in most state maximum hours laws. It is reasonable to conclude, therefore, that, at least for manufacturing, overtime laws both transcended maximum hours laws in their scope of coverage and replaced them as the primary set of standards regulating hours of work.

CHAPTER 4

1. This is one of the three standards of minimum income developed in the New School poverty study to determine the extent of poverty and minimum comfort (Ornati, 1966:11–14). The subsistence budget—used by state agencies dispensing aid to families with dependent children—ties the level of need to the cost of "food, clothing, and shelter, plus a few other needs, such as carfare to work or to seek work. . . . The top level, 'minimum comfort,' represents the threshold of 'comfort,' as comfort is viewed in contemporary terms. This level represents the minimum once considered necessary for 'health and decency' for civil service and other workers."

The modest but adequate budget is "approximately a median between the 'subsistence' and 'minimum comfort' levels." Such standards are highly subjective. For example, the food components of the budgets are based on estimates of "what minimum diet an adult or a child 'ought' to have." There is substantial disagreement over this item, however, among food experts. Furthermore, typical diets vary by socioeconomic class: "Families with low incomes . . . customarily select more beans and less meat, more hamburger and less steak, more potatoes and less fresh corn." Standards upon which these budgets are based also change over time: "As the general U.S. income level has risen, living standards have risen. Expectations have risen. . . . Thus, through the years, standards of sufficiency, however defined, have generally risen." Finally, "minimum needs are related both to the productivity of our society and to the earning patterns and levels of those recognized as working in the least skilled and lowest paid occupations."

The modest but adequate income is a reasonable standard for assessing the minimum wage rate. For 1966, for example, if you divide the annual income level constituting the poverty line—or the lowest of the three standards—into an hourly wage rate using the assumptions specified in the text, you arrive at $1.60 an hour—the 1966 minimum wage rate. This is only partially surprising given that, before 1938, state wage boards generally developed subsistence budgets for women before entering into negotiations with representatives of employers and employees to arrive at the hourly or weekly minimum wage. Oscar Ornati, the head of the New School poverty study, remarks that "the wages of unskilled male labor since the early 1900's have been roughly equal to the 'minimum subsistence' level of the poverty band. Since the Depression of the mid-1930's, men's low wages—as represented by this index—have slightly exceeded this standard" (1966:15).

Yet, this standard is not without its problems. First, the assumptions made in the preceding calculation of a minimum wage rate necessary to earn a modest but adequate income contain some problems. The assumption of no deductions probably results in a slight underestimation of the minimum wage necessary to provide a modest but adequate income. On the other hand, the assumption concerning a constant income definition over time probably leads to an overestimation of the requisite minimum wage—at least for the earlier points. Clearly, such definitions have been revised upward since the 1940s. It is not clear whether these two assumptions cancel each other out.

Second, the average legal standard for minimum wage legislation is not a direct measure of all minimum wage standards established through governmental channels. Provisions that established administrative procedures were coded as if the minimum wage rate was $0.01 per hour. This procedure resulted in underestimating the effective legal standard, especially between 1920 and 1945. Despite these inadequacies, the average legal standard assessed as a percentage of the modest but adequate budget offers a base from which to assess the growth and change in the minimum wage rate over time.

2. For example, 0 percent specifies that there is no law or that the hours threshold is eighty-four (that is, that in effect there is no legal protection). At the opposite

extreme, complete legal protection is achieved when the standard requires that *all* work be subsidized at a higher than normal rate of pay. It is important to keep in mind that a law providing 45 to 55 percent of complete legal protection calls for the payment of overtime benefits after an employee has worked approximately forty to forty-two hours per week.

3. Unfortunately, these laws were honored, more often than not, in the breach. Employers often required employees to sign contracts superceding the legal hours regulations. In New Hampshire, for example, the legislature passed a legal day's work law which applied to employees in the absence of a contract. "On the day that law became operative . . . all the operatives in the New Hampshire textile mills were fired, and then re-hired only if they consented to sign a contract agreeing to the old hours (of thirteen to fourteen hours a day). Any girl who refused to sign such a contract was blacklisted" (Josephson, 1949:282). Such contracts rendered these laws virtually ineffectual. Yet eventually male employees secured a ten- and then an eight-hour day by means of these contracts.

4. The simplifying assumption obscures changes in coverage attributable to the changing industrial distribution of the labor force between these two points in time.

5. The test used to determine whether two betas of the regression line differed significantly are found in Cohen and Cohen (1975:52–53).

6. Compare the immediate response of Frances Perkins to labor's dissatisfaction with the FLSA with the campaign for an enforceable ten-hour law in Massachusetts discussed in Chapter 3. By the 1930s, organized labor had become part of the institutionalized network of interest groups with direct access to bureaucratic and legislative political elites. This development shortened the time lag between the formulation of demands and their acknowledgment by government representatives.

7. The reconstruction of the Supreme Court appears to be integrally related to the pressure to enact legislation providing labor standards. In his message to Congress on January 6, 1937, Roosevelt called for "an 'enlightened view' on social legislation from the judiciary in order that democracy might be made to function successfully. Reports of the President's first press conference of the year indicate that plans were being formulated to 'do something' about minimum wages as well as judicial opposition to his program." It is not entirely coincidental that the reversal of the Supreme Court stand on minimum wage legislation (and other labor matters) immediately preceded a decrease in Roosevelt's efforts to achieve the enactment of his court bill, which would have increased the number of justices sitting on the Supreme Court (Forsythe, 1939:464–465).

8. The 1936 electoral outcome is the national extension of the realignment first observed in the New England states in the 1928 presidential election, which V. O. Key called a "critical election." In a critical election, "voters are, at least from impressionistic evidence, usually deeply concerned . . . the extent of electoral involvement is relatively quite high, and . . . the decisive results of the voting reveal a sharp alteration of the pre-existing cleavage within the electorate. . . . All such characteristics cumulate to the conception of an election type . . . in which more or less profound readjustments occur in the relations of power within the community,

and in which new and durable groupings are formed" (1955:4). Similarly, E. E. Schattschneider contends that the 1932 presidential election revealed a realignment which, in turn, spurred "a profound change in the agenda of American politics" (1960:88).

9. Roosevelt, however, suspended Order 16 for a lengthy period during the war because he feared it contributed to high inflation (Chafe, 1972:156).

CHAPTER 5

1. Cramer's V is one of several statistics used to measure the strength of a relationship found to exist by the chi-square statistic, such as the coefficient contingency C, Tschuprow's T, and ϕ. The coefficient contingency C was less desirable than the other three measures because it is not standardized. Furthermore, T, ϕ and V are equivalent measures of the strength of the relationship for chi-square tables where one of the categories is dichotomous, as was the case for this set of data. Finally, the V-statistic is insensitive to the number of columns in a table.

2. Equal pay legislation constitutes an exception to this pattern. It is unclear whether equal pay is a separate case because of some special meaning attached to this law or because changes in variations in employee coverage were only measured for ten years.

CHAPTER 6

1. The term "imprinting" is borrowed from the literature on animal behavior. It refers to a primary socialization process in young animals in which patterns are established that remain with the animal throughout life. This term points to "a relatively limited period in early life"—termed a critical period—during which the animal forms social bonds and attachments that continue "to exist and [that] form the basis of later social preferences" (Hess, 1968:109–115).

2. In a study relating seventy-seven pieces of legislation, Walker found that states demonstrated a consistent ranking with respect to the time of adoption. In other words, some states were consistent trend setters and others consistent laggards. Moreover, he concluded that "larger, wealthier, more industrialized states adopt new programs somewhat more rapidly than their smaller, less well-developed neighbors" (1969:884). In a separate analysis not reported here (Ratner, 1977a), however, it was found that, for wage and hour standards legislation, time of adoption is law specific: a state that adopts one labor standards law early is not necessarily likely to adopt other labor standards laws early.

3. The expected correlation was calculated as follows:

$$\text{Expected } RXY = \frac{\sigma X^2}{\sigma X^2 + \sigma A^2}$$

where X = value of legal dimension at a point in time, t;
  σX^2 = variance of X;
    Y = value of X at $t + i$, where i = 10, 20, 30, 40, or 50;
    A = $(Y–X)$ or value at $t + i$ minus value at t, or the change in the value of the legal dimension;
  σA^2 = variance of A.

CHAPTER 7

1. Roll calls were examined only for the final bill formulated in the Joint Senate and House Conference Committee. The sources for the data on Congressional roll calls are: Senate in 1938, U.S., Congress, Senate, 1938, p. 7957; and U.S., Congress, 1937; House in 1938, U.S., Congress, House, 1938, p. 9627; and U.S., Congress, 1938; Senate and House in 1961, U.S., Congress, 1961, pp. 518–519, 571; Senate and House in 1966, U.S., Congress, 1966, pp. 912, 977.

2. This resulted in dropping eight states (Vermont, Rhode Island, North Dakota, Montana, Delaware, Idaho, New Mexico, and Arizona) from the analysis.

3. The sources of industrialization data are: total number of wage earners in manufacturing and value added in manufacturing and total population, 1937 and 1939, U.S. Department of Commerce, 1945, pp. 9, 829–830; total number of wage earners in manufacturing and value added in manufacturing, total population, 1960 and 1962, U.S. Department of Commerce, 1964, pp. 11, 779; total number of wage earners in manufacturing and value added in manufacturing, 1965, and total population, 1966, U.S. Department of Commerce, 1968, pp. 12, 727; total number of wage earners in manufacturing and value added in manufacturing, 1967, U.S. Department of Commerce, 1971b, p. 697.

4. They expected voting on the FLSA to be affected by unionization, region (considered a proxy measure for the industrial composition of a state), the number of small businesses, the number of low wage workers, and the number of teenage workers. Unionization (as measured by the total campaign contributions of organized labor to a congressman) was expected to exert a positive impact on the FLSA. Region was predicted to have an uneven influence on the voting of congressmen, yet congressmen from states in more industrialized regions were expected to vote favorably on the FLSA. The number of small businesses and the number of teenage workers were expected to exert a negative influence on congressional voting. Finally, Silberman and Durden remained unsure of the effect of low-wage workers: "The effect of the minimum wage on their jobs is a function of the market wage rate . . . more and more labor units will find it in their interests to oppose such an increase in the minimum wage." Low-wage workers would then put pressure on their congressmen to oppose an increase in the minimum wage (1976:319–321). Using N-chotomous multivariate probit analysis, these authors found that the variables representing unionization, small businesses, region, and teenage workers were

all statistically significant and had "the predicted direction of influence on explaining the variation in the dependent variable. Each variable, moreover, added significantly to the combined explanatory power of the equation." Low-wage workers exerted "a positive influence." This indicates that workers earning below the proposed minimum wage "exert positive pressure on Congressmen" because the relative intensity of preferences of the expected beneficiaries under the proposed legislation outweigh those of the expected losers (Silberman and Durden, 1976:325–326).

5. We also arrived at these conclusions on the basis of a separate analysis not reported in the text of this chapter. A stepwise regression was run in an attempt to predict the 1961 and 1966 congressional votes on the FLSA. For 1961, the congressional vote was regressed on the percentage of employees covered under minimum wage laws in 1960, the percentage of employees unionized in 1953, and the percentage of the labor force in manufacturing in 1961. For 1966, a somewhat more complicated model was introduced: congressional vote was regressed on the percentage of employees covered in 1965, the percentage of employees unionized in 1965, the percentage of the labor force in manufacturing in 1966, the percentage of a state's delegation affiliated with the Democratic party, and the congressional vote in 1961. The one variable that "predicted" congressional vote in both 1961 and 1966 was the extent of coverage under preexisting minimum wage laws.

CHAPTER 8

1. Marx's analysis is a special case of the more general interest group perspective. Political scientists and political sociologists argue, for example, that constituencies organize for and against particular political issues in terms of their interests as they perceive them. These interests need not be narrowly economic ones, and interest groups frequently organize around noneconomic issues. (See Alford, 1975.)

2. Data on unionization were not available for the domestic service and clerical categories. In accordance with the current census classification system, clerical workers were included under one of the other seven SICs.

3. Time series data on the extent of unionization are only available up to 1960. Furthermore, the analysis was restricted to five-year changes in the data because of the legal data.

4. Sociologists and economists have undertaken cross-national studies of the structural correlates of the adoption of or the level of expenditures in social security legislation. (See, for example, Aaron, 1967:13–48; Pryor, 1968; Wilensky, 1975: 1–14.) Political scientists have studied the correlates of the level of expenditures for public policies across states. Hofferbert (1974) reviews this literature. Perhaps the best systematic study on the changing parameters of existing legislation I have encountered is Heclo's (1974) comparative case study of social security legislation in Great Britain and Sweden.

5. We also correlated each of the four variables leading each of the other vari-

ables by ten and fifteen years. The results of these calculations further support the finding that all the processes of change being observed occur fairly rapidly. In general, very few of the correlations were strong and significant when one of the variables led another by ten or fifteen years.

BIBLIOGRAPHY

AARON, HENRY
  1967 "Social Security: International Comparisons." In *Studies in the Economics of Income Maintenance,* ed. Otto Eckstein, pp. 13–48. Washington, D.C.: The Brookings Institution.

ALFORD, ROBERT
  1975 "Paradigms of Relations between State and Society." In *Stress and Contradiction in Modern Capitalism: Public Policy and the Theory of the State,* ed. Leon N. Lindberg, Robert Alford, Colin Crouch, and Clause Offe, pp. 145–172. Lexington, Mass.: Lexington Books.

ANDERSON, H. DEWEY, AND DAVIDSON, PERCY E.
  1940 *Occupational Trends in the United States.* Stanford, Cal.: Stanford University Press.

AUERBACH, MORTON
  1968 "Business Cycles: General." In *International Encyclopedia of the Social Sciences,* ed. David Sills, vol. 2, pp. 221–226. New York: Macmillan and The Free Press.

AVINERI, SHLOMO
  1968 *The Social and Political Thought of Karl Marx.* Cambridge: University Printing House.

BABCOCK, BARBARA ALLEN; FREEDMAN, ANN E.; NORTON, ELEANOR HOLMES; AND ROSS, SUSAN C.
  1975 *Sex Discrimination and the Law: Causes and Remedies.* Boston: Little, Brown and Company.

BACHRACH, PETER, AND BARATZ, MORTON S.
  1970 *Power and Poverty: Theory and Practice.* London: Oxford University Press.

BAER, JUDITH A.
  1978 *The Chains of Protection: The Judicial Response to Women's Labor Legislation.* Westport, Conn.: Greenwood Press.

BAILEY, STEPHEN KEMP
  1950 *Congress Makes a Law: The Story behind the Employment Act of 1946.* New York: Columbia University Press.

BAIN, GEORGE SAYERS, AND ELSHEIKH, FAROUK
  1976 *Union Growth and the Business Cycle: An Econometric Analysis.* Oxford: Basil Blackwell.

BAKER, ELIZABETH FAULKNER
  1925 *Protective Labor Legislation.* New York: Columbia University Press.

1929 "At Crossroads in the Legal Protection of Women in Industry." *Annals* 275 (May): 34–40.

1964 *Technology and Women's Work.* New York: Columbia University Press.

BAUER, RAYMOND, ED.

1966 *Social Indicators.* Cambridge, Mass.: Massachusetts Institute of Technology Press.

BELL, DANIEL

1973 *The Coming of Post-Industrial Society: A Venture in Social Forecasting.* New York: Basic Books.

BENDIX, REINHARD

1964 *Nation-Building and Citizenship.* New York: John Wiley and Sons.

BERK, RICHARD A.; BRACKMAN, HAROLD; AND LESSER, SELMA

1977 *A Measure of Justice: An Empirical Study of Changes in the California Penal Code, 1955–71.* New York: Academic Press.

BERNSTEIN, IRVING R.

1954 "The Growth of American Unions." *American Economic Review* 44 (June): 313.

1960 "Union Growth and Structural Cycles." In *Labor and Trade Unionism: An Interdisciplinary Reader,* ed. Walter Galenson and Seymour Martin Lipset, pp. 73–101. New York: John Wiley and Sons.

1971 *The Turbulent Years: A History of the American Worker, 1933–1941.* Boston: Houghton Mifflin Company.

BEYER, CLARA

1929 *History of Labor Legislation for Women in Three States.* Women's Bureau Bulletin no. 66. Washington, D.C.: U.S. Government Printing Office.

BLALOCK, ROBERT M.

1960 *Social Statistics.* New York: McGraw-Hill Book Company.

BLOCH, FARRELL E.

1975 "Political Support for Minimum Wage Regulation." Working paper no. 71. Industrial Relations Research Section, Princeton University.

BLOCK, FRED

1977a "Beyond Corporate Liberalism." *Social Problems* 24 (February): 352–361.

1977b "The Ruling Class Does Not Rule: Notes on a Marxist Theory of State." *Socialist Revolution* 7 (May–June): 6–28.

BLUMER, HERBERT

1972 "Early Industrialization and the Laboring Class." In *Organizational Issues in Industrial Society,* ed. Jon M. Shepard, pp. 10–16. Englewood Cliffs, N.J.: Prentice-Hall.

BOLI-BENNETT, JOHN, AND MEYER, JOHN W.

1978 "The Ideology of Childhood and the State: Rules Distinguishing Children in National Constitutions, 1870–1970." *American Sociological Review* 43 (December): 797–812.

BOONE, GLADYS

1942 *The Women's Trade Union Leagues in Great Britain and the United States of America*. New York: Columbia University Press.

BRADY, DOROTHY S.

1947 "Equal Pay for Women Workers." *Annals* 251 (May): 53–60.

BRANDEIS, ELIZABETH

1935 *Labor Legislation. History of Labor in the United States: 1896–1932*, vol. 3, ed. John R. Commons. New York: Macmillan Company.

1972 "Organized Labor and Protective Labor Legislation." In *Labor and the New Deal*, ed. Milton Derber and Edwin Young, pp. 195–237. New York: DaCapo Press.

BRAVERMAN, HARRY

1974 *Labor and Monopoly Capital: The Degradation of Work in the Twentieth Century*. New York: Monthly Review Press.

BRECHER, JEREMY

1972 *Strike*. San Francisco: Straight Arrow Books.

BRECKNER, EARL R.

1929 *A History of Labor Legislation in Illinois*. Chicago: University of Chicago Press.

BRIDGES, AMY

1974 "Nicos Poulantzas and the Marxist Theory of the State." *Politics and Society* 4 (2): 161–190.

BROWN, BARBARA A.; FREEDMAN, ANN E.; KATZ, HARRIET N.; AND PRICE, ALICE M.

1977 *Women's Rights and the Law: The Impact of the ERA on State Laws*. New York: Praeger Publishers.

BUREAU OF NATIONAL AFFAIRS

1949 *The New Wage and Hour Law*. Washington, D.C.: Bureau of National Affairs.

1961 *Labor Relations Reporter*. Washington, D.C.: Bureau of National Affairs.

1964 *State Fair Employment Laws and Their Administration*. Washington, D.C.: Bureau of National Affairs.

1967 *Labor Relations Reporter*. Washington, D.C.: Bureau of National Affairs.

BURSTEIN, PAUL

1978 "A New Method for Measuring Legislative Content and Change." *Sociological Methods and Research* 6 (February): 337–364.

BURTT, EVERETT JOHNSON, JR.

1963 *Labor Markets, Unions and Government Policies*. New York: St. Martin's Press.

CAHILL, MARION COTTER

1932 *Shorter Hours: A Study of the Movement since the Civil War*. New York: Columbia University Press.

CHAFE, WILLIAM H.

1972 *The American Woman: Her Changing Social, Economic and Political Roles, 1920–1970*. New York: The Century Company.

CLARK, COLIN

1940   *The Conditions of Economic Progress.* London: Macmillan and Company.

CLARK, LINDLEY D.

1922   *Labor Laws That Have Been Declared Unconstitutional.* Bureau of Labor Statistics Bulletin no. 321. Washington, D.C.: U.S. Government Printing Office.

CNUDDE, CHARLES F., AND MCCRONE, DONALD J.

1969   "Party Competition and Welfare Parties in the American States." *American Political Science Review* 63 (September): 858–866.

COHEN, JACOB, AND COHEN, PATRICIA

1975   *Applied Multiple Correlation/Regression Analysis for the Behavioral Sciences.* New York: John Wiley and Sons.

COHEN, SANFORD

1975   *Labor in the United States.* 4th ed. Columbus, Ohio: Charles E. Merrill Publishing Company.

COLEMAN, JAMES SAMUEL

1974   *Power and the Structure of Society.* New York: W. W. Norton Company.

COLLIER, DAVID, AND MESSICK, RICHARD E.

1975   "Prerequisites versus Diffusion: Testing Alternative Explanations of Social Security Adoption." *American Political Science Review* 69 (December): 1299–1315.

COLLINS, RANDALL

1972   "A Conflict Theory of Sexual Stratification." In *Recent Sociology No. 4: Family Marriage and the Struggle of the Sexes,* ed. Peter Dreitzel, pp. 53–79. New York: Macmillan Company.

COMMONS, JOHN R.

1968   *The Legal Foundation of Capitalism.* Madison: University of Wisconsin Press.

COMMONS, JOHN R., AND ANDREWS, JOHN B.

1936   *Principles of Labor Legislation.* 4th rev. ed. New York: Harper and Brothers.

CORWIN, R. D., AND GRAY, LOIS

1971   "Of Republicans and Recessions: Why Does Big Business Vote for Them." *Social Policy* 2 (November–December): 41–43.

COWART, ANDREW T.

1969   "Anti-Poverty Expenditure in the American States: A Comparative Analysis." *Midwest Journal of Political Science* 13 (May): 219–236.

CROXTON, FREDERICK E., AND COWDEN, DUDLEY J.

1955   *Applied General Statistics.* 2d ed. Englewood Cliffs, N.J.: Prentice-Hall.

CUTRIGHT, PHILLIPS

1965   "Political Structure, Economic Development, and National Social Security Programs." *American Journal of Sociology* 70 (March): 537–550.

DAHRENDORF, RALF

1959 *Class and Class Conflict in Industrial Society.* Stanford, Calif.: Stanford University Press.

1964 "Towards a Theory of Social Conflict." In *Social Change: Sources, Patterns, Consequences,* ed. Amitai Etzioni and Ava Etzioni, pp. 98–111. New York: Basic Books.

DAVIDSON, ELIZABETH H.

1939 *Child Labor Legislation in the Southern Textile Industries.* Chapel Hill: University of North Carolina Press.

DAVIDSON, KENNETH M.; GINSBURG, RUTH BADER; AND KAY, HERMA HILL

1974 *Sex-Based Discrimination: Text, Cases and Materials.* St. Paul, Minn.: West Publishing Company.

DAVIS, H. B.

1941 "The Theory of Union Growth." *Quarterly Journal of Economics* 55 (August): 611–637.

DAVIS, OTTO A.; DEMPSTER, M. A. H.; AND WILDAVSKY, AARON

1966 "A Theory of the Budgetary Process." *American Political Science Review* 60 (September): 529–547.

DAWSON, RICHARD E.

1967 "Social Development, Party Competition, and Policy." In *The American Party Systems: Stages of Political Development,* ed. William N. Chambers and Walter D. Burham, pp. 203–237. New York: Oxford University Press.

DAWSON, RICHARD E., AND ROBINSON, JAMES A.

1963 "Interparty Competition, Economic Variables, and Welfare Policies in the American States." *Journal of Politics* 25 (May): 265–289.

DILLARD, DUDLEY

1967 *Economic Development of the North American Community: Historical Introduction to Modern Economics.* Englewood Cliffs, N.J.: Prentice-Hall.

DOLBEARE, KENNETH N.

1974 *Political Change in the United States: A Framework for Analysis.* New York: McGraw-Hill Book Company.

DOWNEY, E. H.

1910 *History of Labor Legislation in Iowa.* Iowa City: State Historical Society of Iowa.

DURAND, JOHN

1948 *The Labor Force in the United States, 1890–1960.* New York: Social Science Research Council.

DYE, THOMAS R.

1965 "State Legislative Politics." In *Politics in the American States,* ed. Herbert Jacob and Kenneth N. Vines, pp. 493 ff. Boston: Little, Brown and Company.

1966 *Politics, Economics and the Public: Policy Outcomes in the American States.* Chicago: Rand McNally & Co.

1978   *Understanding Public Policy.* 3rd ed. Englewood Cliffs, N.J.: Prentice-Hall.

1979   "Politics versus Economics: The Development of the Literature on Policy Determination." *Policy Studies Journal* 7 (Summer): 652–661.

EASTERLIN, RICHARD A.

1960   "Interregional Differences in Per Capita Income, 1840–1950." In *Trends in the American Economy in the Nineteenth Century,* pp. 73–140. Studies in Income and Wealth, vol. 24. Princeton, N.J.: Princeton University Press.

1971   "Regional Income Trends, 1840–1850." In *The Reinterpretation of American Economic History,* ed. Robert W. Fogel and Stanley L. Engerman, pp. 38–49. New York: Harper and Row.

EAVES, LUCILLE

1910   *A History of California Labor Legislation,* vol. 2. University of California Publications in Economics. Berkeley: University of California Press.

EDELMAN, MURRAY

1967   *The Symbolic Uses of Politics.* Urbana, Chicago, and London: University of Illinois Press.

EDWARDS, RICHARD

1979   *Contested Terrain: The Transformation of the Workplace in the Twentieth Century.* New York: Basic Books.

ELAZAR, DANIEL

1966   *American Federalism: A View from the States.* New York: Crowell Company.

FENTON, JOHN H.

1966   *Midwest Politics.* New York: Holt, Rinehart and Winston.

FINE, SIDNEY

1953   "The Eight-Hour Day Movement in the United States, 1888–1891." *Mississippi Valley Historical Review* 40 (December): 441–462.

1976   *Laissez Faire and the General Welfare State; A Study of Conflict in American Thought, 1865–1901.* Ann Arbor: University of Michigan Press.

FLEXNER, ELEANOR

1971   *Century of Struggle: The Women's Rights Movement in the United States.* New York: Atheneum.

FOGEL, ROBERT W., AND ENGERMAN, STANLEY L., EDS.

1971   *The Reinterpretation of American Economic History.* New York: Harper and Row.

FONER, PHILIP S.

1979   *Women and the American Labor Movement: From Colonial Times to the Eve of World War I.* New York: The Free Press.

FORSYTHE, JOHN S.

1939   "Legislative History of the Fair Labor Standards Act." *Law and Contemporary Problems* 6 (Summer): 464–490.

FRIEDHEIM, JERRY WARDEN
1968   *Where Are the Voters?* Washington, D.C.: The National Press.
FRIEDMAN, LAWRENCE H.
1973   *A History of American Law.* New York: Simon and Schuster.
FRIEDMAN, LAWRENCE H., AND LADINSKY, JACK
1967   "Social Change and the Law of Industrial Accidents." *Columbia Law Review* 67 (January): 50–82.
FRY, BRIAN R., AND WINTERS, RICHARD R.
1970   "The Politics of Redistribution." *American Political Science Review* 64 (June): 508–522.
FUCHS, VICTOR
1968   *The Service Society.* New York: Vantage Books.
GALLMAN, ROBERT, AND HOWLE, EDWARD S.
1971   "Trends in the Structure of the American Economy since 1840." In *The Reinterpretation of American Economic History,* ed. Robert E. Fogel and Stanley L. Engerman, pp. 25–37. New York: Harper and Row.
GAMSON, WILLIAM
1968   *Power and Discontent.* Homewood, Ill.: Dorsey Press.
GARNER, ROBERTA ASH
1977   *Social Change.* Chicago: Rand McNally & Co.
GILBERT, DAVID
1966   "A Statistical Analysis of the Right-to-Work Conflict." *Industrial and Labor Relations Review* 19 (July): 533–537.
GOLD, DAVID LO; CLARENCE, Y. H.; AND WRIGHT, ERIK OLIN
1975   "Recent Developments in Marxist Theories of the Capitalist State, Parts 1 and 2." *Monthly Review* 27 (October and November): 36–51.
GOLDFARB, ROBERT
1974   "The Policy Content of Quantitative Minimum Wage Legislation." *Proceedings of the Twenty-Seventh Conference of the Industrial Relations Association,* pp. 261–268. Madison, Wis.: Industrial Relations Research Association.
GORDON, DAVID M.
1972   "From Steam Whistles to Coffee Breaks." *Dissent* (Winter): 197–210.
GOUGH, IAN
1979   *The Political Economy of the Welfare State.* London: The Macmillan Press.
GOULDNER, ALVIN
1948   "Comment: Industrial Sociology: Status and Prospects." *American Sociological Review* 13 (June): 396–400.
GRAY, VIRGINIA
1973   "Innovation in the States: A Diffusion Study." *American Political Science Review* 67 (December): 1174–1185.
1979   "Conclusion by the Symposium Co-editor." *Policy Studies Journal* 7 (Summer): 799–803.

GREENSTONE, J. DAVID
1969 *Labor in American Politics*. New York: Vantage Books.

GREY, RALPH, AND PETERSON, J.
1974 *Economic Development of the United States*. New York: Irwin.

HAMILTON, WALTON
1931 "Freedom of Contract." In *Encyclopaedia of the Social Sciences*, ed. Edwin R. A. Seligman, vol. 6, pp. 451–455. New York: Macmillan Company.

HANDLER, JOEL F.
1978 *Social Movements and the Legal System: A Theory of Law Reform and Social Change*. New York: Academic Press.

HANNA, HUGH S.
1917 *Labor Laws and Their Administration in the Pacific*. Bureau of Labor Statistics Bulletin no. 211. Washington, D.C.: U.S. Government Printing Office.

HARRINGTON, MICHAEL
1976 *The Twilight of Capitalism*. New York: Simon and Schuster.

HAYS, SAMUEL P.
1957 *The Response to Industrialism, 1885–1914*. Chicago: University of Chicago Press.

HECLO, HUGH
1974 *Modern Social Politics in Britain and Sweden*. New Haven: Yale University Press.

HEILBRONER, ROBERT L.
1973 "Economic Problems of a 'Postindustrial' Society." *Dissent* (Spring): 163–176.

HERNES, GUDMUND
1976 "Structural Change in Social Processes." *American Journal of Sociology* 82 (November): 513–547.

HESS, ECKHARD
1968 "Imprinting." In *International Encyclopedia of the Social Sciences*, ed. David Sills, vol. 7, pp. 109–115. New York: Macmillan and The Free Press.

HICKS, ALEXANDER; FRIEDLAND, ROGER; AND JOHNSON, EDWIN
1978 "Class Power and State Policy: The Case of Large Business Corporations, Labor Unions and Governmental Redistribution in the American States." *American Sociological Review* 43 (June): 302–315.

HILL, ANN CORINNE
1979 "Protection of Women Workers and the Courts: A Legal Case History." *Feminist Studies* 5 (Summer): 247–273.

HOFFERBERT, RICHARD I.
1966 "The Relation between Public Policy and Some Structural and Environmental Variables in the American States." *American Political Science Review* 60 (March): 73–82.

1974   *The Study of Public Policy*. Indianapolis and New York: The Bobbs-
         Merrill Company.
HOFSTADTER, RICHARD
1965   *The Age of Reform: From Bryan to FDR*. New York: Alfred A. Knopf.
HURST, JAMES WILLARD
1956   *Law and Conditions of Freedom in the Nineteenth Century United States*.
         Madison: University of Wisconsin Press.
1971   "Legal Elements in United States History." In *Law in American History*,
         ed. Donald H. Fleming and Bernard Bailyn, pp. 3–94. Boston: Little,
         Brown and Company.
JACKMAN, ROBERT W.
1975   *Politics and Social Equality: A Comparative Analysis*. New York: John
         Wiley and Sons.
JEWELL, MALCOLM
1962   *The State Legislature*. New York: Random House.
JOHNSON, BRUCE C.
1972   "The Democratic Mirage: Notes toward a Theory of American Politics."
         In *The Political Economy of American Social Problems*, ed. Milton
         Mankoff, pp. 362–390. New York: Holt, Rinehart and Winston.
JOSEPHSON, HANNAH
1949   *The Golden Threads, New England's Mill Girls and Magnates*. New
         York: Russell and Russell.
KAITZ, HYMAN
1970   "Experience of the Past: The National Minimum Wage." Youth Employ-
         ment and Minimum Wages, Bureau of Labor Statistics, Bulletin no. 1957,
         pp. 30–54. Washington, D.C.: U.S. Government Printing Office.
KANOWITZ, LEO
1969   *Women and the Law: The Unfinished Revolution*. Albuquerque: University
         of New Mexico Press.
KELLER, MORTON
1977   *Affairs of State: Public Life in Late Nineteenth Century America*. Cam-
         bridge, Mass.: Harvard University Press, Belknap Press.
KERR, CLARK; DUNLOP, JOHN T.; HARBISON, FREDERICK; AND MYERS, CHARLES A.
1964   *Industrialism and Industrial Man: The Problems of Labor and Manage-
         ment in Economic Growth*. New York: Oxford University Press.
KEY, V. O.
1949   *Southern Politics*. New York: Vintage Books.
1955   The Theory of Critical Elections. *Journal of Politics* 17:3–18.
KOCHAN, THOMAS A.
1973   "Correlates of State Public Employment Bargaining Laws." *Industrial
         Relations* 12 (October): 322–337.
KOCHAN, THOMAS A., AND WHEELER, HOYT N.
1975   "Municipal Collective Bargaining: A Model and Analysis of Bargaining
         Outcomes." *Industrial and Labor Relations Review* 29 (October): 46–66.

KOLKO, GABRIEL

1963   *The Triumph of Conservatism: A Reinterpretation of American History, 1900–1916.* Chicago: Quadrangle Books.

1965   *Railroads and Regulations, 1877–1916.* Princeton, N.J.: Princeton University Press.

KORPI, WALTER

1978   *The Working Class in Welfare Capitalism: Work, Unions, and Politics in Sweden.* London: Routledge and Kegan Paul.

KUZNETS, SIMON

1946   *National Product since 1869.* New York: National Bureau of Economic Research.

1971   "Notes on the Pattern of U.S. Economic Growth." In *The Reinterpretation of American Economic History,* ed. Robert W. Fogel and Stanley L. Engerman, pp. 17–24. New York: Harper and Row.

LAND, KENNETH C., AND FELSON, MARCUS

1976   "A General Framework for Building Dynamic Macro Social Indicator Models: Including an Analysis of Changes in Crime Rates and Police Expenditures." *American Journal of Sociology* 82 (November): 565–604.

LAND, KENNETH C., AND SPILERMAN, SEYMOUR, EDS.

1975   *Social Indicator Models.* New York: Russell Sage Foundation.

LASSWELL, HAROLD

1958   *Politics: Who Gets What, When, and How.* Cleveland: World Publishing.

LEBERGOTT, STANLEY

1964   *Manpower in Economic Growth: The American Record since 1800.* New York: McGraw-Hill Book Company.

LEMONS, J. STANLEY

1973   *The Woman Citizen: Social Feminism in the 1920's.* Urbana, Chicago, and London: University of Illinois Press.

LEMPERT, RICHARD

1966   "Strategies of Research Design in the Legal Impact Study: The Control of Plausible Rival Hypotheses." *Law and Society Review* 1 (November): 111–132.

LENSKI, GERHARD

1976   "History and Social Change." *American Journal of Sociology* 82 (November): 548–564.

LIPSET, SEYMOUR MARTIN

1960   *Political Man: The Social Bases of Politics.* Garden City, N.Y.: Doubleday.

LOCKARD, DUANE

1968   *Toward Equal Opportunity: A Study of State and Local Antidiscrimination Laws.* New York: Macmillan Company.

LOETHER, HERMAN J., AND MCTAVISH, DONALD G.

1974   *Descriptive Statistics for Sociologists: An Introduction.* Boston: Allyn and Bacon.

LOWI, THEODORE J.

1969 *The End of Liberalism: Ideology, Policy, and the Crisis of Public Authority.* New York: W. W. Norton and Company.

MC VOY, EDGAR

1940 "Patterns of Diffusion in the United States." *American Sociological Review* 5 (April): 219–227.

MARGLIN, STEPHEN A.

1974 "What Do Bosses Do? The Origins and Functions of Hierarchy in Capitalist Production." *Review of Radical Political Economics* 6 (Summer): 60–112.

MARSHALL, T. H.

1965 *Class, Citizenship, and Social Development.* Garden City, N.Y.: Anchor Books.

1967 *Social Policy.* London: Hutchinson University Library.

MARTIN, GEORGE

1976 *Madam Secretary, Frances Perkins.* Boston: Houghton Mifflin Company.

MARX, GARY, AND WOOD, JAMES L.

1975 "Strands of Theory and Research in Collective Behavior." *Annual Review of Sociology* 1: 363–428.

MARX, KARL

1906 *Capital: A Critique of Political Economy.* Translated by Samuel Moore and Edward Aveling. New York: Modern Library.

MARX, KARL, AND ENGELS, FRIEDRICH

1955 *The Communist Manifesto.* Translated by Samuel H. Beer. New York: Appleton-Century-Crofts.

MILIBAND, RALPH

1969 *The State in Capitalist Society: An Analysis of the Western System of Power.* New York: Basic Books.

MOORE, WILLIAM; NEWMAN, ROBERT J.; AND THOMAS, WILLIAM R.

1974 "Determinants of the Passage of Right-to-Work Laws: An Alternative Interpretation." *Journal of Law and Economics* 17 (April): 197–211.

NEWMAN, PAUL CHARLES

1943 *The Labor Legislation of New Jersey.* Washington, D.C.: American Council on Public Affairs.

NONET, PHILIPPE

1969 *Administrative Justice: Advocacy and Change in a Government Agency.* New York: Russell Sage Foundation.

NOZICK, ROBERT

1974 *Anarchy, State and Utopia.* Oxford: Basil Blackwell.

OBENAUER, MARIE L., AND VON DER NIENBURG, BERTHA

1915 *The Effect of Minimum Wage Determination in Oregon.* Bureau of Labor Statistics Bulletin no. 176. Washington, D.C.: U.S. Government Printing Office.

O'CONNOR, JAMES

1973 *The Fiscal Crisis of the State.* New York: St. Martin's Press.

OGBURN, WILLIAM F.

1912   *Progress and Uniformity in Child-Labor Legislation: A Study in Statistical Measurement.* New York: Columbia University Press.

1964   "Progress and Uniformity in Child-Labor Legislation." In *William Ogburn: On Culture and Social Control,* ed. Otis D. Duncan, pp. 110–130. Chicago: University of Chicago Press.

ORNATI, OSCAR

1966   *Poverty amid Affluence: A Report on a Research Project Carried out at the New School for Social Research.* New York: Twentieth Century Fund.

PALOMBA, NEIL A., AND PALOMBA, CATHARINE A.

1971   "Right-to-Work Laws: A Suggested Economic Rationale." *Journal of Law and Economics* 14 (October): 475–483.

PATTERSON, JAMES T.

1969   *The New Deal and the States.* Princeton, N.J.: Princeton University Press.

PAUL, ARNOLD M.

1969   *Conservative Crisis and the Rule of Law: Attitudes of Bar and Bench, 1887–1895.* New York: Harper and Row.

PEACOCK, ALAN T., AND WISEMAN, JACK

1961   *The Growth of Public Expenditures in the United Kingdom.* Princeton, N.J.: Princeton University Press.

PERLOFF, HARVEY, AND DODDS, VERA W.

1963   *How a Region Grows: Area Development in the U.S. Economy.* Supplementary Paper no. 17. New York: Committee for Economic Development.

PETERSON, JOHN M.

1959   "Employment Effects of State Minimum Wages for Women: Three Historical Cases Re-examined." *Industrial and Labor Relations Review* 12 (April): 406–422.

PIVEN, FRANCES FOX, AND CLOWARD, RICHARD

1971   *Regulating the Poor: The Functions of Social Welfare.* New York: Pantheon Books.

POLANYI, KARL

1957   *The Great Transformation: The Political and Economic Origins of Our Time.* Boston: Beacon Press.

POULANTZAS, NICOS

1973   "The Problem of the Capitalist State." In *Ideology in Social Science,* ed. Robin Blackburn, pp. 238–253. New York: Random House.

1975   *Political Power and Social Classes.* Translated by Timothy O'Hagan. Atlantic Highlands, N.J.: Humanities Press.

POUND, ROSCOE

1909   "Liberty of Contract." *Yale Law Journal* 18 (May): 454–487.

PRYOR, FREDERICK

1968   *Public Expenditures in Communist and Capitalist Nations.* Homewood, Ill.: Richard D. Irwin.

PRZEWORSKI, ADAM, AND TEUNE, HENRY
1970   *The Logic of Comparative Analysis.* New York: John Wiley and Sons.

RATNER, RONNIE STEINBERG
1977a "A Modest Magna Charta: The Rise of Wage and Hours Standards Laws in the United States, 1900–1973; A Social Indicators Approach." Ph.D. dissertation, New York University.

1977b "To Them That Hath Shall Be Given: A Quantitative Analysis of the Relationship between Unionization and Social Reform Legislation." Paper presented at the annual meeting of the Eastern Sociological Society, New York City.

1980   "The Paradox of Protection: Maximum Hours Legislation in the United States." *International Labour Review* 119 (March–April): 185–198.

RAYBACK, JOSEPH G.
1966   *A History of American Labor.* Rev. ed. New York: The Free Press.

RIMLINGER, GASTON
1971   *Welfare Policy and Industrialization in Europe, America and Russia.* New York: John Wiley and Sons.

ROMANYSHYN, JOHN M.
1971   *Social Welfare: Charity to Justice.* New York: Random House.

ROSS, SUSAN DELLER
1970   "Sex Discrimination and 'Protective' Labor Legislation." Unpublished manuscript.

RYAN, FREDERICK LYNNE
1932   *A History of Labor Legislation in Oklahoma.* Norman: University of Oklahoma Press.

SCHATTSCHNEIDER, E. E.
1960   *The Semisovereign People.* New York: Holt, Rinehart and Winston.

SCHEINGOLD, STUART A.
1974   *The Politics of Rights: Lawyers, Public Policy, and Political Change.* New Haven and London: Yale University Press.

SHABECOFF, PHILIP
1977   "Washington and Business: Reincarnation of Taft's Minimum Wage." *New York Times,* pp. 53, 61.

SHARKANSKY, IRA
1968   "Economic Development, Regionalism, and State Political Systems." *Midwest Journal of Political Science* 12 (February): 41–61.

SHARKANSKY, IRA, AND HOFFERBERT, RICHARD I.
1969   "Dimensions of State Politics, Economics, and Public Policy." *American Political Science Review* 63 (September): 867–879.

SHELDON, ELEANOR B., AND MOORE, WILBERT E., EDS.
1968   *Indicators of Social Change: Concepts and Measurements.* New York: Russell Sage Foundation.

SILBERMAN, JONATHAN I., AND DURDEN, GAREY
1976   "Determining Legislative Preferences on the Minimum Wage: An Economic Approach." *Journal of Political Economy* 84 (April): 317–329.

SMELSER, NEIL

1959   *Social Change in the Industrial Revolution: An Application of Theory to the British Cotton Industry.* Chicago: University of Chicago Press.

1969   "Mechanisms of Change and Adjustment to Change." In *Industrial Man,* ed. Tom Burn, pp. 43–68. Baltimore: Penguin Books.

STEPHENS, JOHN D.

1979   *The Transition from Capitalism to Socialism.* London: The Macmillan Press.

STETSON, D. M., AND WRIGHT, G. C., JR.

1975   "The Effects of Laws on Divorce in American States." *Journal of Marriage and the Family* 37: 537–547.

STINCHCOMBE, ARTHUR L.

1965   "Social Structure and Organization." In *Handbook of Organizations,* ed. James G. March, pp. 142–193. Chicago: Rand McNally & Co.

SWEEZY, PAUL

1942   *The Theory of Capitalist Development.* New York: Monthly Review Press.

THOMPSON, E. P.

1975   *Whigs and Hunters: The Origin of the Black Act.* New York: Pantheon Books.

TILLY, CHARLES

1975   "Western State-making and Theories of Political Transformation." In *The Formation of National States in Western Europe,* ed. Charles Tilly, pp. 601–638. Princeton, N.J.: Princeton University Press.

TILLY, CHARLES; TILLY, LOUISE; AND TILLY, RICHARD

1975   *The Rebellious Century, 1830–1930.* Cambridge, Mass.: Harvard University Press.

TROY, LEO

1957   *Distribution of Union Membership among the States: 1939 and 1953.* Occasional Paper no. 56. New York: National Bureau of Economic Research.

1965   *Trade Union Membership, 1897–1962.* National Bureau of Economic Research Occasional Paper no. 92. New York: Columbia University Press.

ULMAN, LLOYD

1955   *The Rise of the National Trade Union: The Development and Significance of Its Structure, Governing Institutions, and Economic Policies.* Cambridge, Mass.: Harvard University Press.

U.S. BUREAU OF LABOR STATISTICS

1916   *Summary of the Report on the Condition of Women and Child Wage Earners in the United States.* Bulletin no. 175. Washington, D.C.: U.S. Government Printing Office.

U.S. CONGRESS

1937   *Congressional Directory.* Washington, D.C.: U.S. Government Printing Office.

1938   *Congressional Directory.* Washington, D.C.: U.S. Government Printing Office.

1961   *Congressional Quarterly Almanac.* Vol. 17. Washington, D.C.: U.S. Government Printing Office.

1966   *Congressional Quarterly Almanac.* Vol. 22. Washington, D.C.: U.S. Government Printing Office.

U.S. CONGRESS, HOUSE

1938   *Congressional Record.* 75th Cong., 2d sess., vol. 83, pt. 8.

U.S. CONGRESS, SENATE

1938   *Congressional Record.* 75th Cong., 1st sess., vol. 81, pt. 7.

U.S. DEPARTMENT OF COMMERCE, BUREAU OF THE CENSUS

1904   *Occupations of the Twelfth Census of the United States, 1900: Special Reports.* Washington, D.C.: U.S. Government Printing Office.

1911   *Statistical Abstract of the United States.* No. 32. Washington, D.C.: U.S. Government Printing Office.

1913   *Thirteenth Census of the United States: 1910 Occupation Statistics.* Vols. 3–4. Washington, D.C.: U.S. Government Printing Office.

1923   *Fourteenth Census of the United States: 1920 Occupation.* Vol. 4. Washington, D.C.: U.S. Government Printing Office.

1932   *Statistical Abstract of the United States.* No. 53. Washington, D.C.: U.S. Government Printing Office.

1933   *Fifteenth Census of the United States: 1930 Occupations by State.* Vol. 4. Washington, D.C.: U.S. Government Printing Office.

1936   *Statistical Abstract of the United States.* No. 57. Washington, D.C.: U.S. Government Printing Office.

1941   *Statistical Abstract of the United States.* No. 62. Washington, D.C.: U.S. Government Printing Office.

1943   *Sixteenth Census of the United States: 1940 The Labor Force.* Vol. 3. Washington, D.C.: U.S. Government Printing Office.

1945   *Statistical Abstract of the United States.* No. 66. Washington, D.C.: U.S. Government Printing Office.

1948   *Statistical Abstract of the United States.* No. 69. Washington, D.C.: U.S. Government Printing Office.

1951   *Statistical Abstract of the United States.* No. 72. Washington, D.C.: U.S. Government Printing Office.

1952   *Seventeenth Census of the United States: 1950 Population.* Vol. 2. Washington, D.C.: U.S. Government Printing Office.

1961   *Eighteenth Decennial Census of the United States: 1960 Population.* Vol. 1. Washington, D.C.: U.S. Government Printing Office.

1963   *County Business Patterns: 1962 U.S. Summary.* Pt. 1. Washington, D.C.: U.S. Government Printing Office.

1964   *Statistical Abstract of the United States.* No. 85. Washington, D.C.: U.S. Government Printing Office.

1968 *Statistical Abstract of the United States.* No. 89. Washington, D.C.: U.S. Government Printing Office.

1971a *County Business Patterns: 1970 U.S. Summary.* Pt. 1. Washington, D.C.: U.S. Government Printing Office.

1971b *Statistical Abstract of the United States.* No. 92. Washington, D.C.: U.S. Government Printing Office.

1972 *Nineteenth Decennial Census of the United States: 1970 Population.* Vol. 1. Washington, D.C.: U.S. Government Printing Office.

1975 *Historical Statistics of the United States: Colonial Times to 1970.* 2 vols. Washington, D.C.: U.S. Government Printing Office.

U.S. DEPARTMENT OF LABOR

1941 *Compilation of Labor Laws.* Washington, D.C.: U.S. Government Printing Office.

1950 *Strengthening the Economy: Thirty-eighth Annual Report of the Secretary of Labor.* Washington, D.C.: U.S. Government Printing Office.

U.S. DEPARTMENT OF LABOR, BUREAU OF LABOR STANDARDS

1967 *The Growth of Labor Laws in the United States.* Washington, D.C.: U.S. Government Printing Office.

U.S. DEPARTMENT OF LABOR, BUREAU OF LABOR STATISTICS

1974 *Handbook of Labor Statistics.* Washington, D.C.: U.S. Government Printing Office.

U.S. DEPARTMENT OF LABOR, EMPLOYMENT STANDARDS ADMINISTRATION

1974 *Federal Labor Laws: A Looseleaf System Containing Laws Administered by the Wage and Hour Division with Regulations and Interpretations.* Washington, D.C.: U.S. Government Printing Office.

U.S. DEPARTMENT OF LABOR, WAGE AND HOUR AND PUBLIC CONTRACTS DIVISION

1948 Annual Report.

1964 Annual Report.

1967 Annual Report.

1970 "Estimates of Coverage under the Minimum Wage and Overtime Standards of the Fair Labor Standards Act and State Labor Standards Laws as of February 1, 1970."

1974 Annual Report.

U.S. DEPARTMENT OF LABOR, WOMEN'S BUREAU

1921 *Some Effects of Legislation Limiting Hours of Work for Women.* Bulletin no. 15. Washington, D.C.: U.S. Government Printing Office.

1938 *The Effect of Minimum Wage Determination in Service Industries.* Bulletin no. 166. Washington, D.C.: U.S. Government Printing Office.

VALE, VIVIAN

1971 *Labour in American Politics.* New York: Barnes and Noble.

WAHLKE, JOHN C.

1966 "Organization and Procedure." In *The American Assembly on State Legislatures,* ed. John C. Wahlke, pp. 126–153. Englewood Cliffs, N.J.: Prentice-Hall.

WALKER, JACK
1969 "The Diffusion of Innovations among the American States." *American Political Science Review* 63 (September): 880–889.

WARE, NORMAN
1958 *The Labor Movement in the United States, 1860–1895: A Study in Democracy.* Gloucester, Mass.: Peter Smith.
1964 *The Industrial Worker, 1840–1860.* Chicago: Quadrangle Books.

WEDDERBURN, DOROTHY
1965 "Facts and Theories of the Welfare State." In *The Socialist Register,* ed. Ralph Miliband and John Seville, pp. 127–146. London: Merlin Press.

WEINSTEIN, JAMES
1968 *The Corporate Ideal in the Liberal State: 1900–1918.* Boston: Beacon Press.

WERTHEIMER, BARBARA MEYER
1977 *We Were There: The Story of Working Women in America.* New York: Pantheon Books.

WHITIN, E. STAGG
1908 *Factory Legislation in Maine.* New York: Columbia University Press.

WIEBE, ROBERT
1967 *The Search for Order: 1877–1920.* New York; Hill and Wang.

WILCOX, LESLIE D.; RALPH, M.; BEAL, GEORGE M.; AND KLONGLAN, GERALD E.
1972 "Social Indicators: Recent Trends and Selected Bibliography." *Sociological Inquiry* 42 (Winter):37–50.

WILDAVKSY, AARON
1964 *The Politics of the Budgetary Process.* Boston: Little, Brown and Company.

WILENSKY, HAROLD L.
1975 *The Welfare State and Equality: Structural and Ideological Roots of Public Expenditures.* Berkeley: University of California Press.
1976 *The "New Corporatism," Centralization and the Welfare State.* Beverly Hills, Cal.: Sage Publications.

WILENSKY, HAROLD, AND LEBEAUX, CHARLES
1965 *Industrialization and Social Welfare: The Impact of Industrialization on the Supply and Organization of Social Welfare Services in the United States.* New York: The Free Press.

WINSLOW, MARY NELSON
1928 *The Effects of Labor Legislation on the Employment Opportunities of Women.* Women's Bureau Bulletin no. 65. Washington, D.C.: U.S. Government Printing Office.

WITTE, EDWIN E.
1932 "Labor Legislation." In *Encyclopaedia of the Social Sciences,* ed. Edwin R. A. Seligman, vol. 7, pp. 657–667. New York: Macmillan Company.

WOLFSON, THERESA
1929 "Trade Union Activities of Women." *Annals* 143 (May): 120–131.
1943 "Aprons and Overalls in War." *Annals* 229 (September): 46–55.

WOLMAN, LEO

  1924   *The Growth of American Trade Unions, 1880–1923*. New York: National
         Bureau of Economic Research.
  1936   *Ebb and Flow in Trade Unionism*. New York: National Bureau of Eco-
         nomic Research.

YELLOWITZ, IRWIN

  1977   *Industrialization and the American Labor Movement, 1850–1900*. Port
         Washington, N.Y.: Kennikat Press.

INDEX